Between Prison
and Probation

BETWEEN PRISON AND PROBATION

Intermediate Punishments in
a Rational Sentencing System

NORVAL MORRIS
MICHAEL TONRY

New York   Oxford
OXFORD UNIVERSITY PRESS
1990

Oxford University Press

Oxford   New York   Toronto
Delhi   Bombay   Calcutta   Madras   Karachi
Petaling Jaya   Singapore   Hong Kong   Tokyo
Nairobi   Dar es Salaam   Cape Town
Melbourne   Auckland

and associated companies in
Berlin   Ibadan

Published by Oxford University Press, Inc.,
200 Madison Avenue, New York, New York 10016

Oxford is a registered trademark of Oxford University Press

Library of Congress Cataloging-in-Publication Data
Morris, Norval.
Between prison and probation:
intermediate punishments in a rational sentencing system/
Norval Morris, Michael Tonry.
p.   cm.   Includes bibliographical references.
ISBN 0-19-506108-X
1. Corrections—United States.
2. Sentences (Criminal procedure)—United States.
I. Tonry, Michael H.   II. Title.
HV9469.M67   1990   364.6'5'0973—dc20
89-23230

9 8 7 6 5 4 3 2 1

Printed in the United States of America
on acid-free paper

To Elaine and Penny
For putting up with us

⊞⊞⊞⊞⊞ Acknowledgments

We are grateful to the Edna McConnell Clark Foundation and to the National Institute of Corrections for financial support. They allowed us time to work on the manuscript and funds to convene five conferences to guide our work.

The first four conferences brought together practitioners in various "intermediate punishment" projects and a few scholars to share information with one another and with us; the fifth was a two-day criticism of the first draft of this book by, among others, Todd Clear of Rutgers, Mark Corrigan of the National Institute of Sentencing Alternatives at Brandeis University, Dan Freed of Yale, Judith Greene of the Vera Institute, Andrew von Hirsch of Rutgers, Jim Jacobs of New York University, Kay Knapp then of the United States Sentencing Commission, George Keiser of the National Institute of Corrections, Lloyd Ohlin of Harvard, Joan Petersilia of the Rand Corporation, Albert J. Reiss, Jr., of Yale, Kenneth Schoen of the Edna McConnell Clark Foundation, and Franklin Zimring of Berkeley. Guided, chastened, and reinvigorated by that last conference we produced this book for which we alone take the blame though they deserve much of any credit that may accrue.

⧈⧈⧈⧈⧈ Contents

Between Prison and Probation

Introduction

Effective and principled punishment of convicted criminals requires the development and application of a range of punishments between imprisonment and probation. Imprisonment is used excessively; probation is used even more excessively; between the two is a near-vacuum of purposive and enforced punishments.

Our plea is for neither increased leniency nor increased severity; our program, if implemented, would tend toward increased reliance on punishments more severe than probation and less severe than protracted imprisonment. At present, too many criminals are in prison and too few are the subjects of enforced controls in the community. We are both too lenient and too severe; too lenient with many on probation who should be subject to tighter controls in the community, and too severe with many in prison and jail who would present no serious threat to community safety if they were under control in the community.

There are many reasons for this inefficient and expensive situation. Some are to be found in community attitudes to punishment and the history of punishment practice in this country, others in the jerky evolution of sentencing practice and the shifts of sentencing discretion among legislature, prosecutor, judge, and parole board that have characterized sentencing reform in this country. The aim of this book is to help bring order to the use of "intermediate punishments"; central to that task is the fashioning of sentencing guidelines that give principled and appropriate place to such punishments.

Brief commentary on the title of our book may help clarify our purposes and define our frame of reference.

Why in the title to this book do we refer to "intermediate punishments," rather than to "alternative punishments" or "alternative sanctions?" Use of the word "alternatives" assumes that these punishments are substitutes for real punishments. It assumes that the norm of punishment is imprisonment, against which all other punishments are to be measured. This is true neither historically nor in current practice. Most felonies never were and are not now punished by imprisonment. Prison may be the norm of punishment in the minds of some citizens, but it is not that to those acquainted with the operation of our criminal justice systems.

Further, "alternatives" gives false promise of reducing the present overcrowding in American prisons and jails. The "alternatives" movement has indeed offered that as a main argument for its support. But the truth is that "intermediate punishments"—intensive probation, substantial fines, community service orders, residential controls, treatment orders—tend at present to draw more from those who otherwise would be placed on unenforced probationary supervision or on suspended sentence than from those who otherwise would go to prison or jail.

The excellent 1987 report of the Canadian Sentencing Commission prefers the phrase "community sanctions" to describe all non-custodial punishments, dividing the world of punishment for crime into custodial sanctions and community sanctions. This is entirely acceptable terminology, but it tends to conceal that many community-based sentences impose and enforce considerable restrictions on the offender's freedom of movement, approximating to the custodial, and coercively limit other aspects of his autonomy. The usage we have preferred, therefore, involves a threefold division of all punishments into those that are incarcerative (prison and jail), those that conform to current "ordinary" probation and to suspended sentences, and those that, covering all the rest, are "intermediate punishments."

Why "punishments" and not "sanctions"? This is almost, but not entirely, a question of taste rather than analytic substance. One of the reasons why American criminal justice systems have failed to develop a sufficient range of criminal sanctions to apply to convicted offenders is that the dialogue is often cast in the pattern of punishment or not, with prison being punishment and other sanctions being seen as treatment or, in the minds of most, "letting off." And, sadly, the popular view proves on closer inspection to be broadly accurate, with widespread nonenforcement of such noncustodial sentences.

It is better to be direct about the matter. Convicted criminals should not be spared punitive responses to their crimes; there is no point in imposing needless suffering, but effective sentencing will normally involve the curtailment of freedom either behind walls or in the community, large measures of coercion, and enforced diminutions of freedom; this is entirely properly regarded as punishment. The language of treatment, reform, and rehabilitation has been corrupted by unenforced and uncritically evaluated good intentions. We fool ourselves—or worse, pretend—if we fail to acknowledge that the intrusions into people's lives that result from criminal punishment are unpleasant and painful. We will do better if we are more blunt about these matters.

Hence *Intermediate Punishments in a Rational Sentencing System*.

All efforts at scientific analysis require artificial isolation of a topic to be studied, and intermediate punishments are no exception. Here is what we are not including within our frame of reference.

We shall not discuss capital punishment. Neither proponents nor abolitionists can be happy with the uneasy and unprincipled compromises that have been reached in the application of this punishment in the United States; but we have enough to do without addressing that ancient and bitter controversy.

We shall not discuss punishments designed only to stigmatize: the stocks, the branding of the adulteress's "A" on the forehead, the public meeting à la Chinoise to harangue the culprit. These punishments seem more romantic than real in the urban agglomerations where crime flourishes.

We shall not discuss corporal punishments, the lash, the birch, the chopping of hands and tongues, the slitting of lips and noses, the slicing of ears. They are less romantic than brutalizing, not only to those who suffer such punishments but—and the historical record is clear on this—to the society that applies them.

Nor shall we deal at any length with normal or ordinary probation, which for state and local crime in many cities has degenerated into ineffectiveness under the pressure of excessive caseloads and inadequate resources. To be sure, there may well be many times when nominal probation, giving the appearance but not the reality of punishment, is exactly what's wanted. Sometimes, for some offenses and offenders, prosecution itself, or the entry of conviction, may be punishment enough. As one scholar aptly put it in the title of a book on lower criminal courts, the process often *is* the punishment. We might augment this to suggest that the lawyers and their fees are often the punishment. For some offenses and offenders, the anxiety and the disruption resulting from prosecution and conviction may be so unpleasant that any punishment more than nominal probation is overkill.

Although we acknowledge that ordinary probation may often be the appropriate aftermath to a conviction, we exclude it from discussion here by defining it and imprisonment as the poles of the punishment continuum between which intermediate punishments are arrayed.

And though there is a lot in common between properly shaped and determinedly enforced "intermediate punishments" and effective release procedures from prison, that topic too will for convenience for the most part be excluded from our coverage. We cannot, however, be rigid in this exclusion because of the near indistinguishability in practice and in principle between, for example, house arrest as a condition of probation, as in Florida, and house arrest as an "institutional placement" by a state correctional department, as in Oklahoma. However, our focus is on sentencing rather than release from prison and on the sentencing choices available in the aggregate to policymakers and to sentencing judges.

What, then, is left? Intensive probation, the fine, the community service order, and a wide variety of treatments and controls to give bite and reality to intermediate punishments.

"Intensive probation" is a general phrase covering the enforcement of a variety of restrictions on freedom in the community and a diversity of programs designed to reduce future criminality by the convicted offender. In the 1950s and 1960s, experimentation with the effects of differential caseloads began. This was soon followed by efforts to classify probationers for risk and to make assignments accordingly. More recently, in many states, probation programs have been developed that are designed to be punitive and to subject offenders to close scrutiny and to close residential controls, augmented in some cases by the provision of services facilitative of self-restoration. Prominent features of orders for intensive supervision now include house arrest, conditions of residence, treatment programs for drugs, alcohol, and mental illness, and the use of electronic controls on movement so that pervasive supervision can be achieved. Such programs, in our view, will be of increasing importance to crime control policies.

Another set of intermediate punishments is the fine and the other financial sanctions that may be imposed on convicted offenders. It is a paradox that this country, so generally confident of the financial incentive, places such little reliance on the financial disincentive and has such a poor record of collecting those fines that are imposed.

And the final broad heading of intermediate punishments is the community service order, turning convicted offenders to useful work in the community.

These intermediate punishments do not function in isolation from one another. The fine is often combined with other punishments. So too are house arrest and the community service order. Electronic monitoring is really a technique or a technology; it is seldom intended to serve as a punishment in itself. All are sometimes allied to brief periods of prison or jail. But separately or in combination, intermediate punishments raise difficult jurisprudential and political problems which we shall address. How can they be made credible and enforced in practice? How can they justly and fairly be applied so that class and race bias is avoided, so that these "lesser" punishments are not applied to privileged criminals while the underclass, particularly the black and Hispanic underclass, goes to prison? How can they be related to sentencing policy so that judicial discretion is controlled in their imposition to minimize disparity and injustice?

We do not shrink from urging the serious consideration of complex intermediate punishments. For some offenders, a substantial fine may well be combined with an order that the offender make restitution to the victim, pay court costs, and be subject to a protracted period of house arrest, monitored electronically, for which too the offender pays the costs. For others, intensive probation involving regular and close supervision by a supervising officer playing a police role and also by a caseworker may be combined with a defined period of residence in a drug treatment facility, followed by regular urinalyses to ensure the offender remains drug free, and also an obligation to fulfill a set number of hours of community service—all strictly enforced. Too complex? Too expensive? Not at all—such sentences in appropriate cases serve the community, the victim, and the criminal better and more economically than the prison terms they supplant.

It will be appreciated that the just and efficient application of such a wide-ranging armamentarium of punishments raises issues of complexity at the sentencing stage if the sentence is to be tailored to the threat that the offender presents to the community and to his social and psychological needs, if recidivism is to be reduced, and unjust disparity in sentencing is to be avoided. Hence the centrality of sentencing theory in our consideration of intermediate punishments.

A glance at the Contents will reveal the sequence in which we consider these problems. This book has two parts. Part I discusses sentencing in practice and in principle to demonstrate how and why intermediate punishments should be integrated into comprehensive sentencing systems. Part II then surveys the prospects for serious development of promising intermediate punishments in the United States. The purpose of our book is to contribute to the development of principled and effective sentencing policy in the many criminal justice systems in this country, with an enriched range of punishments better suited to the diversity of crime and criminals to be sentenced, and with intermediate punishments being more extensively imposed and more determinedly enforced for the better protection of the community and the larger achievement of justice.

2

Toward a Comprehensive Punishment System

When this book is published, there will be more than 1,000,000 Americans aged 18 and over in prison and jail, and more than 2,500,000 on parole or probation. If one adds those on bail or released awaiting trial or appeal and those serving other punishments such as community service orders, the grand total under the control of the criminal justice system exceeds four million, nearly 2 percent of the nation's adult population.

The pressure of these numbers on insufficient and mostly old penal institutions and on sparsely staffed probation offices has sharpened interest in all punishments lying between the prison and the jail at one end and insufficiently supervised probation at the other—there is general agreement about the need to develop and expand "intermediate punishments" but the path to that end is far from clear.

There are two main lines of argument in this book. First, it is submitted that there has been a failure in this country to develop and institutionalize a range of punishments lying between incarceration and probation. That argument can stand alone and would support an expansion of intermediate punishments without considering any questions of sentencing processes. The selection between those properly committed to prison and those sentenced to intermediate punishments cannot be based *alone* on the gravity of their crimes or the lengths of their criminal records, nor can the choice between probation and an intermediate punishment. We deal at length in Chapters 3 and 4 with this inconvenient reality.

The second line of argument takes the matter further: for certain categories of offenders now in prison, some though not all could better be sentenced to intermediate punishments, and for certain categories of offenders now on probation, some though not all could be better subjected to more intensive controls in the community than probation now provides.

The first argument is obvious enough and does not deny the conventional wisdom; indeed, such is the extent of current experimentation with intermediate punishments that the ground is fertile and the time precisely right for their growth. The second argument will meet with more opposition since it seems to contradict the intuitive sense that like cases should be treated alike, that crimes of equal severity committed by criminals with equal criminal records should be punished identically. We regard this position as an erroneous application of principles of "just desert." A comprehensive and just sentencing system requires principled "interchangeability" of punishment of "like" cases, some going to prison, some receiving an intermediate punishment. Similarly, there must be principled interchangeability of punishment of like cases, with some being put on probation while others receive the more intensive control or qualitatively different experience of an intermediate punishment.

We take the definition of "intermediate punishments" from the introduction and provide a bare statement of our recommendations, the rationale forming the rest of this book:

- Intermediate punishments should be applied to many criminals now in prison and jail and to many criminals now sentenced to probation or a suspended sentence.
- Intermediate punishments must be rigorously enforced; they should not, as is too often the present case, be ordered absent adequate enforcement resources.

- Breaches of conditions of intermediate punishments must be taken seriously by the supervising authority and, in appropriate cases, by the sentencing judge, if these punishments are to become credible sanctions.
- The fine should be greatly expanded, in amount and in frequency, both as a punishment standing alone and as part of a punishment package. Fines must be adjusted to the offender's financial capacity (to be achieved by a system of "day fines") and must be collected; this requires innovative assessment and enforcement arrangements, since at present fines are set too low, do not sufficiently match the means of the offender, and are too often not collected.
- The use of community service orders, standing alone or as part of a punishment package, should be greatly increased. Such punishments are applicable to the indigent and to the wealthy; they have much to contribute provided, as for other intermediate punishments, they are vigorously supervised and enforced.
- Intensive probation is a mechanism by which reality can be brought to all intermediate punishments. Allied to house arrest, treatment orders, residential conditions up to house arrest, buttressed by electronic monitoring where appropriate, and paid for by fees for service by the offender where that is realistic, intensive supervision has the capacity both to control offenders in the community and to facilitate their growth to crime-free lives.
- Current sentencing reforms, both proposals and developments, devote inadequate attention to intermediate punishments. Sentencing guidelines, legislative or voluntary, shaped by a sentencing commission or by a court system, must provide better guidance to the judiciary in the use of intermediate punishments if a comprehensive sentencing system is to be developed. In particular:

  1. there is a range of offense–offender relationships in which incarcerative and intermediate punishments are equally applicable;
  2. there is a range of offense–offender relationships in which intermediate punishments and lesser community-based controls are equally applicable;
  3. the sentencing judge requires adequate information about the offender and his financial and personal circumstances to decide on the applicability to each convicted offender of a fine, of a com-

munity service order, of a treatment or residential order, of intensive supervision, or of a split sentence involving incarceration and an intermediate punishment—or a mixture of several of these punishments;

4. the judge should retain ultimate responsibility for the decision on the "back-up" sentence, that is, on what should be done if the conditions of an intermediate punishment are not adhered to.

• As intermediate punishments become part of a comprehensive sentencing system, their efficacy must be critically evaluated so that, in time, an effective treatment classification may emerge.

So curt a summary of recommendations takes a great deal for granted and glosses over many difficulties. To tease out the realities behind these proposals, the discussion in this chapter will examine the following:

• The overuse of imprisonment and probation;
• The underuse of intermediate punishments;
• The enforcement of intermediate punishments:
  —resources and cost,
  —the "back-up" sentence;
• Sentencing to intermediate punishments:
  —present guidance,
  —a comprehensive sentencing system,
  —justice, fairness, and interchangeability of punishments.

The Overuse of Imprisonment and Probation

The figures again: 1,000,000 in prison and jail, over 2,500,000 on probation. How many of these would be better subjected to intermediate punishments cannot be precisely calculated but that the number is large can be confidently affirmed.

Who among the sentenced offenders now in prison or jail need not be there? One way to get at this question is to define the criteria that justify incarceration and then to ask how many in prison and jail do not meet those criteria.

Some years ago, one of us argued in *The Future of Imprisonment* that prison is an appropriate punishment only when one or more of the following three conditions is fulfilled:

- Any lesser punishment would depreciate the seriousness of the crime or crimes committed.
- Imprisonment is necessary for deterrence, general or special.
- Other less restrictive sanctions have been frequently or recently applied to this offender.

We hope it is not stubborn persistence in error that leads us to reaffirm allegiance to those propositions. They track ideas offered by the American Law Institute's *Model Penal Code* and by the American Bar Association's *Standards for Criminal Justice*. Both of these organizations and many other commentators on sentencing have expressed a preference for parsimony in incarceration with a presumption against that punishment unless it be necessary for one or more of these three purposes: to affirm the gravity of the crime, to deter the criminal and others who are like-minded, or because other sanctions have proved insufficient.

Judged by these criteria there are many in prison and jail who need not be there, who are at a shallow end of severity of crime and have criminal records that do not trigger any one of these selecting criteria. How many is a matter of guesswork. Prison wardens differ in their estimates, but it is common to hear talk of 10 to 15 percent. And there are other straws in the wind of this assessment.

In practice, there is another reason, and an increasingly popular reason, why convicted criminals are imprisoned. The sentencing judge may be skeptical that imprisoning a given criminal is necessary to reaffirm any behavioral standards, may doubt that it will have either a general or special deterrent effect, and may doubt that imprisonment will prove any more effective, whatever its purposes, than any other punishment. But this, at least, the judge knows: an offender who is in prison will not be committing any crimes against other than the prison community. Incapacitation plays an increasing role in the sentencing decision and may in considerable part account for the present overcrowding of penal institutions.

Incapacitation is a function of risk-assessment. This becomes clear when "caps" are put on prison populations or on jail populations by court orders pursuant to Eighth Amendment suits. Those running the prisons or jails have frequently had to arrange, and have arranged, early release programs, freeing many who otherwise would be in prison or jail. Wisely they select for such release the lower-risk offenders, those who seem most likely to avoid crime, at least during the remainder of the period to which they had been sentenced. This, of course, is exactly what parole boards do, particularly when they are guided by parole prediction tables such as the "salient factor score" developed for the federal parole system. There are many now in prison who have a low likelihood of future criminality, particularly if that prediction is confined to crimes of personal violence.

In the broad, then, there are certainly prisoners who in terms of risk to society or other punitive purpose need not serve the prison terms now imposed. Within that group a number need never have been so sentenced had there existed a sufficient range of intermediate punishments to provide community protection from them.

Even more certainly, of the more than 2 million convicted offenders now sentenced to probation there are many who should be under closer supervision than ordinary probation provides and also many who by fines or by community service should make larger amends for their crimes than ordinary probation now provides. It would be misleading to suggest with any attempt at precision what that number might be, since it is in large part a function of what community-based treatment and control resources are available. But when one finds caseloads of 200 and more per probation officer in some of our cities, it is clear both that probation is often a merely token sanction providing scant community protection and that the number of probationers meriting middle-range intermediate punishment is large.

We have, in short, created a punishment system that is polarized and ill-adapted to the gradations of severity of crime and magnitude of future threat that are the grist of the mill of our criminal courts. Between overcrowded prisons and even more overcrowded probation, there is a near-vacuum of appropriate and enforced middle-range punishments which are the subject of this book. Unless and until such intermediate punishments are developed and institutionalized, there can be no comprehensive punishment system suited to the realities of crime and criminals in this country.

The Underuse of Intermediate Punishments

At last, there is an experiment with a day-fine system in this country, decades after it became entrenched in many European punishment systems. At last, federal fines have been raised to realistic levels, decades after the threats of white-collar crime and organized crime were understood. Some countries now treat the fine as their main punishment for quite serious crime; such a thought is brushed aside in the United States, a country otherwise dedicated to the power of the economic incentive. Why not, then, let the fine serve as a powerful penal disincentive rather than a mere adjunct to other punishments?

The reasons for the neglect of the fine as a weapon against other than minor crime are not clear. That the fine is an insufficiently used punishment is, however, clear beyond argument. It is seen as ineffective against the wealthy and inapplicable to the poor. Far too often, when a fine is imposed it is not collected, and this holds true in federal as well as state and local courts.

Facts to support these broad allegations of current underuse of the fine are offered in Chapter 5. All that is now affirmed is that a system of fines graduated to the severity of the crime and the capacity of the criminal to pay, if imposed and collected, is an essential part of a comprehensive punishment system. The knowledge base exists to develop and implement such a system. Widespread experimentation has taken place in this country with various methods of assessing, imposing, and collecting fines and other countries have moved toward implementing such systems.

Unlike the other intermediate punishments we shall consider, the development of an effective system of fines could be achieved cheaply, without the development of any large-scale enforcement mechanisms. This is one area of the criminal justice system to which the private sector can make a significant contribution—and to its own profit. Private financial institutions are good at collecting debts; the courts are not.

All who have studied criminal punishments in this country, be they from the bleeding-hearted left or the lantern-jawed right, lament the state of the fine. There is less unanimity concerning the underuse of the other punishments in the middle range between prison and probation, but in our view the cases are equally strong.

The community service order is analogous to the fine, clearly applicable to the indigent, for whom a fine may be inappropriate, but also suited, either alone or as an adjunct to other punishments, to many who can and should pay fines. Later we tell the story of experimentation with this punishment in this country and abroad; for the time being all that is being suggested is that one important way in which the criminal can make amends to the community he has wronged—make a contribution to it given that he has inflicted injury on it—is by his providing some form of community service that is needed and that otherwise would not be provided. In the destroyed inner-city areas there is much need for rehabilitation of otherwise unusable housing; there is unlimited work to be done to preserve our heritage of natural resources; our hospitals and all our community services stand in need of assistance—it seems obvious that there is ample opportunity here for some offenders, as part of their punishment or as their punishment, to give of their labor and skills to our benefit and possibly also to theirs.

Intermediate punishments encompass a wide diversity of community-based treatments and controls of the convicted offender, ranging from house arrest, to halfway houses, to intensive probation with conditions of treatment or control vigorously enforced and, if appropriate, backed up by the emerging technology of electronic and telephonic monitoring. It is arguable whether probation originated in the work of Mathew Davenport Hill in London or with John Augustus in Boston. Whatever the historical priority, the probation order has become the punishment of choice for a wide swath of crimes. Like prison, inadequately supplied with the resources to fulfill its mission, probation has been overwhelmed by numbers. But, this reality apart, it has come to be realized that many offenders require closer supervision than the usual probation order provides. Hence the development of these more intensive controls, combining elements of police supervision and casework assistance. Later we tell the story of their emergence and the experimentation that has been pursued. Here our submission is the modest and obvious one that for some criminals, as a punishment standing alone, for others, as part of a larger punishment package, community-based punishments stand in urgent need of further development as a necessary and integral part of a comprehensive punishment system.

The Enforcement of Intermediate Punishments

As we surveyed experimentation with intermediate punishments, one pattern emerged which may go far to explain their small role in punishment policy and practice: an enthusiastic reformer, a judge as in the origins of the community service order, or an agency as in much experimentation with intensive supervision probation, seeks and finds funds to launch an experimental program of intermediate punishments. It "works well": the early enthusiasm of a new initiative leads the sentencing court and the community in which it is established to be satisfied with its observed results. It does not have a high failure rate; it is hard to know, however, whether the failure rate would have been higher or lower if some other punishment had been imposed on the same offenders. There is always the possibility that the new initiative skimmed the least threatening offenders from the pool of convicted offenders possibly suited to this new punishment; at any event, those who launch it and those who are subject to it feel well about it. It is written up in some popular literature and often featured on local or national television, usually with excessive claims of success. Then the task of building it into the larger punishment system in the city or state where it was established begins—and usually ends. The enthusiasm of the early reformers dissipates; they move on to other pastures. The other punishment agencies, prison and probation, are not excited by this new competition for their clientele, even though they recognize their overload. Bureaucratic inertia dominates. The "reform" is allowed quietly to die.

We draw two morals from this oft repeated experience. First, the designers and administrators of new initiatives must face and overcome daunting organizational, political, financial, and bureaucratic problems if new programs are to be institutionalized and their promised benefits achieved. Second, and more important for our purposes here, the development of a comprehensive punishment system requires the dedication of appreciable resources of men and women, money and materials, to the implementation and enforcement of a range of intermediate punishments if we are to move beyond experimentation.

A parallel in the treatment of mental illness will illustrate the point we are trying to make about the punishment of crime. The deinstitutionalization movement of the sixties, allied with the development of antipsychotic drugs, was heralded as a breakthrough to more humane, less expensive community-based treatment for the mentally ill. The deinstitutionalization movement seemed to promise only good. Few doubted the desirability of alleviating the miseries of life of those confined in the crowded back wards of the huge mental institutions that existed in every state. Few doubted the wisdom and decency of moving many of the mentally ill into the community where they could work in sheltered workshops, be treated in outpatient clinics, and be housed in nurturant group homes. But the community-based treatment, the clinics and shelters and group homes, never appeared in anything like adequate numbers. The emptying was achieved, the providing denied. It is to this extent the same with intermediate punishments: they require resources for their implementation and particularly their enforcement, and not the transitory resources of soft experimental money and of support systems standing outside the established punishment agencies of the state.

It may be true that, in the long run, a punishment system making appropriate use of a range of punishments from probation through the middle range of punishments and on to imprisonment may be less expensive than one that relies excessively on prison; but that will be true, if at all, in the very long run. Community-based controls are labor intensive if they are to be effective. If the convicted offender is to be supervised effectively, with or without the assistance of electronic or similar monitoring, with or without, for example, regular drug testing, supervising officers cannot carry a large caseload. The "alternatives to imprisonment" movement sailed under false colors when it claimed immediate savings; prison budgets decline only when substantial numbers are taken out of the prison so that a prison or a wing of a prison may be closed— and that does not seem an immediate likelihood in most American jurisdictions.

And there is another aspect of reality that is not usually stressed by those who advocate this type of development of our punishment system: the intermediate punishment must be rigorously enforced, it must be "backed up" by enforcement mechanisms that take seriously indeed any breach of the conditions of the community-based sanction. This does not mean, for example, that the addict who once relapses in a treatment program must by that fact and without more be incarcerated; but it does mean that this relapse must be taken seriously and that there is a real possibility of the imposition of a prison term because of the relapse.

If a fine is imposed, adjusted to the criminal's financial circumstances and potential, and time given to pay if necessary, it is of the first importance that an effective and determined enforcement machinery be in place. It seems unnecessary to make such a point, but the record of failure to collect fines in the federal system, and similar experience in state and local fining practice, compel such a stressing of the obvious.

Here too the law must keep its promises. The promise of intermediate punishments demands for its fulfillment resources adequate to their support and sufficient for their determined enforcement.

Sentencing to Intermediate Punishments

Concerns for justice and fairness in sentencing will lead, in time, probably within 25 years, to the creation in most American states of comprehensive systems of structured sentencing discretion that encompass a continuum of punishments from probation to imprisonment, with many intermediate punishments ranged between. These systems may take the form of the sentencing guidelines now in place in Minnesota, Washington, and elsewhere, or they may take some other form, but they will all provide for interchangeability of punishments for like-situated offenders. They will establish ranges of interchangeable punishments, bounded by considerations of desert, that are presumed to be applicable to the cases governed by each range, subject to the right of the judge to impose some other sentence if he provides written reasons for so doing; the adequacy and appropriateness of those reasons will be subject to review by appellate courts that will consult a body of case law, a common law of sentencing, for guidance.

These predictions may seem millenarian, but they are the foreseeable extension of developments and practices that are already in place. Anyone who in 1970 predicted the radical changes in American sentencing practices that have taken place since that date would have seemed even more romantic than we do now. The developments that underlay the past two decades of evolution in American sentencing practices will continue to shape reform for decades to come in the directions that we have identified. To explain why this is so, in the next few pages we describe indeterminate sentencing as it ubiquitously stood in this country in 1970, summarize the developments that led to its rejection, and briefly identify the innovations that have displaced or modified it since 1970.

In 1970 the indeterminate sentencing systems in the United States, federal and state, had continued virtually unchanged from at least 1930 and looked much the same everywhere. Premised at least in theory on commitment to the values of individualized sentencing and rehabilitative correctional programs, indeterminate sentencing systems gave officials wide-ranging discretion and freedom from external controls over their decisions. Criminal statutes and common law doctrines defined the elements of crimes. Statutes established maximum terms of probation and imprisonment, and maximum amounts of fines, that could be imposed. Occasionally, but rarely, the statutes established mandatory minimum prison terms for persons convicted of particular crimes. Prosecutors had complete control over charging and plea bargaining. Judges had little-fettered discretion to "individualize punishment" in deciding who received probation and who was sentenced to jail or prison, and, for those to be confined, to set minimum or maximum terms, and sometimes both. Parole boards, subject only to statutory provisions on parole eligibility, generally when a third of the maximum term had been served, decided who was released from prison prior to the expiration of their terms, when, and under what conditions.

None of these decisions—charging and plea bargaining, sentencing, paroling—was governed by legal or administrative decision rules and only rarely did these decisions raise issues cognizable in the appellate courts. Well-established doctrines based on notions of separation of powers and deference to administrative expertise led appellate courts to refuse to review prosecutorial and parole decisions on the substantive merits. Equivalent notions of comity between judges and deference to the better information of the trial judge caused appellate courts to accord extreme deference to the discretionary sentencing decisions of the trial judge.

When courts did consider appeals from parole and prosecutorial decisions, which was uncommon before 1970, the cases generally involved procedural issues. When appellate courts considered sentence appeals in the few states where such appeals were allowed, few sentences were overturned and they tended to be such gross departures from standard practice that the appeals courts felt comfortable concluding that they constituted an "abuse of discretion" or that they "offended the conscience."

In effect, prosecutors, judges, and parole boards were accountable for their decisions in individual cases only to their political constituencies and their consciences. Few would have guessed in 1970 that nearly every facet of indeterminate sentencing in theory and in practice would be decisively repudiated within a decade.

The developments that undermined indeterminate sentencing seem likely to continue to shape sentencing reform for decades to come. There were at least seven major themes.

First, as Kenneth Culp Davis, one of America's leading administrative lawyers, noted in his 1969 book *Discretionary Justice,* the criminal justice system was unique in its failure to hold public officials accountable for decisions affecting individual liberty or property. Much more demanding constitutional safeguards then attended the repossession of a refrigerator than applied to the filing of criminal charges or the denial of release on parole. Davis proposed that prosecution and parole offices establish rules and policies governing their decisions in individual cases and then establish administrative systems and management controls to assure that those rules and policies were fairly and consistently applied.

Second, as a Working Party of the American Friends Service Committee observed in 1971 in *Struggle for Justice,* its report on prison conditions, the vast and unregulated discretions of the criminal justice system often produced decisions that were inconsistent or arbitrary, and too often produced decisions that appeared to be and frequently were racially biased. The proposition that too great unguided discretion frequently operated to the disadvantage of members of minority groups was put forward by many critics of sentencing and corrections. The Working Party's proposals for reform included calls for the abolition of parole and reduction in the scope of the discretions granted to public officials.

Third, numerous empirical research reports demonstrated beyond peradventure of doubt the existence of substantial unwarranted disparities in the sentences imposed by judges and the release dates set by parole boards. Sentencing disparities were by no means a new discovery in the seventies—during the 1950s, the director of the U.S. Bureau of Prisons, James V. Bennett, regularly testified before Congress about the existence of disparate sentences in the federal prisons—but in the context of other seventies developments, they received renewed attention.

Fourth, catalyzed by the success of *pro se* prisoner plaintiffs and prisoners' rights lawyers in persuading federal judges to abandon the "hands-off doctrine" of nonintervention in matters of prison management, throughout the criminal justice system judges became less deferential to the expertise of administrators and more aggressive in demanding decent and constitutionally adequate treatment of convicted offenders. The longstanding notion that the criminal justice system and its constituent parts were worlds unto themselves lost support. Numerous traditional practices could not withstand the scrutiny of impartial outside eyes and countless administrators, and some judges, began to look for ways to make criminal justice practices and processes more consonant with concern for justice and fairness.

Fifth, related to several of the preceding points, there was a heightened appreciation throughout the legal system of the value of procedural safeguards. Although appellate courts continued to defer to the substantive decisions of judges and parole boards, they began to insist on increased observance of procedural rules— notice of charges and of the evidence on which they rest, opportunities to confront accusers and to question adverse witnesses, requirements that reasons be given for decisions and that opportunity be available to seek review of challenged decisions.

Sixth, unregulated sentencing discretion came under attack from many quarters and for many reasons. Political attacks from the right focused on alleged lenient sentencing by softhearted judges; political attacks from the left focused on racial and class bias and arbitrariness. The most influential and powerful critique came from Marvin Frankel, then a U.S. district court judge, in his 1972 book *Criminal Sentences: Law Without Order.* Judge Frankel argued that sentencing decisions were unique among the important decisions made by judges in that they were "lawless." Every other important decision that trial judges make, Judge Frankel argued, is governed by rules of law and is subject to review as to its correctness in law and in fact. When announcing most decisions, judges describe the rule on which the decision is based and the supporting findings of fact; sometimes a judge decides that the seemingly applicable rule is wrong, or should be changed, or that an exception to its reach should be recognized, and explains why. The adequacy and persuasiveness of those explanations can be appealed to a higher court. Thus, said Judge Frankel, trial judges are accountable to rules and higher judicial authority for all of their decisions except those that affect the liberty and property of persons convicted of crimes.

Seventh, the rehabilitative rationales of indeterminate sentencing, its theoretical and empirical justifications, were undermined. The most devastating empirical attack—the claim that we lack any good reason to believe that rehabilitative correctional programs do rehabilitate offenders—was offered by writers of reviews of research on the effectiveness of treatment programs. The best known of these was Robert L. Martinson's article in the *Public Interest* called "What Works?—Questions and Answers About Prison Reform"; Martinson concluded that it cannot be demonstrated that correctional treatment programs rehabilitate offenders as measured by their subsequent recidivism rates. On the completion of comparable reviews of the state of knowledge, other scholars, including the Panel on Rehabilitative Techniques of the National Academy of Sciences and S. R. Brody, for the British Home Office, reached comparable conclusions.

The theoretical attacks were most influentially advanced by Francis Allen in his 1964 book, *The Borderland of Criminal Justice,* and in 1974 by Norval Morris in *The Future of Imprisonment.* Their arguments had two major elements. First, from an ethical perspective, it is simply wrong to take or extend the state's criminal law powers over individuals for, ostensibly, their own good, especially in light of pessimistic findings on the correctional systems' abilities to rehabilitate offenders. Second, from a psychological perspective, it defies common experience to imagine that coerced participation in treatment programs will often facilitate personal growth and change. Generally, self-improvement is voluntary; coupling participation in treatment programs with a likelihood of earlier release motivated prisoners to participate, but often it did not motivate them to change.

Taken together, these critiques greatly undermined indeterminate sentencing and the practices and institutions that went with it. It is not easy to defend a major set of social institutions that are portrayed as based on unsound empirical, ethical, and psychological premises, as characterized by racial and class bias, by arbitrariness, by lawlessness, and by unfairness, and as conspicuously ineffective at achieving the larger social purposes of reducing crime and rehabilitating offenders—and few tried.

Hence American sentencing institutions and practices underwent more extensive and more radical changes between 1975 and 1985 than in any other decade in our history. Most of the changes attempted to structure or eliminate the discretionary decisions exercised by public officials. Although new initiatives affecting decision making by judges and prosecutors were not uncommon, it was the parole boards, the institutions that in theory based their decisions on rehabilitative predictions and assessments, that experienced the most drastic changes.

In 1975 Maine abandoned parole release and established the first determinate sentencing system in which the prisoner's release date could be calculated on the day of sentencing, assuming he was well-behaved in prison and received the standard amount of time off for good behavior. At least 12 other states later abandoned parole release in favor of determinate sentencing. In 1973 the U.S. Parole Board adopted a system of parole guidelines to structure its own decision making and established an administrative law system within the parole board so that prisoners could challenge adverse decisions. At least 20 states subsequently established parole guidelines.

Extensive efforts were also made to structure the sentencing decisions of judges. Forty-nine states adopted mandatory sentencing laws for selected offenses. Many states enacted statutory determinate sentencing laws in which the criminal code itself establishes a sentence or range of sentences to guide the trial judge's decisions in most cases. In nearly every state, efforts were made to develop voluntary guidelines for sentencing. A number of states, most notably Minnesota and Washington, and the federal government established sentencing commissions and directed them to establish presumptive guidelines for sentencing; these guidelines are called "presumptive" because the sentences that they specify are presumed to be appropriate for the cases to which they apply and offenders may appeal to a higher court for review of the reasons given by judges to justify the imposition of any other sentence. We explain later why this approach to sentencing reform has most completely achieved its objectives of all the new initiatives and why sentencing commissions and sentencing guidelines are the most promising approach to continued improvement of American sentencing practice.

Prosecutors were not immune from reform efforts that derived from the same influences that underlay parole and sentencing changes. In 1976 the attorney general of Alaska "abolished" plea bargaining in that state, as did a number of county prosecutors, including Michael Bradbury of Ventura County, California. Most well-run urban proescutors' offices—for example, those in King County (Seattle), Washington, and in Hennepin County (Minneapolis), Minnesota—established internal guidelines on charging, plea negotiation, and dismissal policies and established management systems to assure that they were followed except when supervisory officials approved case-by-case exceptions.

The state of Washington, for many years an exemplar of indeterminate sentencing, has adopted the most extensive set of sentencing innovations of any American jurisdiction. Until the mid-1970s, offenders sentenced to prison in Washington received a sentence of "one year to the statutory maximum"; the judge had no influence over the maximum sentence; the parole board, guided by its assessment of each prisoner's rehabilitative progress, set release dates on a case-by-case basis. Today, by contrast, parole release has been eliminated and sentencing is guided by a detailed and comprehensive set of sentencing guidelines established by a sentencing commission. The sentencing commission, carrying out a statutory mandate, promulgated standards for prosecutors for filing of criminal charges, for plea negotiation, and for dismissal of charges. (Unfortunately, for political reasons the prosecutorial standards were made recommendations rather than obligations, and probably don't offer real constraints on prosecutors' behavior.) In addition, most county prosecutors' offices have their own plea bargaining guidelines; the guidelines in Seattle have been in place since 1975. From being the state that most fully implemented indeterminate sentencing, Washington has become the state that has most fully repudiated it.

Many of the sentencing innovations since the midseventies have not achieved their proponents' aims. Mandatory sentencing laws, for example, had at best a modest short-term deterrent effect on the crimes they affect and usually produced very little change in sentencing practices. For serious crimes, the one- or two-year minimum sentence usually prescribed was generally less than would normally be imposed even without a mandatory sentencing law. For less serious offenses and offenders, lawyers and judges could usually devise a method for circumventing the mandatory sentence when its imposition seemed to them unduly harsh.

Voluntary guidelines for sentencing fared little better. Voluntary guidelines were voluntary in two senses; their development by judges was self-initiated and not in furtherance of a statutory directive, and whether and to what extent judges followed them was entirely in the hands of each individual judge. In most jurisdictions, voluntary guidelines seem to have had little effect on sentencing. Although courts in more than 40 states established voluntary guidelines between 1975 and 1980, in most places they were soon abandoned or soon became dead letters.

Statutory determinate sentencing laws did somewhat better and in some states, notably North Carolina and California, they seem to have reduced sentencing disparities and made sentencing somewhat more predictable. In other states, however, like Illinois and Indiana, the new laws offered no meaningful constraints on judicial discretion and proved to be no improvement on the indeterminate sentencing systems they replaced.

Parole guidelines in some jurisdictions, such as Minnesota and the federal system, accomplished much of what their creators had in mind. Consistently applied, they made release dates more predictable and served to even out disparities in the lengths of prison sentences meted out by judges. Their major shortcoming from a reform perspective was that they affect only those offenders who are sent to prison and accordingly have no effect whatever on the question of who is sentenced to prison or on what happens to those who are not imprisoned.

The sentencing reform initiative of the future is the combination of the sentencing commission and presumptive sentencing guidelines that Judge Frankel first proposed in 1972 as a solution to the lawlessness that he decried, that Minnesota first implemented in 1980, and that other jurisdictions have elaborated as the years have passed. Presumptive sentencing guidelines establish presumptions that govern judges' decisions whether to imprison an offender and, if so, for how long. The judge may conclude that special circumstances justify some other sentence or, in other words, that the presumption should be rejected. If so, the judge must explain his reasoning and its adequacy is subject to review by appeal of sentence to a higher court. Careful evaluations of the experience in Minnesota and later Washington showed that presumptive sentencing guidelines could reduce sentencing disparities, reduce differences in sentencing patterns associated with race, increase consistency in sentencing statewide, and make sentencing much more predictable, so that state sentencing policies could be related in a meaningful way to the availability of prison beds and other correctional resources.

Presumptive sentencing guidelines appear to be a way to address most of the major critiques of indeterminate sentencing. They reduce disparities and the potential for decisions based on invidious considerations of race and class. They provide decision rules to guide the sentencing choices judges make. Judges are made accountable because they must comply with the guidelines' presumptions or give reasons for doing something else. Sentence appeals become meaningful because appellate judges have some basis for assessing the correctness of the trial judge's decisions and the reasons that are invoked to justify them.

The wisdom of Judge Frankel's proposal, and the core of the sentencing commission idea, was its combination of the sentencing commission, sentencing guidelines, and appellate sentence review.

All three elements were crucial. The creation of an administrative agency responsible for formulation of sentencing policy provided an institution much better situated than any legislature to accumulate specialized expertise to develop comprehensive sentencing policies and sufficiently removed from the glare of day-to-day legislative politics to approach these often controversial matters in a principled and thoughtful way. The resulting sentencing guidelines for the first time provided an instrument for the expression of finely tuned standards for exercise of the punitive powers of the state, and their presumptive character required that judges give reasons for their decisions to depart from the guidelines' presumptions. Those reasons, in turn, for the first time in this country provided the material for development of principled appellate review of sentences.

Not all sentencing commissions have been successful; some failed dismally. Nor were the commissions in Minnesota and Washington successful in everything they set out to do. Both, for example, failed to establish controls on plea bargaining, which in a system of regulated and predictable sentencing can be used to manipulate sentencing, and neither of them made serious efforts to establish guidelines for the use of nonincarcerative punishments.

Our aim in this book is to demonstrate how the lessons learned to date can guide this country to the creation of comprehensive systems of punishment that are principled and practical, that can be applied with fairness and with justice to all the offenders who come before the court for sentencing. The sentencing commission, coupled with presumptive sentencing guidelines and appellate sentence review, provides the mechanism, and the need is to develop ways to extend that mechanism to encompass all crimes, all criminals, and all punishments.

A comprehensive sentencing system must provide guidance to judges in choosing among all available sentencing options, including probation, prison, and all the intermediate punishments that fall between them in severity and intrusiveness. We will set out the elements of a comprehensive sentencing system later. There is, however, one threshold that must be crossed before such a system becomes a viable possibility—the prison or probation, something or nothing, simplicities of too much present thought must be rejected. Even the sentencing guidelines systems of Minnesota and

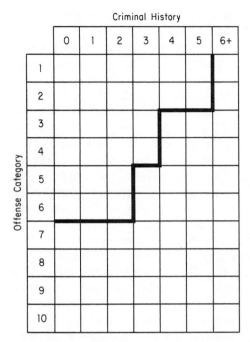

Figure 1. Simplified sentencing guidelines grid.

Washington, which we greatly admire, make this mistake. Figure 1 sets out a simplified version of the sentencing grid of the Minnesota sentencing guidelines system. Across the top of the grid are arrayed six categories of offenders' criminal histories; along the side are ten categories of offenses ranked in terms of their severity. To find the presumptive sentencing range for any offender, a judge would look to the cell of the grid in which the applicable offense severity row intersects with the applicable criminal history column. A jagged black line crosses the Minnesota grid. Below that line are the cells in which a term of state imprisonment is the presumptive sentence. Above the black line are cells in which state imprisonment is not the presumptive sentence: the judge may impose any other sentence, including probation, community service, restitution, a fine, and up to 12 months in a local jail.

The jagged black line across the Minnesota sentencing guidelines grid is an error. It exaggerates the divide that separates imprisonment from all other punishments. Under the guidelines, an offender whose circumstances place him in a cell just above the line is an "out." An offender whose circumstances place him in a cell just below the line is an "in." In reality, those clear bright lines cannot be drawn. It is precisely those cases that would fall near the "in/out" line that present the greatest punitive ambiguity. These are the cases where reasonable judges are likeliest to differ in their views of what is appropriate. These are the cases in which factors and governing penal purposes peculiar to the individual case are likeliest to tip the balance in favor of one punishment or another.

If that black line were erased, and various interchangeable punishments were made presumptively appropriate for the cases falling within each cell, the punishment system, like criminal offenses, could be seen as a continuum ranging from the least to the most severe. We believe that such guidelines systems will soon be established and that they will become as prevalent in American jurisdictions in the twenty-first century as was indeterminate sentencing in the twentieth century. In such systems, punishments will be made proportionate in punitiveness and intrusiveness to the severity of the offenders' crimes, disparity and discrimination in sentencing will be greatly reduced, judges will be made fully accountable for the sentences they impose, and the rule of law will at last be made fully applicable to the criminal courts.

In later chapters we describe the components of a comprehensive sentencing system. Here we simply set them out:

1. The principle of interchangeability of punishments must be recognized.
2. The "in/out" line must be erased to eliminate the false dichotomous prison-or-nothing simplicities.
3. In place of a two-part in-or-out sentencing grid, there should be at least four graded categories of punishment presumptions: "out," "out unless . . . ," "in unless . . . ," and "in."
4. Within the governing purposes *of* sentencing established by policymakers, the guidelines should permit the judge to look to the applicable purposes of punishment to be served *at* sentencing in choosing among the available interchangeable punishments.
5. The principle of interchangeability should be recognized for all

crimes for which the presumptive prison sentence (for those cases where the applicable purposes at sentencing will best be served by incarceration) is two years or less.

6. The system should provide guidance for all sentencing decisions for all felonies and misdemeanors.

7. The choice among interchangeable punishments is for the judge to make, not the offender.

The preceding list does not address all of the issues our proposals raise. For example, it does not explain how the exchange rates between different punishments are to be determined or calculated, or how judges are to know what the governing purposes are *at* sentencing. We discuss such problems later. We believe, however, that they are simpler than at first appears and that their apparent difficulty results mainly from their novelty.

Our mission in this book is to explain how in principle and in practice a comprehensive sentencing system, which incorporates a rich variety of intermediate punishments linked to one another and to probation and prison by a principle of interchangeability, can be established and implemented. Before we turn to that fuller explication and justification, a critical issue of justice as fairness must be mentioned and its implications noted.

Fitting intermediate punishments into a principled sentencing system has proved to be the Achilles heel of both sentencing reform proposals and practice. The central reason for this is (somewhat unexpectedly given the general human capacity to tolerate the sufferings of others with a degree of equanimity) a sense of unfairness when it is suggested that two equally undeserving criminals should be treated differently—since differently here means that one will be treated more leniently than the other.

The conceptual keystone of the argument in this book, its central thesis, is that a developed punishment theory requires recognition that precise equivalency of punishment between equally undeserving criminals in the distribution of punishments is in practice unattainable and is in theory undesirable. We argue that all that can be achieved is a rough equivalence of punishment that will allow room for the principled distribution of punishments on utilitarian grounds, unfettered by the miserable aim of making suffering equally painful. For the time being we ask you to take this on trust—the thesis is fully developed in Chapters 3 and 4—and turn to some of the consequences of this argument.

The first consequence is that it now becomes possible to move appreciable numbers who otherwise would be sentenced to prison into community-based intermediate punishments, having a roughly equivalent punitive bite but serving both the community and the criminal better than the prison term. It also becomes possible to move appreciable numbers who otherwise would be sentenced to token probationary supervision into intermediate punishments that exercise larger controls over them and provide us with larger social protection from their criminality. The advantages are obvious; it is a liberating idea—but it has its problems, theoretical and practical.

First, the theoretical problem. If appropriate guidance is to be given the sentencing judge under such a system of punishment, some "exchange rates" between punishments to achieve this rough equivalence must be stated in advance. There exist a few fledgling efforts to state these exchange rates; we believe that a principled system of punishment can be defined in which rough equivalence of punitive bite and identity of process in relation to stated purposes of punishment provide the necessary guidance to the judge and also give both the appearance and the reality of fairness to the community and to the convicted offender.

Among the practical problems that accompany such a purposive introduction of intermediate punishments into the body of a punishment system, none is more troublesome than its impact on existing class and race biases.

At present black adult males per hundred thousand are more than seven times as likely to be in prison as white adult males. The reasons for this are deeply rooted in history, social structure, and social attitudes; but it also seems clear that the criminal justice systems of this country—federal, state, and local—make some contribution to this sad result. Are we really proposing the introduction of a punishment system that by its expansion of intermediate punishments will make this racial skewing worse? At first blush it would appear so.

Take two addict-criminals convicted of selling relatively small amounts of cocaine on a number of separate occasions. Each has once before been convicted of illegal possession of marijuana.

Each is aged 20. Criminal A is in college, the son of a loving and supportive middle-class family, living in a district where space is available in drug treatment programs. Criminal B has never met his putative father, lives in a high-rise apartment in a slum area with his mother and his two much younger siblings, welfare being their major financial support. The waiting list at the available drug treatment center is long, the waiting time three months.

You know the pigmentation of the two hypothetical but far from unreal criminals.

Are we really suggesting that Criminal B serve a jail or prison term with the hope that thereafter he can be fitted into a drug treatment program, while Criminal A should pay a substantial fine, be under intensive probationary supervision with a condition of regular attendance at a drug treatment program where he is tested regularly to ensure that he is drug-free, and be subjected possibly to house arrest in the evenings and weekends—electronically monitored if that be necessary? This will, of course, be the likely result. Is it unprincipled? We think not.

The criminal justice system lacks both resources and capacity to take on the task of rectification of social inequalities of race or class. It will do well if it does not exacerbate them. To insist that Criminal A go to jail or prison because resources are lacking to deal sensibly with Criminal B is to pay excessive tribute to an illusory ideal of equality. That is not the way equality of opportunity and equality of punitive pain is to be achieved; it is to be achieved by efforts to provide within the criminal justice system for Criminal B what exists for Criminal A, and to intercede by means other than the criminal justice system to eradicate the inequalities that generate the present discrimination.

The comprehensive punishment system we propose will, we believe, in the longer run reduce the impact of race and class on sentencing practice. The more clearly the exchange rates between punishments and the purposes each is to serve can be articulated in advance, the more possible it will be to reduce race and class biases in the selection of sanctions. Strong racial and class prejudices, conscious and less perceived, already drive sentencing practice; the substitution of purposive principles framed independently of race and class but necessarily having race and class correlates will make matters better, not worse.

PART I

Just and principled sentencing is the foundation of a fair and effective punishment system. Hence we give priority of consideration to the question, neglected in the existing literature, of the part that intermediate punishments should play in a comprehensive system of criminal sanctions.

Since H. L. A. Hart's 1959 lecture to the Aristotelian Society, "Prolegomenon to the Philosophy of Punishment," there has been widespread agreement that neither a retributivist, or a "just deserts," scheme of sentencing, as it is usually advanced, nor a purely utilitarian philosophy, aiming unambiguously at crime reduction, can alone shape an acceptable philosophy of punishment. Sentencing purposes are inexorably mixed, combining concepts of desert and of crime prevention. Where intermediate punishments should fit in such a scheme has, as we say, been neglected, their role too often being phrased in terms of more lenient and less costly alternatives to other more severe punishments. This is, to us, a fundamental mistake.

In Part I, therefore, we discuss the relationship between intermediate and other punishments in terms of their interchangeability at the sentencing stage and the jurisprudential issues of justice and community protection that such interchangeability raises.

Put in its sharpest form, the question is this: given two

35

equally undeserving criminals convicted of equally severe crimes and with equal criminal records, is it proper, is it just, is it wise social policy that one should serve a prison term and the other an intermediate punishment? We offer an answer in the affirmative and seek to defend that response in practice and in theory. If we are right, intermediate punishments can be released to play a major role in American sentencing practice.

3

Interchangeability of Punishments in Practice

These are the best of times and the worst of times for intermediate punishments. Prison crowding and fiscal concerns have forced attention on the development of punishments that do not require provision of more prison beds. Across the country, many jurisdictions are responding by creating sentencing programs aimed at preventing or reducing crowding by keeping newly convicted criminals out and by releasing previously sentenced prisoners. From the perspective of institution-building, narrowly conceived, these are good times for intermediate punishments. They are bad times, though, because the crowding impetus gives only a negative reason for new programs—to avoid prison crowding and the resulting court orders—rather than positive reasons; programs aimed at avoiding something are less likely to endure than are programs aimed at achieving something. We wish to make our case for a substantial expansion of intermediate punishments independent of the fact that our prisons have become crowded beyond capacity of control. Quite apart from the availability of cells, far too many criminals are sentenced to prison and to jail as punishments—too many felons and too many misdemeanants.

A just and efficient sentencing system should include a range of punishments and not merely a choice between imprisonment and probation. A variety of intermediate punishments, along with appropriate treatment conditions, should be part of a comprehensive, integrated system of sentencing and punishment. Much has been learned over the last decade of innovation with intermediate punishments. Knowledge exists about the implementation of such programs and about methods for establishing their integrity and punitive credibility in the eyes of judges and the public. Although these developments are heartening, they can be but part of the story since the intellectually challenging task remains of blending them into a principled system of punishments. The task is to devise a system of sentencing guidelines that can structure sentencing discretion and regularize the use of intermediate punishments within a comprehensive system of punishment.

We take it as given that the current movement toward development and implementation of systems of presumptive sentencing guidelines will continue. Most thoughtful practitioners, including most judges, and most scholars now accept that indeterminate sentencing as was implemented in this country throughout most of this century resulted in unacceptable, unwarranted sentencing disparities—in appearance and in fact. The broad and unguided discretions indeterminate sentencing afforded judges and parole boards also created unacceptable risks that decisions would be influenced by invidious considerations like race, class, or cultural stereotypes. Judge Marvin Frankel's then novel proposition in 1972 that the rule of law should govern sentencing decisions—which after all involve the ultimate conflicts between state powers and human liberty and autonomy—is now widely accepted. This means at minimum that in sentencing, as in any other kind of judicial decision making, there must be standards that govern judges' decisions, reasons for disregarding these standards must be given, and the adequacy of these reasons must be subject to review by appellate judges.

Presumptive sentencing guidelines have been shown to be an effective way to establish standards, to reduce sentencing disparities, to assure judicial accountability, and to provide a basis for appellate sentence review. The Minnesota sentencing guidelines commission showed the way and at least 15 states have created sentencing commissions, as has the federal government. Although some of these commissions have failed and others have been but partially successful, still others have succeeded. Two or three states create sentencing commissions each year.

Outside the United States, recommendations for establishment of sentencing commissions were made in Canada in 1987 by the Canadian Sentencing Commission and in Australia in 1980 by the Australian Law Reform Commission. The subject has been widely discussed in England, as is demonstrated by a recent book, *Sentencing Reform: Guidance or Guidelines,* edited by Ken Pease and Martin Wasik.

To date, however, even the best sentencing guidelines do no more than set standards governing the decisions whom to imprison and, for the prison-bound, for how long. For nonimprisonment decisions, with minor partial exceptions, the unguided judicial discretions of indeterminate sentencing survive.

Until recently, policymakers have shied from efforts to structure discretion over nonimprisonment sentencing decisions because of the complexity of the practical, conceptual, and implementation issues that are raised. We believe the tools now exist for addressing these issues.

Americans tend to equate criminal punishment with prison. To the public, to the public official, even to the judge, sentencing is often seen as a choice between prison and nearly nothing. Researchers build mathematical models of the correlates of decisions to imprison and of variations in lengths of imprisonment, but not of variations in the imposition of sanctions other than prison. Scholars have at times developed numerical scales of punishment that treat anything other than prison as "zero" and assign positive value only to increments of imprisonment.

Why sentences other than imprisonment have received so little sustained attention is a complex question.

Partly the answer lies in the rehabilitative rationales of indeterminate sentencing and the associated notion that nonprison sentences, probation especially, must be tailored by a thoughtful judge and a compassionate probation officer to the individualized needs of each offender; though to the public and the press probation is often seen as a "letting off," which, when one considers the sizes of probation caseloads in our metropolitan courts, it often is.

Partly the answer lies in the political and institutional fragmentation of most states' criminal justice systems: the mixture of state, county, and local institutions; of elected and appointed officials; of varying traditions governing the distribution of responsibility for various programs among judges, sheriffs, county boards, and prosecutors; of diverse patterns of public funding. Prison is a state-financed function. Probation and community-based sanctions tend to be funded by local court systems and local communities.

Partly the answer also lies in the absence in this country of a jurisprudence of sentencing or of a tradition of thinking about sentencing generally, from a comprehensive system-wide perspective, rather than specifically, as a series of individual decisions. Concern for fairness and justice requires that both the general and the specific dimensions of sentencing be addressed. Fairness requires that general standards apply to all offenders; justice requires that decisions concerning each offender be made in light of general punitive purposes as they interact with each offender's individual circumstances.

So far, much prevailing thought and practice concerning the relations between imprisonment and other punishments have been constrained by prison-or-nothing simplicities, and most scholarly analysis of the exercise of sentencing discretion and of disparities in the exercise of that discretion has confined itself to two issues: disparities between those who are and those who are not sentenced to prison, and disparities in the lengths of prison terms imposed. Comprehensive analysis, however, requires recognition of the need for a continuum of punishments and for the principled exercise of discretion in sentencing which covers that entire range of punishments.

A continuum of punishments should range from warnings and restitution through a diversity of community-based punishments, including probation and intensive probation, fines and community service orders, and a variety of restrictions and obligations in the community, the range of punishments then moving on to jail and prison terms, the whole to be adjusted to sentencing purposes and the particular conditions of the offender—the threat he presents, the needs he has to minimize that threat. Under such a system, some offenders with similarly severe crimes and similar criminal records will receive one punishment while others receive another. Sometimes this will involve the incarceration of some and community-based punishments for others. This is not only current practice; it is also hard to conceive of a system of guided discretion in which this result did not obtain. At present we leave this choice, relatively unguided, to the individual discretion of the sentencing judge in each particular case. It would be illusory to expect even-handed dispositions from the current system. All the pressures and principles that have produced guidelines for the in/out decision and for the decision as to the duration of the prison term (whether parole or sentencing guidelines) apply with at least equal force to the wise selection of intermediate punishments.

There can be no rational or workable hierarchy of punishments in which incarcerative and intermediate punishments do not over-lap—there must be interchangeability of punishments within this overlap. Important jurisprudential issues are raised by the notion of interchangeability (how interchangeability between imprisonment and other punishments is to be justified, how the limits of interchangeability are to be set, whether rough equivalence be-tween punishments is to be measured in suffering, intrusion on autonomy, or function); to these issues we turn in the next chapter. For purposes of this chapter, we assume, as we believe, and we ask you at least for the time being to assume that interchange-ability between incarcerative and intermediate punishments can be made part of a just system of sentencing.

In sentencing there is an inexorable tension between general and specific considerations. Concern for fairness and even-handed-ness and respect for the values of equality and proportionality urge that there be general standards governing all sentences imposed, and that punishments be meaningfully commensurate with the nature and severity of the offender's behavior, and be proportion-ately severe for offenses of significantly different gravity. Much of the impetus for presumptive sentencing guidelines and statutory determinate sentencing came from these general concerns to reduce unwarranted disparities and to eliminate sentencing that is idio-syncratic or capricious.

At the same time, much of the opposition to these initiatives came, and still comes, as a 1988 *Harvard Law Review* article by

Charles Ogletree demonstrates, from people who fear that structured sentencing discretion would prove to be too rigid and mechanistic to take account of significant differences between offenders. Mandatory sentencing laws, for example, are often circumvented because judges and lawyers believe that their observance would result in unjustly severe punishments in many cases.

Any system of rules or guidelines requires that people or phenomena be classified into groups. Although in the abstract this is easy to understand, it creates for most of us a sense of unease. The notions of human freedom, autonomy, and individuality are precious to us. As William James noted of efforts at classification in his 1902 book, *The Varieties of Religious Experience:*

> The first thing the intellect does with an object is to class it along with something else. But any object that is infinitely important to us and awakens our devotion feels to us also as if it must be *sui generis* and unique. Probably a crab would be filled with a sense of personal outrage if it could hear us class it without ado or apology as a crustacean, and thus dispose of it. "I am no such thing," it would say; "I am MYSELF, MYSELF alone."

A comprehensive sentencing system must harness the tension between the requirement of fairness that there be general standards that apply to all and the requirement of justice that all legitimate grounds for distinguishing between individuals be taken into account when decisions about individuals are made.

In this chapter, we summarize the antecedents and course of modern efforts to establish comprehensive systems of sentencing, describe the gradual evolution of efforts to include nonprison punishments within systems of structured sentencing discretion, and set out our proposal for incorporating intermediate punishments within a comprehensive system of sentencing standards.

Sentencing Reform: 1969–1989

Sentencing institutions, philosophies, and practices in the United States have changed radically since 1970. Perhaps ironically, however, most of the charges that were laid against American sentencing during these years continue to apply with unabated force to sentences other than to imprisonment. The influential critique that Judge Marvin Frankel offered in 1972 of sentencing generally—gross unwarranted disparities, "lawlessness" in the sense that no standards govern decisions, lack of judicial accountability—currently applies to nonprison punishments in nearly every jurisdiction. Even in those states that have established finely tuned sentencing guidelines or statutory sentencing criteria, the standards apply mainly to decisions about imprisonment. Judicial discretion over sentences other than imprisonment remains unfettered.

For a variety of reasons that we develop elsewhere in this book, we believe that intermediate punishments should be, and will be, developed much more extensively than ever before in this country. Their use, we believe, should be guided by established, published standards, and judges should be accountable for the decisions they make. In other words, the modern efforts to bring consistency, justice, and fairness to sentencing should now be broadened in focus to encompass nonprison sentences.

Until recently, American jurisdictions did not establish jurisdiction-wide standards for sentencing. Since the midseventies, however, new initiatives have moved toward creation of such systems and have now reached a stage at which it is both wise and necessary to develop meaningful standards for nonprison sentences. In the Sentencing Reform Act of 1984, for example, the U.S. Sentencing Commission was charged to do exactly that when the Congress directed it to develop guidelines governing the imposition and amounts of fines and the imposition, duration, and conditions of probation.

Had the U.S. Sentencing Commission begun work 20 years earlier, it would have had little experience on which to draw in this country or abroad. Although base expectancy tables for parole failure were first developed in the 1920s, they were seldom used. Parole and sentencing guidelines were as yet unheard of. Structured plea bargaining was an innovation even further away in time. The abolition of parole was, to most, unthinkable.

Between the late sixties and today, however, much has changed. It may help lay a foundation for what follows if we devote a few paragraphs to describing how the legal environment had changed by the time the U.S. Sentencing Commission set to work. Like most stories having to do with the modern criminal law, this one

begins with publication in 1962 of the American Law Institute's
Model Penal Code.

The *Model Penal Code* marked a turning point not only in the
substantive criminal law in this country but also in the movement
toward fairer and more predictable punishment. Substantively, it
has brought principled, coherent, and reasonably comprehensive
criminal codes to many states, though regrettably not yet to the
federal system; the history of its impact on sentencing is less clear.

Paul Tappan and Herbert Wechsler, the main architects of the
Model Penal Code's sentencing provisions, accepted the broad
pattern of indeterminate sentencing that had prevailed in this
country throughout the twentieth century. The trial judge determined whether the convicted offender should be imprisoned, and
in most cases the maximum of that imprisonment, and left the
determination of the term actually to be served to the parole
board, which was to be guided in fixing the release date by the
prisoner's behavior in prison and likely later avoidance of crime.

Though accepting the broad sweep of this allocation of sentencing powers, the *Code* sought in Section 305.9 to establish a
presumption favoring the prisoner's release at the initial parole
eligibility date, to bring some order to the "in/out" decision, and
to reduce the categories of felonies and misdemeanors to five and
three respectively and attach maximum terms to each. There was
provision, however, for extended terms for certain categories of
particularly confirmed or threatening offenders, as well as special
provisions for youthful offenders.

As to the choice between imprisonment and other punishments,
the *Model Penal Code* in Section 7.01(1) articulated a strong
preference for nonincarcerative punishments—"the court shall deal
with a person who has been convicted of a crime without imposing sentence of imprisonment *unless* . . ."—and permitted the
imposition of sentences of probation rather than imprisonment for
most offenses. Indeed, even a crime as serious as murder could,
and in the exceptional case should, attract a punishment less than
imprisonment; mercy killings where motive is not in doubt and the
agony of observing the sufferings of a loved one led to a facilita-
tion of a desired death may properly be so punished, if at all. And
there is no difficulty in thinking of a variety of other sometimes
serious felonies which in particular cases should not be punished

by imprisonment. For this, the *Model Penal Code* not only allowed room but fashioned a presumption.

The *Code* has had much more success in its substantive provisions than in its provisions regarding sentencing. While the former attracted steadily increasing legislative acceptance, and indeed judicial acceptance when legislatures were heedless (much of the federal criminal law as enunciated by federal courts has been greatly influenced by the *Model Penal Code*), the sentencing provisions encountered increasing criticism and have not much influenced legislative or judicial practice. In the years of the acceptance of the philosophy that underlay the substantive provisions of the *Model Penal Code,* the philosophical basis of its provisions on punishment was in substance rejected. Indeterminacy of punishment was rejected in many states. The proposition that punishments should be defined by the offender's rehabilitative needs was rejected in most states. The existence of unprincipled and excessive disparity of punishment was recognized everywhere.

The social turbulence of the midsixties led to a stress on "fairness," so far as it could be achieved in the relationship between government and the citizen, even the convicted criminal citizen. Numerous studies established that gross disparities existed between the punishments of offenders convicted of nearly identical offenses with nearly identical records. Another line of studies established the incapacity of parole boards to predict the later conduct of offenders significantly better than could a prediction made at the time of sentencing. The whole structure came to be seen as both unfair and hypocritical; unfair in its randomness of punishment, hypocritical in its claim that future behavior could be predicted by observing prison behavior. A series of books attracted substantial attention and drove home the point. Among these were Kenneth Culp Davis's *Discretionary Justice* in 1969, Marvin Frankel's *Criminal Sentences* in 1972, Norval Morris's *The Future of Imprisonment* in 1974, the Twentieth Century Fund's *Fair and Certain Punishment* in 1976, and Andrew von Hirsch's *Doing Justice,* also in 1976.

A further line of criticism of then predominant sentencing practice rejected the mendacity of a system in which judges announced prison punishments quite other than the terms to be served. The 10-year maximum sentence celebrated in newspaper headlines often in reality resulted in release on parole after 18 months. The judges barked more loudly than prison bit and the belief arose that this diminished the deterrent and punitive credibility of the criminal sanction. Truth-in-sentencing came to be seen as no less laudable than truth-in-lending or truth-in-advertising.

Though many areas and shades of disagreement remained, a broad consensus emerged among scholars and policy analysts that criminal sentences should either be defined by, or at least limited by, the "deserved" punishment; that they should be roughly uniform in the sense that gross disparities between "like" offenders should be avoided; and that purposes of crime control by means of deterrence, rehabilitation, or incapacitation should be subordinate to these larger considerations of justice.

These were the main lines of scholarly criticism that led to sentencing reform. The popular criticisms were quite different. The years from 1965 to 1980 were a time of rapidly and steeply rising crime rates, particularly of those types of street crime which in our society attract prison terms, such as robbery, burglary, assaults, and theft. For example, the rate of robberies known to the police increased from 61.8 per 100,000 inhabitants in 1963 to 258.7 per 100,000 inhabitants in 1981. For other serious crimes, the increases in rates between these dates were comparable.

Although a variety of causes, not all involving increased incidence of crime, contributed to these increases, the press, the public, and many public officials found a scapegoat in lenient sentencing as a cause of the increase. Leniency had, of course, very little indeed to do with the matter, but it played well on the hustings and had a profound effect on the lines of sentencing reform. The scholarly criticisms of then existing sentencing practice came from the political left; the popular criticisms came from the political right and center. It was a powerful if, in the long term, an inherently unstable combination. As a result, by the late 1970s indeterminacy of punishment was on the way out in many states, and sentencing reform was on the way in.

A quite different line of criticism of sentencing practice also fueled the movement to sentencing reform. Prison was said to be used excessively and other punishments insufficiently for purposes both of crime control and of social welfare. Prison, it was argued, should be seen as a scarce and expensive resource to be reserved for those who most largely threatened social welfare. The "alternatives" movement found its largest support in the National Council on Crime and Delinquency and its call for a moratorium on prison construction and greater use of alternative punishments.

The alternatives movement led to much experimentation with community service, restitution, intensive supervision probation, and a variety of community-based control and treatment methods; though many such programs were launched, it was hard to demonstrate that they served to any significant extent to limit increases in prison and jail populations, which rose steeply despite the extension of such alternatives. In 1963 there had been 214,336 sentenced prisoners in state and federal institutions, not counting jails; this level was not reached again until 1974 when there were 218,466 state and federal prisoners. Since 1974 prison populations have continuously increased, reaching nearly 700,000 by December 31, 1989.

This apparent paradox of expanded use of alternative sanctions that did not measurably decrease use of incarceration is not difficult to explain. These programs tended to draw their subjects from those who had previously been sentenced less not more severely, from those who would otherwise be on "ordinary" probation rather than in prison or jail. The net of punishment was widened by the alternative punishment; in practice, as the Canadian Sentencing Commission demonstrated in its 1987 report, *Sentencing Reform: A Canadian Approach,* they were often not alternatives but additives. And this pattern of increasing use of midlevel punishments between probation and imprisonment accompanied the most rapid increase in prison populations in the years 1975 to 1990 that the United States has ever seen, despite declining or stable crime rates for the latter half of that period. Between 1980 and 1988, for example, the population of federal and state prisons nearly doubled; homicide, robbery, and burglary rates declined by nearly a quarter in the same period.

The failure of the alternatives movement to reduce prison populations was widely recognized. The condition was diagnosed, but the paths to a cure remained obscure. What also came to be appreciated was the need to link efforts to develop credible nonincarcerative sentences with the contemporary sentencing reform movement.

Three broad patterns of sentencing reform emerged: voluntary sentencing guidelines developed by the judiciary; legislatively prescribed, fixed-term sentencing; and systems of presumptive sentencing guidelines. Each of the three major approaches has been tried in several jurisdictions and carefully evaluated. The results of these evaluations were summarized by the National Academy of Sciences Panel on Research on Sentencing in 1983 and again by Michael Tonry in *Crime and Justice* in 1988. The voluntary guidelines approach has generally been found ineffective at reducing sentencing disparities or significantly altering the patterns of sentences that judges impose. The statutory approach has been ineffective in many jurisdictions. There is no need here to add to the existing commentary on statutory determinate sentencing laws since they had little or no impact other than on prison sentences, though it seems clear that in many states such laws achieved increases in the proportion of convicted offenders sent to prison, in the lengths of the prison terms they served, or in both. In two jurisdictions, North Carolina and California, however, such laws have been shown to have succeeded in reducing sentencing disparities and changing patterns of sentencing outcomes. The systems of presumptive sentencing guidelines developed by a sentencing commission gradually seem to be winning the day; we must turn to them if a fair and comprehensive range of punishments is to be developed and justly applied.

The idea of a sentencing commission to establish presumptive sentencing guidelines, to monitor and provide feedback to the sentencing system, owes its origin to a proposal of Judge Marvin Frankel that was first offered in a lecture at the University of Cincinnati Law School. That proposal was elaborated in the Minnesota legislation of 1978 that led to the first working system and brought three ideas into conjunction: presumptive sentences defined by offense–offender characteristics, appellate review when the judge sentenced outside the guidelines, and a permanent commission to establish the guidelines, monitor their implementation, and provide guidance to the courts on their operation, modifying the presumptive sentences as experience and the growth of knowledge might dictate.

Both scholarly analysis and the judgments of most Minnesota criminal justice professionals agree that the Minnesota guidelines system brought greater predictability and larger justice to sentencing in that state than previously obtained.

The sentencing guidelines grids established in Minnesota and elsewhere are both mechanism and metaphor for thinking about sentencing for an entire jurisdiction. The Minnesota system of presumptive sentencing guidelines for the first time required public officials to think comprehensively about sentencing, to think about punishments for any single offense in relation to punishments for all other offenses. Inevitably, this forced attention to scaling of seriousness of crimes, to enunciation of appropriate increments of punishment on account of prior criminality, and, in general, on proportionality in punishment among various combinations of offenses and offenders' circumstances.

The Minnesota sentencing guidelines for felony offenses are expressed in a grid that is seen in Figure 2. Offenses are divided into ten categories of scaled severity, offenders are sorted into seven categories of prior criminality, and the resulting presumptive sentences are arranged proportionately across the grid. The numbers in cells below the bold black jagged line on Figure 2 are presumptive guideline ranges for prison sentences for offenders whose cases fall within those cells. The numbers above the line, however, are presumptive prison sentences to be imposed *only* on revocation of probation or after the offender has otherwise failed successfully to complete a non–state-prison sentence. Above that black line, in other words, the presumptive sentence is to something other than state prison and, except after revocation, a state prison term can be imposed only as a "departure" for which reasons must be given and which can be appealed to a higher court.

The sentencing guidelines developed in Minnesota were unprecedented in the detailed standards they created for judges' decisions of whom to imprison and for how long. No common law jurisdiction had ever before established such strict accountability over judges' sentencing discretion or such finely tuned guidance about sentence lengths.

Many states have now followed in Minnesota's footsteps. Canadian and Australian commissions have urged that those countries do likewise. In England, even, there have been glimmers of interest.This tale has, however, been told by Michael Tonry in numbing detail, in *Crime and Justice* in 1988 and elsewhere, and we won't

Presumptive Sentence Lengths in Months

Italicized numbers within the grid denote the range within which a judge may sentence without the sentence being deemed a departure.

Offenders with nonimprisonment felony sentences are subject to jail time according to law.

Criminal History Score

Severity Levels of Conviction Offense		0	1	2	3	4	5	6 or more
Unauthorized use of motor vehicle Possession of marijuana	I	12*	12*	12*	13	15	17	19 *18-20*
Theft related crimes ($250-$2500) Aggravated forgery ($250-$2500)	II	12*	12*	13	15	17	19	21 *20-22*
Theft crimes ($250-$2500)	III	12*	13	15	17	19 *18-20*	22 *21-23*	25 *24-26*
Nonresidential burglary Theft crimes (over $2500)	IV	12*	15	18	21	25 *24-26*	32 *30-34*	41 *37-45*
Residential burglary Simple robbery	V	18	23	27	30 *29-31*	38 *36-40*	46 *43-49*	54 *50-58*
Criminal sexual conduct, 2nd degree (a) and (b)	VI	21	26	30	34 *33-35*	44 *42-46*	54 *50-58*	65 *60-70*
Aggravated robbery	VII	24 *23-25*	32 *30-34*	41 *38-44*	49 *45-53*	65 *60-70*	81 *75-87*	97 *90-104*
Criminal sexual conduct, 1st degree Assault, 1st degree	VIII	43 *41-45*	54 *50-58*	65 *60-70*	76 *71-81*	95 *89-101*	113 *166-120*	132 *124-140*
Murder, 3rd degree Murder, 2nd degree (felony murder)	IX	105 *102-108*	119 *116-122*	127 *124-130*	149 *143-155*	176 *168-184*	205 *195-215*	230 *218-242*
Murder, 2nd degree (with intent)	X	120 *116-124*	140 *133-147*	162 *153-171*	203 *192-214*	243 *231-255*	284 *270-298*	324 *309-339*

1st degree murder is excluded from the guidelines by law and continues to have a mandatory life sentence.

At the discretion of the judge, up to a year in jail and/or other non-jail sanctions can be imposed as conditions of probation.

Presumptive commitment to state imprisonment.

* One year and one day.

Figure 2. Minnesota sentencing guidelines grid.

repeat it here, for our interest is not in what Minnesota did, but in what it did not do. Minnesota did not attempt to develop guidelines for that vast majority of felony offenders—in that state, 80–85 percent of convicted felons—who are not presumptively bound for prison, nor did it attempt to develop guidelines for misdemeanors.

Despite statutory empowerment to develop guidelines for sentences other than to state prison, the commission elected not to do so. The enabling legislation provided:

> The sentencing guidelines . . . may also establish appropriate sanctions for offenders for whom imprisonment is not proper . . . [and] shall make specific reference to noninstitutional sanctions, including but not limited to the following: payment of fines, day fines, restitution, community work orders, work release programs in local facilities, community based residential and nonresidential programs, incarceration in a local correctional facility, and probation and the conditions thereof.

Instead, as too often happens when American policymakers and scholars think about sentencing, the Commission focused attention on the questions whom to imprison and for how long.

The members of the Minnesota Sentencing Guidelines Commission may have believed that guidelines for imprisonment alone were quite enough to take on. They may well have been right. And in any case, as we now know with many years' more experience to draw on than was available in 1980, it is not easy to design a comprehensive integrated system of punishments that includes nonprison sanctions. We believe it can be done, but we don't fault the Minnesota Commission for not doing it.

If one examines Figure 2 with nonprison sentences in mind, two of its features stand out. First, the grid provides no guidance whatever concerning sentences other than imprisonment. If the offender's criminal history and current offense place him above the bold black line, the presumptive sentence is "out" and the judge may impose a fine, probation, community service, intermittent confinement, up to 12 months in jail, or some combination of these, subject to no guidance at all.

Second, a shift of one cell on the grid makes an enormous difference in the presumptive sentence. To pick an extreme example: for a person with a criminal history score of 2, the presumptive sentence following conviction of an offense of severity level VI is "out." Conviction of that same person for a level VII offense results in a presumptive sentence of 38 to 44 months' imprisonment.

The bold black line starkly partitions the universe of cases between those that warrant imprisonment and those that do not. This presupposes that there is not a range of offense–offender relationships where a choice may justly and appropriately be made between imprisonment and a nonprison punishment. It assumes that there cannot be sufficient equality of punitive severity between such punishments that some offenders might appropriately be imprisoned and others similarly situated receive nonprison punishments. This is a false assumption.

Almost by definition, it is the cases that fall in the cells that abut the "in/out line" that present the greatest punitive ambiguity. They are as a class those offenses that are neither so venial that imprisonment would be unwarrantedly harsh nor so serious that nonimprisonment would generally be seen unduly to depreciate their seriousness. These are the cases where a fair-minded judge is likely genuinely to be undecided about the choice between prison and nonprison and the cases where two fair-minded judges are most likely to differ in their decisions.

Our argument is perhaps best made by considering some hypothetical cases where judges currently divide in their choice between such punishments and then arguing that they are right to do so and that an effective presumptive sentencing system must take account of this.

Let us take a typical case where judges at present divide in practice in choosing between imprisonment and a community-based punishment, and consider how it would be handled under the sentencing guidelines now in effect in Minnesota, Pennsylvania, Washington State, and the federal system. Table 1 shows the presumptive sentencing range that applies under each of these schemes to persons with two prior felony convictions who are convicted of nonresidential burglary or simple robbery. In each case the prior convictions are assumed to be for nonviolent, nonburglary felonies of the lowest severity ranking and the offender is

TABLE 1 Presumptive Sentencing Ranges in Four Jurisdictions
for Selected Offenders

	Nonresidential Burglary	*Simple Robbery*
Minnesota	Out (0–12 months)[a]	Out (0–12 months)[a]
Pennsylvania	2.5–18 months[b] incarceration	2.5–18 months[b] incarceration
Washington	3–9 months incarceration	12–14 months incarceration
Federal	12–18 months[c] incarceration	30–37 months[c] incarceration

a "Out" can include up to 12 months in jail.
b Minimum sentence before parole release eligibility.
c This assumes no prior prison sentence served; otherwise the applicable range is higher.

Sources: Knapp 1984a; Pennsylvania Commission on Sentencing 1981; Washington State Sentencing Guidelines Commission 1985; and U.S. Sentencing Commission 1987.

assumed not to have been on probation, parole, or similar status when the current offense was committed.

The Minnesota Commission allows anything from nominal probation to 12 months in jail for these offenses; Washington and Pennsylvania presume short prison sentences; and the U.S. Sentencing Commission calls for 12–18 months for nonresidential burglary and 30–37 months for simple robbery. Which is right? How could one vote on that question? Data are lacking to determine the differential effects of sentences of this magnitude on the later conduct of the offender or the differential deterrent effects of such sentences on the criminality of others. The decision will have to be based on other grounds. Perhaps it cannot be said that any of these presumptive sentences are right and the others wrong (though of course we have our own personal views). Perhaps— and this is the heart of the matter—it is precisely in cases like these that the trial judge should be directed by sentencing guidelines to *choose* between equivalent appropriate sentences, addressing as well as possible the many individual features of a case that cannot be encompassed within the guideline grid.

None of these guidelines systems is properly designed. They either define a presumed incarcerative punishment, as in Pennsylvania, Washington, and the federal system, or offer no guidance at all on the nature of the sentence, as in Minnesota; they also provide for some fine-tuning on factors that are not within the grid but are nevertheless relevant to sentencing. But the problem is that the point of origin, the original presumption of a choice between imprisonment and other punishments, is flawed.

If a reasonable balance of fairness in sentencing is to be achieved, there must be some sense of rough equivalence in severity between the incarcerative and nonincarcerative punishments that are presumptively appropriate in any given case. Perfect equality is, of course, not achievable; but at least the nonincarcerative punishments must be perceived as not incommensurate in their severity to the prison sentences to which they are alternatives.

Minnesota's bold black line is objectionable because it implies—as much American thought assumes—that the only important choice of punishments is between prison and nonprison. This must be wrong. Crimes fall along a continuum from the most venial to the most venal. Offenders range from the mildest milequetoasts to the most brutal blackguards. Punishments, to be commensurate with the various categories of offenses and offenders, should be similarly graduated.

This idea that the only important punishment questions are whether prison should be imposed and, if so, for how long obscures analysis and impedes efforts to develop nonprison punishments, for it discourages, even precludes, systematic approaches to nonprison sentences. Yet it must be true that the punishment continuum extends downward from prison just as it extends upward in prison in units of months and years. Sensible policies must be developed for regulating and regularizing that lower portion of the continuum that is much the more important in terms of the number of offenders affected.

Sentencing guidelines grids should not have bold black lines running diagonally across their faces. Cells on each side of that line should spell out a variety of types of incarcerative and nonincarcerative presumed sentences scaled in severity to the offenders' culpability but sufficiently flexible to allow judicial choice among sentences of rough punitive equivalence. Only thus can we escape from the net-widening and prison-filling effect of the present systems.

And there is good reason for the net-widening and prison-filling effects of current sentencing systems: when a grid of offense–offender relationships is fashioned, the deserved punishment has to allow for the "worst case" that falls within each cell. Once prison is seen as deserved by *some* in that cell it will be the presumptive sentence to be imposed on *all* who fall within it, unless there is a "departure." It is inevitable that cases of greatly differing character fall within a single cell. Inclusion in any cell depends on various combinations of offenses and past records of criminality. Because of the vagaries of plea bargaining, a single cell will include some whose criminal conduct is much less serious than that generally associated with the conviction offense, others who have committed more serious forms of the crimes encompassed by a single statutory label, and others—beneficiaries of charge reductions—who have committed much more serious crimes altogether. Some of those crimes may involve acts of violence; others, intrusion on property interests. The black line reifies these diverse kinds of offenses and offenders into a single generic type. This must be wrong.

The April 13, 1987 report of the U.S. Sentencing Commission offers a good illustration of this phenomenon. The Commission chose to require incarceration for all but a small proportion of federal offenders. This represented a substantial change from the past practice of extensive use of probation and seemed inconsistent with a congressional directive that the guidelines "reflect the general appropriateness of imposing a sentence other than imprisonment in cases in which the defendant is a first offender who has not been convicted of a crime of violence or an otherwise serious offense." To authorize prison sentences for white-collar crimes that often in the past provoked sentences of probation, the Commission reports, it defined as "serious" a host of offenses that judges clearly had not previously regarded as serious.

To assure prison sentences for some types of white-collar offenses, the Commission required them for many other offenses of diverse types. In the jargon of social scientists, this is an over-aggregation problem. Simple theft and petty embezzlement need not have been lumped together with tax evasion, insider trading, and antitrust offenses. The last three could have been treated one way, the first two another. The point, though, is that the Commission did not do this. Other decisions placed these offenses in the same cell, on the wrong side of the in/out line, and imprisonment for all was the result.

If intermediate punishments are to take their proper place in a comprehensive system of structured sentencing discretion, there must be some interchangeability between incarcerative and non-incarcerative punishments *within* some of the boxes of the guideline grid.

As we have seen, sentencing reforms to date have not incorporated this idea; however, some policies have been articulated to guide the imposition of intermediate punishments and some ambitious reform proposals have been advanced that have incorporated the idea of interchangeability of punishments.

In what follows we discuss first the policies that have been developed in Minnesota, Pennsylvania, Washington, and the District of Columbia and by the U.S. Sentencing Commission, and then the proposals for reform that have been suggested in Delaware and Minnesota and by some staff members and one commissioner of the U.S. Sentencing Commission. We conclude this chapter by advancing our own recommendations as to the elements essential to a comprehensive sentencing system allowing for interchangeability of punishments.

Policies on Interchangeability and Intermediate Punishments

Progress in the development of rules for interchangeability of punishments has been slow. All of the major sentencing guidelines efforts have had to face the problem. The first important commission—in Minnesota—finessed the subject by giving judges unguided discretion to choose between prison and nonprison for many cases. The Washington State and federal commissions took small steps toward establishment of overt exchange rates. The District of Columbia commission went furthest of all and entirely repudiated the notion of an in/out line. In this section we trace these developments to show that the concepts and experience are now in place for incorporation of intermediate punishments into a comprehensive set of sentencing standards.

Under traditional indeterminate sentencing laws and under most statutory determinate sentencing laws, judges are given no guidance whatever in choosing among possible nonprison sentences except for occasional statutes that mandate prison sentences or make persons convicted of certain offenses ineligible for probation. The general question of interchangeability between prison and other punishments has not arisen.

Not much changed under presumptive sentencing guidelines. The Minnesota sentencing guidelines specified whether felony sentence should be "in" or "out," and if in, for how long. For the outs, however, judges could choose from a sentencing buffet varying from nominal supervision to 12 months' jail, and as to this choice, the Commission gave no guidance. The Pennsylvania Sentencing Commission provided slightly more guidance; it did so by limiting the proportion of cases over which judges were authorized to decide *whether* to incarcerate and by limiting the upper bound of the authorized presumptive minimum term of imprisonment in some cases. Figures 3a and 3b show the contrast between the Pennsylvania and Minnesota systems by isolating the lowest levels of both states' guidelines grids.

There are two major contextual differences that distinguish Figures 3a and 3b that must be mentioned before they are compared. First, Pennsylvania retains a parole board and the Pennsylvania guidelines accordingly specify minimum sentences, not, as in Minnesota, determinate sentences. There is no assurance that an offender in Pennsylvania will be released on completion of the minimum term and the guidelines do not set standards for maximum terms. Second, the Pennsylvania guidelines cover misdemeanors and felonies; Minnesota's only felonies.

With this background, one difference between Figures 3a and 3b stands out: Minnesota's guidelines affect a much smaller proportion of criminal offenses than do Pennsylvania's. Minnesota's guidelines apply only to felonies; the guidelines give no direction on sentences even for most felonies in the first six offense levels except that the sentence be no more than 12 months' jail. In Pennsylvania, by contrast, the first three offense levels are mostly misdemeanors. Levels 4 and 5, the lower felony levels, contain only four cells in which the judge is given carte blanche to choose between confinement and other punishments.

Reasonable people can differ about the merits of the Pennsyl-

Offense Level	Criminal History						
	0	1	2	3	4	5	6
I	0-6	0-6	0-6	0-6	0-6	0-6	0-6
II	0-12	0-12	0-12	0-12	0-12	2-12	5-12
III	0-12	0-12	0-12	0-12	3-12	5-12	8-12
IV	0-12	0-12	0-12	5-12	8-12	18-27	21-30
V	0-12	3-12	5-12	8-12	18-27	21-30	24-36
VI	4-23	6-12	8-12	12-29	23-34	28-44	33-49

Figure 3a. Pennsylvania guidelines: Six lowest levels (of ten) felony and misdemeanor sentences (standard range).

Offense Level	Criminal History						
	0	1	2	3	4	5	6 or more
I							18-20
II							20-22
III	Out or in to 12 months in jail				18-20	21-23	24-26
IV					24-26		
V				29-31			
VI				33-35		In	
VII	23-25	30-34	38-44	45-53			

Figure 3b. Minnesota guidelines: Seven lowest levels (of ten) felony sentences.

vania and Minnesota approaches. Those who oppose excessive use of imprisonment will likely prefer the more limited reach of Minnesota's guidelines and the resulting imprecision about all misdemeanor sentences and many felony sentences. Those who are concerned primarily about sentencing disparities will likely prefer the scope of Pennsylvania's guidelines, which offer guidance for

Offense Level	Offender Score							
	(Discretion)		(Partial) (Interchangeability)					(Prison)
	0	1	2	3	4	5	6	7 8 9 or more
I	0-60 days	0-90 days	2-5 months	2-6	3-8	4-12	12+-14	In
II	0-90 days	2-6 months	3-9	4-12	12+-12	14-18	17-22	In
III	1-3 months	3-8	4-12	9-12	12+-16	17-22	22-29	In
IV	3-9	6-12	12+-14	13-17	15-20	22-29	33-43	In
V	6-12	12+-14	13-17	15-29	22-28	33-43	41-54	In
VI	12-14	15-20	21-27	26-34	31-41	36-48	46-61	In

Figure 4. Washington state guidelines: Six lowest levels (of 14) felony sentences.

sentences for a much larger proportion of the universe of cases. For our purpose, however, the two approaches are similar in that neither sets guidelines for use of specific nonprison sentences or establishes exchange rates.

Washington State was the first jurisdiction to grapple with interchangeability. Figure 4 shows the lowest six levels of the Washington grid. The Washington grid, like Minnesota's, addresses only felony sentencing. Washington in effect has three punishment bands or zones: the discretionary in/out band; the interchangeability band; and the in band. Compared with the approaches taken in Minnesota and Washington, this is a significant advance.

Note the upper-left-hand areas in which the top of the range of presumptive sentences is 12 months or less. For these cells, for nonviolent offenders, the guidelines provide: "[T]he court shall consider and give priority to available alternatives to total confinement and shall state its reasons if they are not used," guided by the following conversion rates:

- one day's partial confinement equals one day in prison
- eight hours' community service equals one day in prison (but not to exceed 30 days' credit)

Section 9.94A.380 of the Washington guidelines expressly contemplates hybrid sentences: "As an example, a sentence of total confinement of nine months may be converted to five months of jail time, three months of partial confinement, and one month of community service."

This is an extremely limited approach to exchange rates. Except for three cells setting ranges of 0–60 days or 0–90 days, every cell presumes that incarceration is the appropriate sentence. Community service can be a partial substitute only for confinement terms longer than 30 days, and the only other substitution is of partial confinement up to a year for total confinement for the same period. No provision is made for exchange rates between fines or intensive supervision and total (or partial) confinement. Although this is a small step, it is nevertheless a step in the right direction.

The District of Columbia has taken the multiple-band idea one step further. Rather than develop a single comprehensive grid for all offenses, the D.C. Superior Court Sentencing Guidelines Commission prepared separate grids for "armed," "unarmed," and "drug" offenses. Figures 5a and 5b show the unarmed grid and its schematic version. The proposed District of Columbia guidelines create a system of progressively more tightly constrained discretion. Four bands create presumptions of "out," "out but . . . ," "in but . . . ," and "in." In the first band, the presumptive sentence is to be served in the community and may, along with probation, include a fine, restitution, community service, or "other similar sanctions." In the second, the judge may impose either a community sentence or an incarcerative sentence; in effect the former is rebuttably presumed appropriate because the judge must state for the record the reason "why an alternative sentence has not been selected." In the third, the judge again may impose either type of sentence, but there is no rebuttable presumption in favor of a community sentence and no reason need be given for imposing a prison sentence. Cells in the fourth band specify prison sentences.

Although the D.C. Commission's four bands seem to us a sound approach to structuring sentencing discretion, they represent two steps forward and one back. The four bands of scaled discretion move beyond the Washington State Commission's approach, but the failures to provide exchange rates or any guidance concerning the specific nature or dimensions of community sentences are steps backward.

The most recent guidelines effort to deal with nonprison sentences is that of the U.S. Sentencing Commission. In general, the Commission looks unfavorably on nonprison punishments. Home detention and community service are not recognized as independent punishments at all, but merely as an occasional adjunct of probation. Fines as stand-alone punishments are restricted to the most trifling offenses. Fines are, however, to be imposed in every case, subject to constitutional limits concerning ability to pay; for the most part this means fines are supplements to confinement, and not substitutes for it. The role of probation also has been degraded to be replaced by more use of incarceration.

The Commission allows for limited interchangeability in a pattern that resembles Washington State's. Table 2 sets out the federal guidelines grid. Like those in the state guidelines systems, it is organized on the basis of scales of offense severity and offenders' past involvement with crime. For the lowest 6 of 43 offense levels, where sentencing ranges start at 0, the judge has complete discretion to impose confinement or community sentences. For offense levels 7–10, with a lowest presumptive guideline sentence of one to six months' confinement, the judge has discretion to choose among prison, intermittent or community confinement, and a split sentence including imprisonment *for half of the minimum term or at least one month;* in other words, some confinement is required. For offense levels 11 and 12, with a lowest presumptive guideline sentence of six to ten months, the judge may substitute community or intermittent confinement for imprisonment, *so long as at least half the minimum guideline sentence is satisfied by imprisonment.* For offense levels 13–43, no substitution of nonprison punishments for prison time is presumed appropriate.

The Commission's niggardly provisions for determining substitutes for imprisonment, within the narrow compass described above, thus allow substitution of 30 days intermittent confinement or one month's community confinement in a halfway house or community treatment center for one month's imprisonment. There

Figure 5a. Unarmed grid. Time reported in months. (From D.C. Superior Court, Sentencing Guidelines Commission 1987.)

Criminal History Score

Offense Score	A 0	B 0.5 – 1.5	C 2 – 3.5	D 4 – 5.5	E 6+
1	6 [a]	6 [a]	6 [b]	9 [c] 6–12	15+
2	6 [a]	6 [a]	9 [b]	12 [c] 9–15	18+
3	6 [a]	6 [b]	9 [c] 6–12	15 12–18	21+
4	9 [b]	9 [b]	12 [c] 9–15	18 15–21	24+
5	9 [b]	12 [c] 9–15	18 15–21	24 18–30	33+
6	12 [c] 9–15	18 15–21	24 18–30	30 24–36	42+
7	24 18–30	30 24–36	36 30–42	42 36–48	54+
8	36 30–42	42 36–48	48 42–54	54 48–60	66+
9	48 42–54	54 48–60	60 54–66	66 60–72	78+
10	72 66–78	78 72–84	84 78–90	90 84–96	102+
11	96 84–108	102 90–114	108 96–120	114 102–126	132+

[a] The presumptive guideline sentence for this offense would be served in the community. Along with probation, the court might impose a fine, restitution, a requirement of community service, or a combination of these and other similar sanctions. The number shown is the longest minimum sentence which would be imposed and suspended or imposed after revocation based on non-compliance with the conditions of the community-based sentence.

[b] At the discretion of the judge, a community sentence (as defined above) or an incarcerative sentence may be imposed; the number shown is the longest minimum sentence which may be imposed if the initial sentence is one of incarceration, or the longest minimum sentence which would be imposed if a community sentence is initially imposed and later revoked. Before imposing sentence, the judge shall consider alternatives to incarceration (i.e., intensive probation supervision and other highly structured supervision programs) for cases in this cell. If

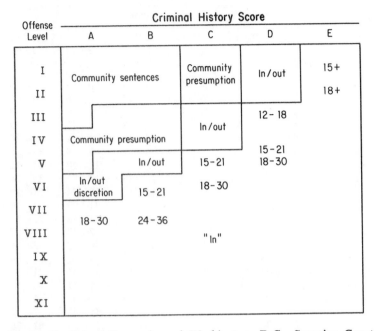

Figure 5b. Schematic version of Washington, D.C., Superior Court proposed "unarmed grid."

is no interchangeability whatever between imprisonment and fines or community service or house arrest or intensive supervision.

That, to our knowledge, is the full extent of existing efforts systematically to address the use of intermediate punishments in a comprehensive sentencing system, although at the time of writing newly created sentencing commissions in a number of states are wrestling with these issues and the commissions in Minnesota and Washington are taking another look at the subject. The developments that appear to us most promising are Washington State's

---

(*Fig. 5a notes, continued*)

an incarcerative sentence is imposed, the judge is required to state on the record why an alternative sentence has not been selected.

c Before imposing sentence, the judge may consider alternatives to incarceration for cases in this cell provided that the conviction offense does not involve use of a gun (including assault with a deadly weapon) or injury to a victim and the offender was not on probation or parole at the time of the offense.

TABLE 2 Sentencing Table

Offense Level	Criminal History Category					
	I	II	III	IV	V	VI
	0 or 1	2 or 3	4, 5, 6	7, 8, 9	10, 11, 12	13 or more
1	0– 1	0– 2	0– 3	0– 4	0– 5	0– 6
2	0– 2	0– 3	0– 4	0– 5	0– 6	1– 7
3	0– 3	0– 4	0– 5	0– 6	2– 8	3– 9
4	0– 4	0– 5	0– 6	2– 8	4– 10	6– 12
5	0– 5	0– 6	1– 7	4– 10	6– 12	9– 15
6	0– 6	1– 7	2– 8	6– 12	9– 15	12– 18
7	1– 7	2– 8	4– 10	8– 14	12– 18	15– 21
8	2– 8	4– 10	6– 12	10– 16	15– 21	18– 24
9	4– 10	6– 12	8– 14	12– 18	18– 24	21– 27
10	6– 12	8– 14	10– 16	15– 21	21– 27	24– 30
11	8– 14	10– 16	12– 18	18– 24	24– 30	27– 33
12	10– 16	12– 18	15– 21	21– 27	27– 33	30– 37
13	12– 18	15– 21	18– 24	24– 30	30– 37	33– 41
14	15– 21	18– 24	21– 27	27– 33	33– 41	37– 46
15	18– 24	21– 27	24– 30	30– 37	37– 46	41– 51
16	21– 27	24– 30	27– 33	33– 41	41– 51	46– 57
17	24– 30	27– 33	30– 37	37– 46	46– 57	51– 63
18	27– 33	30– 37	33– 41	41– 51	51– 63	57– 71
19	30– 37	33– 41	37– 46	46– 57	57– 71	63– 78
20	33– 41	37– 46	41– 51	51– 63	63– 78	70– 87
21	37– 46	41– 51	46– 57	57– 71	70– 87	77– 96
22	41– 51	46– 57	51– 63	63– 78	77– 96	84–105
23	46– 57	51– 63	57– 71	70– 87	84–105	92–115
24	51– 63	57– 71	63– 78	77– 96	92–115	100–125
25	57– 71	63– 78	70– 87	84–105	100–125	110–137
26	63– 78	70– 87	78– 97	92–115	110–137	120–150
27	70– 87	78– 97	87–108	100–125	120–150	130–162
28	78– 97	87–108	97–121	110–137	130–162	140–175
29	87–108	97–121	108–135	121–151	140–175	151–188
30	97–121	108–135	121–151	135–168	151–188	168–210
31	108–135	121–151	135–168	151–188	168–210	188–235
32	121–151	135–168	151–188	168–210	188–235	210–262
33	135–168	151–188	168–210	188–235	210–262	235–293
34	151–188	168–210	188–235	210–262	235–293	262–327
35	168–210	188–235	210–262	235–293	262–327	292–365
36	188–235	210–262	235–293	262–327	292–365	324–405
37	210–262	235–293	262–327	292–365	324–405	360–life
38	235–293	262–327	292–365	324–405	360–life	360–life
39	262–327	292–365	324–405	360–life	360–life	360–life
40	292–365	324–405	360–life	360–life	360–life	360–life
41	324–405	360–life	360–life	360–life	360–life	360–life
42	360–life	360–life	360–life	360–life	360–life	360–life
43	life	life	life	life	life	life

Source: U.S. Sentencing Commission 1987 (April 13, 1987 version).

first tentative steps toward establishment of exchange rates and the District of Columbia's creation of its four bands of changing presumptions for and against the use of nonprison sentences.

Proposals for Interchangeability

When we turn from policy made to policy considered, examples of innovation and creativity are more ambitious. There have been two particularly notable efforts to date to deal systematically with nonprison sentences and interchangeability.

In Delaware for adult sentencing and in Minnesota for juvenile sentencing, attempts have been made to work out the details of sentencing guidelines that incorporate nonprison sentences and that address the interchangeability issue. In addition, the staff of the U.S. Sentencing Commission developed a number of proposals for exchange rates in the federal guidelines; these were not adopted.

Delaware

The Delaware Sentencing Reform Commission in 1983 proposed an integrated system of sentencing standards to govern all correctional placements from sentencing to institutional assignment. The standards would guide decisions by judges about sentencing, by probation officials about degrees of control, and by prison officials about transfers between custody levels. Table 3 is one version of the Delaware proposal.

The proposal, often referred to as the Du Pont proposal after Governor Pierre Du Pont, creates ten "accountability levels" ranging from unsupervised release to maximum security imprisonment. For each level, specific standards for mobility, supervision, special conditions, and financial obligations are set out.

Under the provisions of a separate sentencing guidelines grid, not unlike those in Minnesota and Washington, an offender would be assigned to a specific accountability level for a designated period. Governor Du Pont in 1986 stressed that "the offender's needs will not determine his assignment to a level of punishment—that will be determined by the nature of his offense and his criminal history. But [thereafter] the specific conditions attaching to the

TABLE 3 Accountability Levels in the Delaware Sentencing Approach

Restrictions	I 0–100	II 101–200	III 201–300	IV 301–400	V 401–500
Mobility in the community[a]	100% (unrestricted)	100% (unrestricted)	90% (restricted 0–10 hours/week)	80% (restricted 10–30 hours/week)	60% (restricted 30–40 hours/week)
Amount of supervision	0	Written report monthly	1–2 face-to-face/month, 1–2 weekly phone contact	3–6 face-to-face/month, weekly phone contact	2–6 face-to-face/week, daily phone, written reports/weekly
Privileges withheld or special conditions[b]	(100%) same as prior offense conviction	(100%) same as prior conviction	1–2 privileges withheld	1–4 privileges withheld	1–7 privileges withheld
Financial obligations[c]	Fine/cost may be applied (0–2 day fine)	Fine/costs/restitution/probation supervisory fee may be applied (1–3 day fine)	Same (increase probation fee by $5–10/month) (2–4 day/fine)	Same (increase probation fee by $5–10/month) (3–5 day/fine)	Same (pay partial cost of food/lodging/supervisory fee) (4–7 day/fine)
Examples (these are examples only—many other scenarios could be constructed meeting the requirements of each level)	$50 fine/court cost; 6/months unsupervised probation	$50 fine, restitution, court costs; 6 months supervised probation; $10/month fee; written report	Fine/costs/restitution; 1 year probation; weekend community service; no drinking	Weekend community service or mandatory treatment, 5 hours/day; $30/month probation fee; no drinking; no out-of-state trips	Mandatory rehabilitation skills program, 8 hours/day; restitution; probation fee of $40/month; no drinking; curfew

Accountability Levels in the Delaware Sentencing Approach (continued)

Restrictions	VI 501–600	VII 601–700	VIII 701–800	IX 801–900	X 901–1,000
Mobility in the Community[a]	30% (restricted 50–100 hours/week)	20% (restricted 100–140 hours/week)	10% (90% of time restricted) incarcerated	0% Incarcerated	0% Incarcerated
Amount of Supervision	Daily phone, daily face-to-face, weekly written reports	Daily on-site supervision 8–16 hours/day	Daily on-site supervision 24 hours/day	Daily on-site supervision 24 hours/day	Daily on-site supervision 24 hours/day
Privileges withheld or special conditions[b]	1–10 withheld	1–12 withheld	5–15 withheld	15–19 withheld	20 or more withheld
Financial obligations[c]	Same as V (8–10 day fine)	Same as V (11–12) day fine	Fine, costs restitution payable upon release to VII or lower (12–15 day fine)	Same as VIII	Same as VIII
Examples (these are examples only—many other scenarios could be constructed meeting the requirements of each level)	Work release; pay partial cost of room/board/restitution; no kitchen privileges outside meal time; no drinking; no sex; weekends home	Residential treatment program; pay partial program costs; limited privileges	Minimum security prison	Medium security prison	Maximum security prison

a Restrictions on freedom essentially structure an offender's time, controlling his schedule, whereabouts, and activities for the designated amount of time. To the extent monitoring is not standard or consistent or to the extent that no sanctions for accountability accrue for failure on the part of the offender, the time is *not* structured. It could consist of residential, part-time residential, community service, or other specific methods for meeting the designated hours. The judge could order the hours be met daily (e.g., 2 hours/day) or in one period (e.g., weekend in jail).
b Privileges/conditions: choice of job; choice of residence; mobility within setting; driving; drinking (possible use of Antabuse); out-of-state trips; phone calls; curfew; mail; urinalysis; associates; areas off limits.
c As a more equitable guide to appropriate fine, the amount would be measured in units equivalent to daily income, such as 1 day's salary = 1 "day's fine."

Source: Du Pont 1986, pp. 320–21.

offender's sanction can be individualized as much as possible to his needs (such as drug or alcohol treatment)."

After the offender is assigned an accountability level, he may with the passage of time be promoted or demoted. Thus an offender assigned to level V, which resembles many intensive supervision probation programs, could, after some months of good behavior, look forward to promotion to the lesser restrictions of level IV. Conversely, he might on bad behavior be demoted to a level of tighter control and restriction.

This Delaware proposal offers a graduated, integrated approach to nonprison punishments, but it does not deal with interchangeability. What is proposed is in effect a system of "designer sanctions" to be devised to meet the custody and treatment needs of each offender. Thus, for example, the last row in Table 3 shows sample punishment packages but notes that "many other scenarios could be constructed meeting the requirements of each level."

In the event, Delaware policymakers did not adopt the Du Pont plan, but instead late in 1987 adopted a simpler five-level system of accountability levels; the system is "voluntary and non-binding," which means that judges need not comply with the system.

The full-blown Du Pont proposal seems to us a promising step toward a comprehensive sentencing system but one that is both too specific and not specific enough. It is too specific in that it sets a single amount of supervision or a single set of financial sanctions as appropriate for each level, without allowing for the possibility that there might be tradeoffs between supervision, conditions, and financial payments, so long as the aggregate punishments visited on offenders within a single accountability level are in a meaningful sense equivalent. It is not specific enough in that it leaves entirely to the discretion of the individual official what use is to be made of which different kinds of placements; more guidance is needed to the appropriate bases for choices between different punishments.

Delaware's proposals are, to our knowledge, the first ambitious effort to work out the details of a comprehensive punishment system covering the full array of criminal punishments for an entire jurisdiction and results in part from what Governor Du Pont described as the realization that there is "a yawning gap in Delaware's corrections system" between probation and prison that should be filled with intermediate punishments.

Minnesota Juvenile Court Dispositional Guidelines

The other ambitious attempt to devise comprehensive, integrated standards for both incarcerative and nonincarcerative punishments is the system of juvenile court dispositional guidelines developed for Minnesota by the Minnesota Citizens Council on Crime and Justice. These guidelines were tested in 13 Minnesota counties in 1981–1982, but have nowhere been adopted as court policy.

The guidelines are set out in Figure 6. Like most guidelines grids, the guidelines array punishments in terms of a criminal history score, based on prior adjudications, and an offense severity score, based on offense seriousness. For each cell that results from the intersection of a criminal history column and an offense severity row, the guidelines specify a set of appropriate punishments that fully embody a principle of interchangeability.

How this works can most easily be illustrated by looking at a hypothetical case. Imagine an offender who committed burglary (a level 4 offense) and who has a criminal history score of 3. The appropriate cell on the grid specifies as the appropriate punishment a $320 fine *or* 80 hours' community service *or* 480 days' probation *or* a combination of these *or* a maximum of 120 days' confinement. The authorized combinations are set out in a different table, which is cross-referenced by the number "41" contained in the cell. The sanction combinations for level 41 are shown in Figure 7 and include *either* up to 120 days' confinement *or* any of a number of permutations of fines, community service, and probation.

The Minnesota juvenile court guidelines system is, to our knowledge, the most detailed effort yet made to devise a comprehensive set of sentencing standards. It does, however, have a dauntingly mechanical character, and this may be why it has not been formally adopted anywhere as official court policy. These guidelines were ahead of their time but today provide a useful illustration of one approach to integration of both incarcerative and nonincarcerative punishments in a single comprehensive scheme.

The U.S. Sentencing Commission

Although the U.S. Sentencing Commission's guidelines allow little place for intermediate punishments, the commission's staff and one

Advisory Sanction Levels

Offense Severity Scale – Ranking of Most Serious Current Offense	Offense History	
	0 Previous Offense in Ranking A	1 or More Previous Offenses in Ranking A
A. Habitual Truancy – 260.015, subd. 19 Running Away – 260.015, subd. 20 Juvenile Petty Offenses – 260.015, subd. 21	10 no adjudication, continuance up to 90 days	11 no adjudication, continuance up to 90 days, possible extension up to 90 days

Offense Severity Scale – Ranking of Most Serious Current Offense	Offense History Point Total			
	0	.25	.50	.75 or more
B. Juvenile Alcohol Offenses – 260.015, subd. 22 Juvenile Controlled Substance Offenses – 260.015, subd. 23	20 $40 fine or 10 hrs. work or 60 days prob. or combination	21 $60 fine or 15 hrs. work or 90 days prob. or combination	22 $80 fine or 20 hrs. work or 120 days prob. or combination	23 $100 fine or 25 hrs. work or 150 days prob. or combination

Offense Severity Scale – Ranking of Most Serious Current Offense	Offense History Point Total					
	0-.25	.50-.75	1 - 2.75	3 - 5.75	6 - 8.75	9 or more
C. Misdemeanors – Examples: Assault 4 – 609.224 Theft under $150 – 609.52, subd. 3(5) Disorderly Conduct – 609.72	22 $80 fine or 20 hrs. wk. or 120 days prob. or comb.	23 $100 fine or 25 hrs. wk. or 150 days prob. or comb.	24 $120 fine or 30 hrs. work or 180 days prob. or combination	25 $140 fine or 35 hrs. work or 210 days prob. or combination	26 $160 fine or 40 hrs. work or 240 days prob. or combination	27 $180 fine or 45 hrs. work or 270 days prob. or combination
1. Felonies – Examples: Dangerous Weapon – 609.66 Unauthorized Use of Motor Vehicle – 609.55 Forgery – 609.63	24 $120 fine or 30 hrs. work or 180 days prob. or combination		26 $160 fine or 40 hrs. work or 240 days prob. or combination	28 $200 fine or 50 hrs. work or 300 days prob. or combination	29 $240 fine or 60 hrs. work or 360 days prob. or combination	40 $280 fine or 70 hrs. work or 420 days prob. or combination or maximum of 90 days instit.

Offense Severity Level – Examples					
2. Felonies – Examples: Aggravated Forgery $150–$2500 – 609.625; Damage to Property – 609.595, subd. 1(2) & (3); Terroristic Threats – 609.713, subd. 2	26 $160 fine or 40 hrs. work or 240 days prob. or combination	28 $200 fine or 50 hrs. work or 300 days prob. or combination	29 $240 fine or 60 hrs. work or 360 days prob. or combination	40 $280 fine or 70 hrs. work or 420 days prob. or combination or maximum of 90 days instit.	50 maximum of 120 days instit. or DOC
3. Felonies – Examples: Sale of Marijuana –152.15, subd. 1(2); Theft Crimes $150–$2500 – (See Theft Offense List); Arson 3 Over $300 – 609.563	28 $200 fine or 50 hrs. work or 300 days prob. or combination	29 $240 fine or 60 hrs. work or 360 days prob. or combination	30 $280 fine or 70 hrs. work or 420 days prob. or combination	41 $320 fine or 80 hrs. work or 480 days prob. or combination or maximum of 120 days instit.	51 maximum of 150 days instit. or DOC
4. Felonies – Examples: Burglary – 609.58, subd. 2(3); Receiving Stolen Goods $301–$999 – 609.525, 609.53; Negligent Fires – 609.576(a)	29 $240 fine or 60 hrs. work or 360 days prob. or combination	30 $280 fine or 70 hrs. work or 420 days prob. or combination	41 $320 fine or 80 hrs. work or 480 days prob. or combination or maximum of 120 days instit.	42 $360 fine or 90 hrs. work or 540 days prob. or combination or maximum of 150 days instit.	52 maximum of 180 days instit. or DOC
5. Felonies – Examples: Assault 3 – 609.223; Criminal Sexual Conduct 3 – 609.344 (a)&(b); Burglary – 609.58, subd. 2(1)(a)&(c)	30 $280 fine or 70 hrs. work or 420 days prob. or combination	41 $320 fine or 80 hrs. work or 480 days prob. or combination or maximum of 120 days instit.	51 maximum of 150 days instit. or DOC	52 maximum of 150 days instit. or DOC	60
6. Felonies – Examples: Arson 2 – 609.562; Burglary of Occupied Dwelling – 609.58, subd. 2(2); Criminal Sexual Conduct 2 – 609.343(a)&(b)	41 $320 fine or 80 hrs. work or 480 days prob. or combination or maximum of 120 days instit.	42 $360 fine or 90 hrs. work or 540 days prob. or combination or maximum of 150 days instit.	52 maximum of 180 days instit. or DOC	60	DOC
7. Felonies – Examples: Aggravated Robbery – 609.245; Criminal Sexual Conduct 2 – 609.343 (c),(d),(e)&(f); Burglary with Weapon – 609.58, subd. 2(b)	51 maximum of 150 days instit. or DOC	52 maximum of 180 days instit. or DOC	60	DOC	DOC
8. Felonies – Examples: Assault 1 – 609.221; Criminal Sexual Conduct 1 – 609.342; Manslaughter 1 – 609.20 (1) & (2)	60	60	Department of Corrections	Department of Corrections	Department of Corrections
9. Murder 3 – 609.195; Murder 2 – 609.19; Murder 1 – 609.185	60	Department of Corrections	Department of Corrections	Department of Corrections	Department of Corrections

Figure 6. Minnesota Citizens Council on Crime and Justice (formerly Correctional Services of Minnesota) advisory sanction levels. DOC = Department of Corrections. (From Minnesota Citizens Council on Crime and Justice 1982.)

Adjudication
$320 fine
Or 80 hours work
Or 480 days probation
Or combination:

Fine / Work / Probation								
$320 0 hrs. 0 days	$280 10 hrs. 0 days	$240 20 hrs. 0 days	$200 30 hrs. 0 days	$160 40 hrs. 0 days	$120 50 hrs. 0 days	$80 60 hrs. 0 days	$40 70 hrs. 0 days	$0 80 hrs. 0 days
$280 0 hrs. 60 days	$240 10 hrs. 60 days	$200 20 hrs. 60 days	$160 30 hrs. 60 days	$120 40 hrs. 60 days	$80 50 hrs. 60 days	$40 60 hrs. 60 days	$0 70 hrs. 60 days	
$240 0 hrs. 120 days	$200 10 hrs. 120 days	$160 20 hrs. 120 days	$120 30 hrs. 120 days	$80 40 hrs. 120 days	$40 50 hrs. 120 days	$0 60 hrs. 120 days		
$200 0 hrs. 180 days	$160 10 hrs. 180 days	$120 20 hrs. 180 days	$80 30 hrs. 180 days	$40 40 hrs. 180 days	$0 50 hrs. 180 days			
$160 0 hrs. 240 days	$120 10 hrs. 240 days	$80 20 hrs. 240 days	$40 30 hrs. 240 days	$0 40 hrs. 240 days				
$120 0 hrs. 300 days	$80 10 hrs. 300 days	$40 20 hrs. 300 days	$0 30 hrs. 300 days					
$80 0 hrs. 360 days	$40 10 hrs. 360 days	$0 20 hrs. 360 days						
$40 0 hrs. 420 days	$0 10 hrs. 420 days							
$0 0 hrs. 480 days								

Or maximum of 120 days institutionalization

Figure 7. Sanction combinations for level 41. (From Minnesota Citizens Council on Crime and Justice 1982.)

72

of the commissioners developed a number of interesting and imaginative approaches for dealing with interchangeability.

During the deliberations that preceded the promulgation of the federal guidelines, two sets of proposals were considered (how seriously, we do not know) and rejected; if adopted, they would have constituted major conceptual advances on current approaches to formulation of sentencing policy.

The first, the creation of former commissioner Paul Robinson, was a plan for converting measures of offense severity and criminal history into "punishment units." The core notion was that offenders' culpability, and correspondingly their vulnerability to punishment, can be expressed much more precisely than the archaic federal criminal law permits. Although serious efforts to modernize federal criminal law by adopting a coherent criminal code have been afoot for nearly a quarter century, they have invariably fallen short of adoption. As a result, the federal criminal law consists of a congeries of inconsistent statutes, judge-made common law doctrines, and umbrella crimes like mail fraud, conspiracy, and Racketeer Influenced and Corrupt Organizations violations (RICO), whose labels give no indication whatever of the underlying behavior. Complicating matters further, charging and plea negotiation practices in the federal courts vary substantially between districts and prosecution offices.

Robinson's ingenious "punishment units" plan had two parts. First, to get round the deficiencies and anomalies of the federal criminal law, he proposed to characterize crimes in terms of the factual elements that make up what lawyers call the *actus reus* (the "illegal act") and the *mens rea* (the "illegal mental state") of crimes. What harm did the offender cause? Precisely what kind of physical injury or property loss or damage resulted? What was the degree of injury or the amount of loss? What harm did the offender intend to cause, or know was a probable consequence of his acts under the circumstances known or believed by him? Were his acts intentional or knowing or reckless or negligent? The answers to these and similar questions would yield numbers of punishment units. Added up, all the punishment units for any single crime would give a numerical measure of the seriousness of the crime and the offender's conduct.

Robinson's plan also called for adoption of "real offense sentencing" under which judges would calculate presumptive sentences in terms of punishment units irrespective of the offense of which the offender was convicted. Of course, if the presumptive sentence exceeded the maximum authorized by statute for the conviction offense, that maximum would serve as a trump. Real offense sentencing was seen as a way to compensate both for the inadequacy of the federal criminal law and for the vagaries of plea bargaining. Whether an offender who intentionally killed another person was convicted under a civil rights statute, a conspiracy doctrine, a homicide statute, or RICO laws was seen as normatively irrelevant. What was seen as important was the harm that resulted and the offender's state of mind when he set in motion the events that led to the resulting harm.

For our purposes, however, the conceptual rationale for a punishment units approach is less important than the notion itself. If normative judgments of penal vulnerability can be expressed in generic terms, which is what, in effect, happens when a variety of offense and offender circumstances fall within a single guidelines cell, there is no reason why the other side of the equation, the punishments to be imposed and suffered, cannot also be expressed in punishment units. This next step was taken, in modest form, by members of the Commission's staff.

Through several successive drafts, Robinson and Commission staff worked on development of a fully elaborated system of sentencing guidelines premised on the punishment units concept. The Commission ultimately rejected this approach but the idea was enormously creative and the resulting documents will likely influence the development of sentencing policy for decades to come.

One 1986 staff proposal by Messrs. Hoffman, Tevelin, and Lombardero urged adoption of an interchangeability concept. When the minimum number of months of imprisonment in the guidelines ranged between one and six, they argued, the trial judge should be able to impose either that term or "a sentence of probation that includes a condition or combination of conditions that provide for intermittent confinement, community confinement, home detention, or community service equivalent to the number of months of imprisonment required to satisfy such minimum, as set forth in the following schedule:

One month of imprisonment = 30 days' intermittent confinement
= one month's community service
= two months' home detention
= 100 hours' community service"

This draft proposal applied only to cases in which the minimum term of imprisonment in the guideline range was less than six months; above that, the minimum term of imprisonment must be served. But at the lower end of severity of punishment, "exchange rates" between different punishments were being proposed in order roughly to equalize punitive severity.

A later staff memorandum by David Tevelin in 1987 took the matter further, proposing discretionary interchangeability of sentences by the trial judge, under a scheme in which one month's imprisonment was equivalent to two months' community confinement or three months' home detention. Equivalences were also suggested for fines, based on the criminal's after-tax annual income corrected for his net worth—a variation on the European day-fine systems that we discuss in Chapter 5. That same 1987 memorandum by David Tevelin neatly states the objective of this approach:

> If the Commission can establish reasonable exchange rates, the guideline approach advocated above should result in the imposition of sentences that have a comparable cumulative impact on similarly situated offenders who commit similar crimes, and permit judges to "do justice" in each case.

Little of the creative thinking that underlay the punishment units or interchangeability concepts became part of the federal guidelines. Earlier we described the Commission's ungenerous and unimaginative approach.

Proposal

Although none of the exchange rate policies or proposals we have described calls for a comprehensive system of interchangeability, many of the elements are there. Some jurisdictions have acknowledged the need to move beyond the in/out line to a system of interchangeability. The District of Columbia has shown how the use of changing presumptions can both guide discretion and enrich sentencing options. Various jurisdictions have begun to establish explicit criteria for establishing equivalence between total and partial confinement, community service, fines, and other punishments.

Once the idea of reasonable interchangeability between types of sentences is accepted, the path is clear to fashioning such a system. A comprehensive sentencing system can be envisioned, and established, that is evenhanded, that is constrained by concerns for desert and proportionality, and that integrates incarcerative and nonincarcerative punishments.

We believe that all the elements for such a system are in place and that it is philosophically justified and socially needed; we regret that the U.S. Sentencing Commission did not act on its authorization from Congress to create such a system. The federal system is especially favorably situated to have shown the way, for the federal system does not suffer from some of the practical problems of implementation that impede sentencing reform efforts in most states. In many states, for example, prisons are financed and operated by the state, jails by the county governments, and probation and related services by the judiciary, which itself is sometimes centrally funded, sometimes locally. These variations in financial and administrative responsibility often frustrate innovation because benefits may be statewide and costs local, or vice versa. An intermediate punishment designed to reduce state prison populations may increase local costs; when administration is in local hands, it is not surprising if implementation is less than wholehearted. The federal government, however, does not suffer these handicaps. The courts and probation, and the prisons, jails, and other programs of the Federal Bureau of Prisons, are all centrally funded and centrally managed. The Federal Probation Office, the Bureau of Prisons, and the federal judiciary are professionally managed with talented and well-trained staffs. All of these things make the federal system the most promising of all American jurisdictions for serious sentencing reform efforts. We return to these problems of implementation in Chapter 8. Here we describe the elements we regard as essential to a comprehensive sentencing system.

The Principle of Interchangeability

A comprehensive integrated sentencing system must include a system of interchangeable punishments, particularly covering the middle range of severity of crime and ordinariness of criminal record, that can be tailored to the circumstances presented by individual cases.

Erase the In / Out Line

The division of sentencing standards between prison and everything else, necessary though it may have been in early guidelines systems, is an error that reifies simplistic approaches to sentencing policy.

Use Presumptions Creatively

Most sentencing guidelines create presumptions about who is to receive prison sentences and for how long. Judges may decide that the circumstances of a given case overcome the presumption if reasons to support this decision are given. The District of Columbia Superior Court Sentencing Commission sensibly moved these notions forward by creating presumptions about the choice of intermediate punishments (A 1988 article by Wasik and von Hirsch also proposes a series of successive presumptions as a sensible way to integrate intermediate punishments into sentencing guidelines.) The four bands of presumptive sentences that we described earlier are a substantial step forward that we urge future sentencing commissions to adopt.

Purposes at Sentencing

Sentencing choices from among interchangeable punishments (or packages of punishments) should be governed by the purposes to be served *at* sentencing, not by the purposes *of* sentencing. In the following chapter we develop this distinction between purposes of sentencing and at sentencing at greater length. Within the range of discretion that the guidelines allow, however, judges' decisions should be guided by the purposes they hope to achieve at sentencing in imposing a sentence from among those interchangeable punishments that the guidelines authorize. Once the principle of interchangeability is accepted in a system of structured sentencing discretion, the importance of purposes *at* sentencing becomes unarguable.

The Mechanics of Interchangeability

Simpler is better. Both simple intuition and experience with parole and sentencing guidelines urge that decision rules should be simple and easy to undertand. Minnesota's juvenile court guidelines offer an example of guidelines that spell out the choice of interchangeable punishments presumptively appropriate at sentencing for every offender. Washington State's general rules on exchange rates (for example, that eight hours' community service equals one day's confinement) offer a different approach. No doubt there are others.

The Limits of Interchangeability

Although we recognize that our views perforce are subjective and arbitrary, we would urge that the principle of interchangeability govern all offenders for whom a prison term up to 24 months' *real time* (net of allowable time for good behavior) is presumptively authorized.

There is a point at which imprisonment and other punishments cease to be interchangeable. Exactly where this point is must be determined in each jurisdiction in light of prevailing normative views of policymakers and prevailing public attitudes. This is true at both ends of the punishment continuum. As the District of Columbia's out band attests, there are some offenses for which any amount of imprisonment would be too severe. There are other offenses for which any punishment less than a term of imprisonment would be too lenient and tend to depreciate the seriousness of the offender's conduct. These observations do no more, however, than restate the outer bounds of not-undeserved punishment that are set by concern for the canons of desert that we discuss in the next chapter.

Another unhelpful qualification is that there will always be cases in which the ordinary rules do not apply. Homicide, for example, may be an offense for which the presumptive sentence should always be a substantial term of imprisonment. Most judges will nevertheless often want to impose some other sentence on some persons convicted of mercy killing or on the battered wife whose lethal behavior did not quite rise to the level of an affirmative defense of self-defense. These cases can and should be handled as departures from the ordinary rules, and acknowledgment of their existence therefore does not move the argument forward.

We have several reasons for urging that 24 months' incarceration be the point beyond which intermediate and incarcerative sentences not be interchangeable. First, two years should, in general, be a good proxy for nonviolent or not-very-violent stranger crime. In most jurisdictions, heinous crimes or crimes involving substantial or gratuitous violence are likely to call for sentences in excess of two years' imprisonment.

Second, whether justified in terms of parsimony, or use of the least restrictive alternative, or prevention of "prisonization," we believe that prison should be used sparingly and that, in general, the presumption should be against imposition of short prison sentences.

Third, we can envision punishments that could meaningfully be said to be roughly equivalent to two years' imprisonment. A German-style day-fine system, for example, in which a day fine is calculated as the loss of income associated with a day's incarceration, would permit a fine of 440 day-fine units: the income that would be lost in two years' imprisonment. Such a fine may well be financial devastation for an offender's family, but so would his incarceration for two years. Similarly, we can envision packages of community service, residential controls, treatment conditions, and financial penalties equivalent to two years' imprisonment.

Reasonable people will disagree with the proposed two-year outer bound for prison/nonprison equivalence. We are less concerned with the persuasiveness of our arguments for two years than with the need to set an outer bound that recognizes interchangeability for other than trifling cases.

The Defendant's Veto, Not His Choice

The choice among interchangeable punishments is for the judge, not the defendant. The judge must decide what purposes at sentencing are to be served by the punishments chosen. The defendant may be entitled to a veto of nonincarcerative punishments, as the Minnesota supreme court has held, although we are not confident about this. If credible equivalent community sanctions are less expensive to administer than incarceration, it is not clear why an offender should be entitled to insist that the state impose the most expensive equivalent punishment. Of course, an otherwise prison-bound offender who willfully refuses to comply with the conditions of a community-based punishment will likely soon arrive in prison in any case, perhaps for a longer term than he would originally have received.

Calculating the Exchange Rates

One problem that confronts the establishment of exchange rates looks hard, but in fact is easy. How exactly are the exchange rates to be set? What should they be? The reason these are easy questions to answer is that there are no right answers. There are palpably wrong answers, but there are no right answers. Exactly how days of community service, dollars or day-fine units, months of intensive supervision or home detention, or full or partial incarceration relate to one another must be decided in each jurisdiction in which the question is faced. Setting the exchange rates seems a more daunting task than it need be, mostly because it has so seldom been done. The issues raised are no more difficult than those associated with the scaling of offenses, the assignment of sentencing ranges to particular offense–offender combinations, the development of "criminal history" scores, and decisions about who is to go to prison. In the end, all of these decisions are arbitrary to a degree but justifiable in terms of a consistent internal logic. For example, we earlier described the detailed exchange rates of the Minnesota juvenile court guidelines. These equivalences are inevitably somewhat arbitrary. They are, however, consistent throughout the entire scheme. And so they can be in any comprehensive sentencing system.

In setting out this program for a comprehensive sentencing system including interchangeable punishments, we have purposely set aside the jurisprudential, practical, political, bureaucratic, and other problems that must be overcome for such a system to be established. To those problems of principle and practice we turn in the following chapters.

4

Interchangeability
of Punishments
in Principle

The concept of interchangeability raises serious jurisprudential concerns. In advance and independently of specific cases, can equivalences be set out between different types of punishments so as to satisfy multiple legitimate ends of sentencing policy—including social utility and moral justification? Are there "exchange rates" between punishments that can be expressed or encapsulated in a system of comprehensive sentencing standards? Can a sentencing system fairly and justly impose a prison sentence on one offender and a community-based sentence on his in-all-respects like-situated brother?

Fairness and Justice

The tension between the requirement of fairness—that there be general standards that apply to all—and the requirement of justice—that all legitimate grounds for distinguishing between individuals be taken into account when decisions about individuals are made—was brought into focus by the Congress's mandate to the U.S. Sentencing Commission. Section 3553 of the Sentencing Reform Act of 1984 required the Commission to devise sentencing guidelines:

(A) to reflect the seriousness of the offense, to promote respect for the law, and to provide just punishment for the offense;

(B) to afford adequate deterrence to criminal conduct;

(C) to protect the public from further crimes of the defendant; and

(D) to provide the defendant with needed educational or vocational training, medical care, or other correctional treatment in the most effective manner; . . .

The Congress at the same time affirmed "the need to avoid unwarranted sentence disparities among defendants with similar records who have been found guilty of similar conduct."

Can these diverse legislative directions be fulfilled by a sentencing system that sends one offender to prison and imposes on another offender, convicted of a crime of equal gravity and with an identical criminal record (in the words of the statute, "with similar records who have been found guilty of similar conduct"), a sentence of, say, a fine, residential restrictions, and community service? If the answer is a principled "Yes," then there must be some principled exchange rates between different punishments if "the need to avoid unwarranted sentence disparities" is not to be flouted.

The question of penal equivalence has a very practical political side. Public opinion sees too many intermediate punishments as indulgences to the more privileged convicted criminals, a way by which judges deal leniently with "criminals like us, who have suffered enough" while consigning underclass criminals to crowded and brutal prisons. Indeed, in its April 13, 1987 report to the Congress, the U.S. Sentencing Commission justified a narrow approach to use of nonprison sentences as the product of its objective of assuring that white-collar offenders receive other than nominal punishments. Hence there are two aspects to our inquiry into interchangeability: the practical-political and the jurisprudential. In Chapters 3 and 8 we deal with the practical and political problems associated with taking intermediate punishments seriously; in this chapter we pursue an excursus into the jurisprudence of punishment. Since justificatory arguments about the moral appropriateness of imposition of different but roughly equivalent punishments vary substantially with the punishment philosophy to which one subscribes, the jurisprudential issues though complex are unavoidable.

The Jurisprudence of Interchangeability

For people who espouse teleological or consequentialist punishment philosophies, usually some version of utilitarianism, in which actions are justified by their results, "equality of suffering" by the offender is seldom a paramount aim; the justification must be expressed in terms of crime prevention or achievement of other desirable social ends through such processes as deterrence, incapacitation, and rehabilitation.

For those who espouse deontological punishment philosophies, usually some form of retributivism or "just deserts," the moral justification for imposition of suffering on the offender must relate to the offender's culpability or character and the notion of "equally deserved punishment" often is accorded dominant or substantial importance. In the extreme case, what H. L. A. Hart once called "thoroughgoing retributivism," deserved punishment would be linked closely to the degree of moral misconduct expressed by the offender's actions and two identically culpable offenders would deserve identically severe punishments.

In the abstract, our arguments for a sentencing system that authorizes imposition of different but roughly equivalent punishments on similarly culpable offenders who share comparable personal biographies present few difficulties in principle for the utilitarian. For the retributivist, however, our doctrine of rough equivalence faces obstacles and consequently it is these theories that we principally address.

First, however, some preliminary analytical skirmishing. A thoroughgoing retributivist would claim that the punishment to be imposed on an offender should be "exactly as much as he deserves, no more, no less." A skeptic would respond, however, that mortal minds do not possess moral calipers that can tell us exactly how much punishment any wrongdoer deserves. Of course, the skeptic will concede, any one individual may feel able to make such judgments; the problem, however, is that legal rules must be knowable in advance so that equally virtuous judges will reach identical or at least similar decisions in such matters. Socrates and Maimonides are unlikely to possess identical views about deserved punishment, in general or in specific cases. Therefore, concludes the skeptic, there is no way to determine the single, generally applicable, morally appropriate punishment for any given case, and these decisions of deserved punishment must be made on other grounds.

There are, however, at least two strategies a retributivist could adopt for getting round this dilemma. First, he could urge some sort of democratic solution. Whether by consulting some measure of general public opinion or by relying on the judgments of some body of policymakers, perhaps a legislature or a sentencing commission, people could be asked to declare their views of the single appropriate punishment for a single actual or hypothetical case. The resulting range of answers could then be averaged, giving a mean measure of deserved punishment, or the persons consulted could negotiate a consensual measure of deserved punishment.

The difficulty with these solutions is that the resulting measure of deserved punishment would be supported by a formal logic, but not a moral logic. Research on sentencing disparities, and on exercises in which judges are asked to "sentence" hypothetical cases, compel the conclusion that judges vary widely in their judgments about appropriate punishment, and there is no reason to doubt that a similar diversity of view would characterize any cross section of the general public. What a democratic solution to our inability to specify deserved punishments would provide is mean or consensual measures of deserved punishment that are essentially arbitrary, the product of a wide range and distribution of individual judgments about deserved punishments. Thus the democratic strategy seems not to work, except as a method for identifying the range within which reasonable peoples' judgments about deserved punishments fall, and thereby identifying a range beyond which punishments are generally seen as undeserved.

The second strategy for getting round the dilemma is comparative. Our friend and estimable colleague Andrew von Hirsch has developed this analysis most fully and creatively. In his 1985 book,

Past or Future Crimes, von Hirsch concedes that a notion of "commensurate desert" cannot be a "defining principle" for what he calls "cardinal magnitudes" of punishment. By this, he means to concede that theory cannot tell us precisely what punishment is appropriate in any given case. Nevertheless, argues von Hirsch, theory can provide powerful guidance concerning the relations between punishments for offenses of differing gravity. If two otherwise identical offenders commit, respectively, a minor theft and an armed robbery, notions of deserved punishment should lead to the imposition of a more severe punishment on the armed robber than on the thief. When a sufficiently large number of comparative assessments of offense severity and culpability have been made, von Hirsch argues, the result will be an "ordinal" ranking of offense severity. Persons who commit offense B are more culpable than those who commit offense A and less culpable than those who commit offense C. Once "anchoring points" of amounts of punishment have been fixed and specified as appropriate for the most and least serious offenses, the ordinal ranking of offense severity can serve as a basis for assigning appropriately scaled punishments for all offenses in a way that is consistent with a commensurate deserts starting point. Thus if nominal probation is one end of a punishment continuum and 20 years' imprisonment the other, an ordinal ranking of offense severities will provide a morally persuasive system of proportionate punishments.

Von Hirsch's analysis provides a logic for developing a system of ordinally proportionate penalties for jurisdictions that, as a matter of policy, wish to do so. The question for us, however, is whether the analysis compels that primacy be given to a value of "equality of suffering."

We think not, for four reasons. First, von Hirsch's concession that no theoretical starting point can entail judgments of "cardinal desert" concedes that reasonable people can differ in their judgments about the deserved quantum of punishment in any given case. Reasonable peoples' judgments can tell us much more about punishments that are undeserved because too severe or too lenient than about punishments that are deserved.

Second, although notions of ordinal proportionality provide in theory a mechanism for scaling punishments in such a way as to assure equal punishment for equally culpable wrongdoers, they do not provide a compelling argument for why policymakers should choose to establish such a scheme. If the imprecision of cardinal judgments of deserved punishment gives powerful guidance about undeserved punishments but only slight guidance about deserved punishments, why may policymakers not justly create standards that authorize imposition of any sentence that is not undeserved (that is, that falls within the range of punishments that reasonable people would regard as deserved)?

Third, in practice, judgments of comparative culpability are enormously difficult to make. In mind games or in science fiction's parallel universes two otherwise identical offenders who commit different offenses can readily be imagined. In life, no two offenders are identical and any system of sentencing that takes account only of the statutory labels of the offender's crime alone or together with some measure of his past involvement in crime will be too crude to be morally compelling. Statutory labels simply tell too little about the moral gravity of individual acts. H. L. A. Hart observed, in his classic 1968 book, *Punishment and Responsibility*, that scalings of the gravity of crimes can provide "rough distinctions . . . but cannot cope with any precise assessment of an individual's wickedness in committing a crime (who can?)." Sometimes complexity of moral judgment will result from details of the offender's biography, sometimes from details of the crime; for innumerable reasons in innumerable cases there will be occasions when the penal guidance given by a system of ordinal proportionality will be incomplete. Von Hirsch would likely concede this last point but urge that it is not inconsistent in principle with his position; any system of guided discretion must allow for exceptional cases, he might say, and these, in a guidelines system, should be treated as "departures" for which reasons must be given.

There is, however, a fourth, and for us compelling reason to reject a strong retributivist punishment theory. In practice, few if any policymakers or decisionmakers subscribe to such theories in any strong form. Many view retribution and commensurate desert as appropriate considerations to be taken into account at sentencing; few view these as the *only* appropriate considerations. In our experience, most public officials subscribe to the view that Norval

Morris in *The Future of Imprisonment* in 1974 called "limiting retributivism," in which punishments are seen as justifiable when they are "not undeserved."

In any case, we doubt that much in the world of practical affairs turns on analytical differences of the sort canvassed in the preceding paragraphs. People have been arguing about the justifications for punishment and for the criminal law for thousands of years. Whether it be Aristotle and Plato in classical Greece, Jeremy Bentham and Immanuel Kant early in the nineteenth century, John Stuart Mill and James Fitzjames Stephen in Victorian England, or H. L. A. Hart and Lord Patrick Devlin in modern times, fundamentally opposed punishment philosophies seem to characterize every era in which these matters receive attention.

People have deeply embedded beliefs about punishment, as they do about the death penalty, the exclusionary rule, or abortion, and these tend to be the kind of beliefs that are seldom changed by argument or by the marshaling of evidence. Although some people may, for example, be agnostics concerning capital punishment, there are probably many more who will remain fixed in their views whatever the findings of empirical research concerning deterrent effects or the logic of opponents' arguments.

Harvard philosopher Robert Nozick observed in his 1981 book, *Philosophical Explanations,* that professional philosophers are in this respect like the rest of us:

> When a philosopher sees that premisses he accepts logically imply a conclusion he has rejected until now, he faces a choice: he may accept this conclusion or reject one of the previously accepted premisses. . . . His choice will depend upon which is greater, the degree of his commitment to the various premisses or the degree of his commitment to denying the conclusion. It is implausible that these are independent of how strongly he wants certain things to be true. The various means of control over conclusions explain why so few philosophers publish ones that (continue to) upset them. (pp. 2–3)

If philosophers are little susceptible to persuasion about deeply embedded normative beliefs, it is not surprising that philosophical and ethical arguments often have little persuasive impact on the beliefs of others. One of the characters in Canadian novelist Robertson Davies's *Fifth Business* notes of philosophers addressing a fundamental question that they "answered it in ways highly satisfactory to themselves; but I never knew a philosopher's answer to make much difference to anyone not in the trade."

Given the reality that peoples' views of deserved punishment vary widely, it is unlikely that any comprehensive system of sentencing standards will adopt a rigid scheme of deserved punishments. Retributive considerations can, however, give guidance on undeservedly lenient or severe punishments; within those bounds there is, we believe, ample room for principled interchangeability of punishment.

To return to interchangeability: one way to address the problem of interchangeability is to deny the reality of the problem. If the crime and the offender's criminal record merit imprisonment, then equality of punishment, the need to treat like cases alike—the commensurate deserts argument goes—requires that imprisonment be imposed. Elsewhere, Norval Morris has argued in a 1976 lecture, "Punishment, Desert, and Rehabilitation," that the concept of treating like cases alike has been much exaggerated as a principle of punishment but, whatever the merits of that argument, no one doubts that it is desirable, so far as practicable, to diminish the extent to which like cases are treated differently. Equality in punishment may not be an unassailable principle, but it is at least a desirable goal.

H. L. A. Hart has written in *Punishment and Responsibility* of the "somewhat hazy requirement that 'like cases be treated alike.' " Hart may have found this requirement somewhat hazy because it was inconsistent with his own punishment philosophy in which general prevention provides the justification for criminal punishment as a social institution and which "allows some place, though a subordinate one, to ideas of equality and proportion in the gradation of the severity of punishment."

Hart's notion of haziness is apt, for it expresses the difficulty of knowing in advance or from afar that seemingly like cases are indeed alike. In any case, there are sound reasons in principle and prudence for honoring only a weak version of the adjurations for equality of suffering.

Imprisonment is expensive and unnecessary for some convicted felons who present no serious threat to the community and whose imprisonment is not necessary for deterrent purposes, and yet whose crime and criminal record could properly attract a prison sentence. Are we to allow an excessive regard for equality of suffering to preclude rational allocation of scarce prison space and staff? The path of wisdom, in terms of justice and political accept-ability, requires the enunciation of some rough interchangeabilities between different types of punishments. The aim must be to iden-tify punishments with roughly equal punitive properties that are suited to the variety of social threats and personal conditions that characterize offenders, a diversity of punishments, suited to social needs, that do not result in unwarranted sentencing disparities.

In the preceding chapter we offered a detailed proposal for a sentencing guidelines system based on the notion that, within limits, punishments can be made roughly equivalent in punitive force and social purpose and interchangeable in application. Of three like-situated offenders convicted of similar offenses, under our proposal, one might receive a six-month prison term, one a substantial fine, and the third a fine, intensive supervision, and required participation in a drug treatment program.

Once the principle of rough equivalence between incarcerative and nonincarcerative punishments is accepted, it follows that the choice of punishment should be guided by the purposes sought to be achieved in the individual case. Sentencing choices from among interchangeable punishments (or packages of punishments) should be shaped by governing purposes *at* sentencing, not by the general crime preventive or retributive purposes *of* sentencing (or punish-ment). General purposes may sometimes interpose negative con-straints on judges' choices; they seldom provide positive guidance. Michael Smith, director of the Vera Institute of Justice in New York City, has frequently urged that decisions among punishments in individual cases should reflect the judge's purposes at sentenc-ing. This slight change of preposition from "of" to "at" captures an important insight in respect to nonprison punishments. If, for example, the sole or primary purpose at sentencing is retribution, an appropriately severe package of financial sanctions, including restitution, costs, and a substantial quantum of day fines, may suf-fice. If the purposes at sentencing include both desert and control, depending on the offender's circumstances, a combination of com-munity service, home detention, mandatory drug treatment and testing, and intensive probation supervision may be enough. In still other cases, responding to public sentiment or deterrent or incapacitative concerns may be the governing purposes at sentencing; if so, the principle of rough equivalence permits imposition of a not-undeserved incarcerative sentence.

This helpful distinction between purposes of sentencing and purposes at sentencing is not new conceptually. Since the appearance of H. L. A. Hart's *Punishment and Responsibility* in 1968, most writers have accepted his partitioning of the philosophy of punishment into questions of "What is the justification for the institution of punishment?" (general justifying aim), "Whom do we punish?" (liability), and "How much do we punish?" (amount). Hart wanted to show that there was no reason in logic or principle why one could not simultaneously argue that, for example, utilitarian purposes provide the general justification for punishment while arguing that, for example, liability to punishment must be governed by retributive considerations. The general justifying aim of punishment involves purposes *of* punishment; the question of amount involves purposes *at* sentencing.

Hart's distinction has become newly salient at a time when the rule of law has begun to apply to sentencing. Under indeterminate sentencing systems in which the judge's discretion knew few bounds, it was hard to give operational meaning to the distinction between "at" and "of." After all, it was the individual judge who made both choices. Under presumptive sentencing guidelines, however, the judge's discretion is bounded. Consideration of the purposes of sentencing has shaped the architecture of the guidelines system, the ranking of offenses, the scaling of punishments, the identification of items of information that should and should not be taken into account in classifying offenses and offenders.

Within the range of discretion that the guidelines allow, however, the judge's decision should be guided by the purposes he hopes to achieve at sentencing in imposing a sentence from among those interchangeable punishments that the guidelines authorize. Once the principle of interchangeability is accepted in a system of structured sentencing discretion, the importance of purposes *at* sentencing becomes unarguable.

One main line of criticism that has been offered of this concept of interchangeable punishments, comparably punitive yet adapted to the many other concerns relevant to rational sentencing, is that it is too complex to be workable. This seems to us more a sign of apprehension of the unknown than the recognition of any problem in the sentencing process. Why should the task of sentencing convicted offenders be simple?

Is it that judges cannot cope with complexity? They do so in many other areas of the law; the complexities of a comprehensive, integrated set of sentencing standards are child's play compared with the factual, conceptual, and legal complexities posed by federal tax, securities, or antitrust laws. In the criminal law, judges deal with the arcane glosses of the federal Racketeer Influenced and Corrupt Organizations (RICO) statutes, mail and wire fraud, the law of conspiracy, and many other statutory and common law doctrines of bewildering complexity. There, as here, judges function in a context of complex guided discretion.

Is it that the law's deterrent signals must be clear and unqualified? They are not so now, and at present they are not even truthful, with current "bark and bite" practices, by which the punishment served is often greatly less than the punishment announced—and this is widely known, certainly to potential criminals. Such leniency as exists in current American criminal justice systems largely flows not from sentimentality but from overload: a greater flow of criminals than inadequately funded and staffed police, court, and correctional services can handle.

A complex sentencing system, applied and enforced, is much to be preferred to the relatively simple and often unenforced systems that now obtain.

There have been some efforts to enunciate such exchange rates between punishments. These were discussed in the preceding chapter, where we described the slow, halting, but perceptible movement toward the development of comprehensive sentencing policies that integrate both prison and nonprison into a system of interchangeable punishments. To assist understanding of our present problem, recall the central features of those emerging systems, pertinent to the imposition of intermediate sentences:

1. Rejection of the abrupt distinction between prison and nonprison sentences;
2. Establishment of standards governing choices between prison

and nonprison sentences and among diverse nonprison sentences;
3. Creative use of presumptions for and against use of nonprison sentences to guide, but not straitjacket, the exercise of judicial sentencing discretion;
4. Establishment of "exchange rates" to achieve, for appropriate cases, principled interchangeability between prison and nonprison sentences and among different nonprison sentences.

American sentencing policy can, and should, move forward in its explicit, principled integration of a variety of nonprison sentences into its sentencing armamentarium.

Interchangeable Sentences

Lest it be thought we have in this jurisprudential excursus too obliquely passed over a fundamental incompatibility between our proposals and the moral imperatives of equality and proportionality in sentencing, we now develop two lines of practical argument about criminal justice to support our proposals. First, from a moral perspective, the measure of punishment is not its objective appearance but its subjective impact. Our goal is to achieve a system of interchangeable punishments that the state and the offender would regard as comparable in their punitive effects on him. Second, we believe that nonincarcerative (and partly incarcerative) sentences can be devised that can meaningfully be said to be equivalent to imprisonment, and that these can be deployed within a system of guided discretion that maintains proportionality and rough equivalence among the punishments imposed on different offenders. We do not expect acceptance of these propositions without some discussion.

Differential Impact

Need a system of interchangeable punishments run afoul of concern for achievement of equality and proportionality in the administration of punishment? Even if we cannot precisely calibrate desert to punishment, the argument goes, we can at least ensure

that punishments are scaled in a meaningful way to the comparative gravity (and desert) of different offenses. Thus proportionality
in punishment will, in the nature of things, assure that offenders of
comparable desert (in terms of the seriousness of their crime and
their criminal record) receive comparable punishments. For reasons developed earlier, we believe this search for equality and
proportionality is chimerical; it oversimplifies the complexity of
moral judgments about desert and the need to make such assessments in light of the circumstances of each offender other than his
crime and criminal record.

Those favoring retributive or just deserts systems of punishment
frequently neglect to consider with sufficient precision the coinage
in which their justly deserved punishments are to be paid. It is
taken as axiomatic that two equally undeserving criminals, in terms
of the gravity of their crime and the length and severity of their
criminal records, should be punished equally. The argument frequently stops there; yet a great deal is assumed. One critical assumption is that equality of punishment is now obtained when,
pursuant to a statute or a guideline, two offenders, who are closely
comparable in terms of their current crime and past crimes, each
receive sentences of three years' incarceration. In practice, those
two three-year prison sentences may, both objectively and sub-
jectively, be very different.

At the outset, before discussing these two hypothetical offenders, we reject the approach taken by utilitarian philosophers who
reject "interpersonal comparisons of utilities." By this they mean
that analyses of the incentives and disincentives of social policy
must be assessed by reference to a hypothetical average man. It is
too complex, ultimately impossible, they argue, to take into account in such analyses the predispositions and disinclinations of
every person. In sentencing, however, no generic man stands
before the court, but countless individuals do. We think it axiomatic that questions of fairness and justice in criminal punishment
must be weighed in individual terms.

Is the equality of punishment to be inflicted on our two equally
undeserving criminals an equality of pain or suffering? If it is, how
can that possibly be measured?

Let us put the point aphoristically. A year often is not a year.
A year's imprisonment in one prison may well not equal a year's

imprisonment in another terms of pain and suffering. Every prison administrator knows this, and certainly every prisoner knows this. A year in a minimum security federal prison, security level 1, is a profoundly different experience from a year in a maximum security federal prison, security level 6. A year in a state prison forestry camp is a profoundly different experience from a year in a state maxiprison proximate to a city. Prisons differ dramatically in their levels of violence, fear, social separation, and vocational and developmental opportunities; it would be an expensive and needless exercise in cruelty to seek to equate the suffering of our two criminals, each sentenced to a year's imprisonment. In a dystopia described in Kurt Vonnegut's *Welcome to the Monkey House,* dedication to equality of opportunity requires that the beautiful wear masks, the athletic wear chains and weights, the mentally able wear hearing devices that emit a constant and shrill grinding noise. So it would be if equality in carceral suffering were required, for it is certain that the equality would be achieved by increasing the suffering of the relatively privileged rather than by improving the lot of the disadvantaged. And no responsible prison administrator would join in such a fruitless and expensive exercise.

There is, of course, another variable that prevents a year's imprisonment for one criminal being equal to a year's imprisonment for another equally undeserving and equally justly punishable criminal: one is aged 30, the other is aged 70 (their records of embezzlement are the same). Does the 70-year-old endure more loss from a year's confinement than the 30-year-old? We suppose so. And in a like manner, much of the life histories, personal and family circumstances, and psychological sensitivities of our two antiheroes will condition the quality of the pain and deprivation they suffer from a year in the same prison; subjective equality in this hedonistic calculus is unachievable.

By more subtle psychological measures of pain and suffering, a year's imprisonment may well not be equal to a year's imprisonment. Both A and B will suffer a sense of diminished self-image, a separateness from the flow of their lives; this too differs not only between prisoners but between prisons in the extent to which some prison administrations bolster, as best they can, the personal and community ties of their inmates, while others impose restrictions and degrading ceremonies on all such contacts.

A final comment on this point: many, though not all prisons, provide a safer and more comfortable environment than the environment from which many of our street criminals come. In prison, they are less likely to be assaulted or killed, they eat better, they often begin educational efforts they had previously entirely neglected, they sometimes begin to take hold of their lives and give them shape. Are those from such adverse social circumstances to have extra pains and sufferings inflicted on them to compensate for the advantages that accompany confinement in decent, well-run prisons?

This side of the punishment equation is of great practical importance to a rational and just sentencing system. The assumption that the coinage of punishment is fungible is a gross oversimplification. In practice, prison administrators often have enormous latitude in determining the conditions of life of offenders "in the custody of the state department of corrections." Some "state prisoners" in Oklahoma are "confined" in their homes under house arrest. In many places, prison administrators have discretion to grant work or educational furloughs or to assign prisoners to community-based facilities under partial or intermittent confinement. Thus the contrasts in suffering between two persons each sentenced to two years in prison are often even starker than in our earlier illustrations of confinement in different institutions; in practice, one "two-year sentence" may be served in a maximum security prison and another under terms of nighttime confinement in the prisoner's hometown while he attends college courses.

Three consequences flow from this argument of the nonfungibility of prison punishment expressed in terms of time.

First, further strength is given to our submission that the sensible ideal of justly deserved punishments should limit the boundaries of punishment and should not be thought capable of defining what is the single appropriate punishment in any given case—that definition is to be sought on other grounds. Just as the seemingly equal one-year prison sentences of two like-situated offenders may in practice result in quite different experiences of imprisonment, so, in our view, like-situated offenders can justly receive different but roughly equivalent punishments of great variety.

Second, it is immediately apparent that just as prison and time do not define a fungible punishment, no other criminal sanction does. No matter what we do by way of graduating fines, for example, to the wealth and earning capacities of different offenders, we cannot achieve equal impact between the wealthy and talented and the indigent and untrained.

Third, for us the most important point: the variety of objective and subjective experiences encompassed within the words "you are sentenced to two years' imprisonment within the custody of the Department of Corrections" demonstrates that even seemingly equal terms of imprisonment often result in only "rough equivalence" and sometimes not even that.

Is all this an argument in favor of disparity of punishment? That certainly is not our purpose. What is argued is that all that can in reality be achieved and all that should in practice be sought is a rough and ready equivalence of punishment in terms of preserving a reasonably fair and just punishment system, doing as much good as it can, and avoiding needless suffering and expense where it can. For these purposes it is the public perception of a punishment system as striving for a rough equality that is determinative. That system cannot rectify the underlying social and personal inequalities on which it rests; it does well if it does not exacerbate them.

It is precisely this more modest view of what is involved in a system of equally deserved punishments that more than justifies interchangeability of punishments between those that are incarcerative and those that are community based—it compels it.

Punishments have different impacts on different people. If non-incarcerative punishments are seen as in the main to impose less suffering on the offender than incarcerative punishments, that is no reason to avoid them, provided the punishment imposed is reasonably appropriate to the offense and the conditions of that punishment are determinedly enforced and backed up on breach, if necessary, by incarcerative punishment.

Rough Equivalence

It may be thought that the reiteration of the idea of "rough equivalences" of punishment reveals the weakness of the idea. Why rough equivalence? Why not equivalence? Is it because there cannot in practice be equal punishment between these different types of sentences and that use of "rough" reveals the superficiality of the concept?

It is often asserted that fairness in punishment requires that punishments be "justly deserved" and that this involves equivalency and some would say identity, but certainly more than "rough equivalency" in the punishment of like cases. But in its most difficult form for those who favor an extended and extending use of intermediate punishments, the proposition is this: if offenders A and B be equally deserving of punishment, judged by the gravity of their crime and the seriousness of their criminal records, then if one is justly sentenced to prison, so should the other.

Sometimes an effort is made to sidestep the rigidity of this assertion by stressing the usual "unlikeness" of cases, to make the point that there can be found in all but exceptional cases some differences of moral desert, gravity of crime, or severity of criminal record that will justify sentencing one to prison while imposing a nonincarcerative punishment on the other. This is, of course, one way of constructing sentencing guidelines to favor the extension of intermediate punishments; stress a presumption favoring nonincarcerative punishments and then list an extended series of aggravating and mitigating circumstances that will facilitate the imposition of a prison term on one of our hypothetical miscreants and an intermediate punishment on the other. In practice, this may well be the way sentencing discretion should be guided, but here, for purposes of analysis, we wish to avoid this easy way out, this delegated discretionary sidestep, and take on the hard issue of whether it is proper, assuming for purposes of the argument absolute identity of "desert," to impose a prison term on one offender and a roughly equivalent noncustodial intermediate punishment on the other. If a year's imprisonment is the appropriate sentence for A, how can a substantial nonincarcerative punishment be justified for B?

Before we answer this question, some ground clearing is in order. In the previous chapter we set out the elements of a comprehensive sentencing system that incorporates prison and nonprison punishments and that allows for interchangeability of roughly equivalent punishments for like-situated offenders. It can be worthy of adoption or of consideration only if in principle it is consonant with prevailing notions of justice and fairness.

To further develop the case for a system of roughly equivalent interchangeable punishments, we must introduce a number of notions and distinctions, and a roadmap of the balance of the chapter may help the reader stay the course with us. First, we explain what we mean by the terms exchange rates and equivalency. Second, we address the question "equivalency in what sense?" There are several possibilities: equivalency in pain or suffering, equivalency in intrusiveness or deprivation of autonomy, equivalency in penal purpose. Third, we consider the process by which rough equivalents are to be identified for policymaking purposes and suggest a principled approach for addressing all of these questions.

EXCHANGE RATES AND ROUGH EQUIVALENCY

For a comprehensive system of sentencing to authorize choices among equivalent incarcerative and nonincarcerative punishments for particular categories of offenders, there must be some language for expressing equivalence, some exchange rates for relating periods of incarceration to periods of intensive supervision probation to amounts of money or community service. In the previous chapter we mentioned the State of Washington's exchange rate of one day's community service for one day's confinement and also various federal proposals and the ambitious proposal in the Minnesota juvenile court dispositional guidelines.

Too close an analogy should not be drawn between "penal exchange rates" and monetary exchange rates, for monetary exchange rates involve both too great precision and too great variation for the rough equivalences we believe should guide sentencing policy.

Fixed monetary exchange rates of the sort negotiated at Bretton Woods—for example, 6.2 French francs to the dollar—offer much greater precision than criminal punishment can sustain. Any reasonable set of sentencing standards will authorize ranges of presumptively appropriate punishments, expressed in months of imprisonment, numbers of day fines, periods of intensive supervision probation. Thus there must be both ranges of authorized sanctions of each type and rough equivalence between sanctions of different types. Fixed exchange rates are much too rigid to serve these ends.

By contrast, modern floating monetary exchange rates are too volatile to serve as a guide. No doubt there are good reasons to allow market forces in the world economy deeply to drive down the dollar's value against the yen, but a sentencing system that abruptly and substantially altered the relations between types of punishments would soon lose its moral authority and credibility.

In sentencing policy, exchange rates must provide a basis seen by the public as reasonably acceptable for setting and applying rough equivalence of punishment for like-situated offenders. At any one time, they must be stable and provide meaningful guidance; over time, they must evolve gradually to reflect changing community values and attitudes toward crime and toward punishment. Thus neither Bretton Woods nor modern currency volatility provides a good model for the exchange rates of sentencing; wisdom suggests a middle way.

EQUIVALENCIES IN PAIN, INTRUSION, AND FUNCTION

To say that a sentencing system must be capable of delivering roughly equivalent punishments for like-situated offenders leaves open a central question: equivalent in what sense? There are at least two realms in which equivalence can be sought. The first looks to equivalence from an offender's perspective, equivalence in pain or intrusiveness; the second, from the perspective of the criminal justice system, equivalence in function.

Equivalence from the offender's perspective can be measured either in pain or suffering or in intrusion on autonomy. In theory, no doubt much could be said about differences between measures of pain and measures of intrusiveness. In practice, whether a year's incarceration or an intermediate punishment package is weighed in visceral terms of pain or unpleasantness or in more abstract analytic terms of intrusion on autonomy is not likely to matter. Criminal punishments are unpleasant burdens, however conceptualized, and it is principally in terms of this onus that punishments must be roughly equivalent.

As we have emphasized, differences between prisoners and differences between prisons banish assumed equivalency. Perhaps only in the judgment of the unthinking is a year's imprisonment the deserved equivalent of a year's imprisonment. By "the judgment of the unthinking" we mean the uninformed lay public which receives most of its knowledge of the criminal justice system from evening tabloids and television detective programs. Nonetheless, our dismissive reference may be a clue to lingering unease in the force of this argument that in terms of condign punishment a year for one is not a year for another and hence that the equality of deserved punishment is illusory. Perhaps it is the uninformed public who matter, not the judges and the criminals. Their expectations of the criminal justice system, and in particular of the judge's sentencing role within that system, is of pronouncements of powerful punishments, inflexible and inexorable, treating all alike, recognizing the central symbolic function of the criminal law and its educative and ego-reinforcing roles. Perhaps these are the attitudes and values that define the range of punishments acceptable for a given criminal with a given record, these are the measures of rough equivalence that will help to define the interchangeability of sentences between the incarcerative and the rest. If so, our thesis holds, though it has to be slightly differently phrased. Within existing public tolerances, there has already been clear demonstration of the public acceptability of intermediate sanctions in many jurisdictions where such sentences have supplanted some prison sentences. Perceived inequality does not seem to be a bar.

One reason for this is that public interest tends to be confined to the most serious or most sensational cases. These are not the cases where intermediate punishments are likely to have their greatest impact. In practice, adequate community acceptability has already been demonstrated of the diversity of punishments we seek. The difficulty of institutionalizing these ideas lies less with community opposition than with an inadequacy of resources and the lack of sufficiently refined jurisprudential principles, a lack to which we now return.

Can a sentencing system take account of such realities and preserve both an *appearance* and the *reality* of evenhanded punishment of the equally undeserving? Within the view of just punishment we adopt, we believe it can. Pain or suffering is a measure of the deserved punishment, to us only in the sense that the punishment imposed must not depreciate the severity of the crime and the criminal's prior record by leniency nor impose pain or suffering in excess of that justified by the crime and the record; within this definable range it seems to us perfectly proper for Mr. A to be sentenced to a prison term while Mr. B is sentenced to an intermediate punishment.

Is there another measure of equivalence of punishment more apt than pain or suffering? Is loss of autonomy the measure? There is certainly a larger measure of restriction of freedom in the prison than in any intermediate sentence, including electronically monitored house arrest. Is this why it is thought unfair to send A and not B to prison? In every physical sense, A may be better off for a year than his cloned friend B, but B remains more of a choosing, self-determining adult, and this is a decisive difference.

We have no complete answer to an equivalency so demanded. Obligations are, of course, imposed on B that severely restrict his autonomy, but the sharp difference remains. All that can be replied to those who would insist on equality of punitive restriction so defined is that it is not achieved now and its achievement would require a revolution in the community's judgment of fair punishment, which seems achievable, if at all, only in a society of far more sensitive punitive instincts than those that now obtain.

So what looks on the tidy face of a guidelines grid to be a single equal sentence of, say, 12 months' imprisonment may, in practice, vary substantially in its impact on the offender. Even rough equivalence in pain and suffering is not achieved by present prison practice, and it would be a most undesirable purpose to pursue.

Rough equivalences, both in fact and in the view of judges and the public, are all that we can hope to achieve no matter how we seek properly guided discretionary sentencing suited both to community needs and community expectations. Put affirmatively, we can well achieve equivalence in sentencing in terms of the functions it serves, evenhandedness in that sense between criminal and criminal.

But this question merits more than dismissal by demonstration of the impossibility of achieving equality of imposed suffering. There is a strong moral sense that this is an insufficient defense of our position. Let us take on the hard case, eschewing not even its racial overtones.

Two young offenders are convicted of robbery; both have a record of drug addiction. Posit equal severity of crime and of criminal record. The sentencing guideline, expressed or customary, in the jurisdiction of their crime suggests a prison term of one year. Criminal A, aged 19, is black, has been unemployed for the past six months, reads at a fifth-grade level, lives in a crowded apartment with his unmarried mother who has two other younger children with her on welfare. Criminal B, also 19, is white, has steady employment which need not be terminated if he is not sent to prison, graduated from high school, is now involved in trade training, and lives with his parents in a middle-class neighborhood. Are the following sentences justified? For Criminal A, one year's imprisonment with a recommendation to the correctional authorities that he be given the opportunity to participate in a drug treatment program while in prison and a release procedure that may assist him to avoid his present drug dependency. For Criminal B, two years' intensive supervision probation with the following conditions: an appropriate period in a residential drug treatment facility, thereafter at least weekly outpatient contacts with that facility with regular urine testing to ensure that he is free of drugs, and an obligation of at least weekly contacts with the probation officer. Restitution and a fine may also be appropriate; he must certainly work and contribute from his current earnings to the cost of his probation supervision and his drug treatment. If he lacks funds and cannot find work, add or extend an obligation of community service.

This is not an unreal hypothesis. The fact of a responsible home and a job and an education makes a dramatic difference to the possibilities of imposing a more socially protective punishment on B than on A. And these realities become even more significant when electronic controls and telephonic reporting are thought appropriate; the underclass is in effect excluded.

In the world as it is these two will certainly be sentenced differently. Is it necessary that in the sentencing world we would bring to pass that they be treated identically?

To insist on equal suffering by Criminal B because of the adverse social conditions of Criminal A is to purchase an illusory equality at too high a price. It is a leveling down and benefits neither Criminal A nor the community. The criminal law cannot rectify social inequalities; those inequalities will inexorably infect rational punishment policies. But this hypothetical situation leaves an uneasy sense of moral imbalance and forces us to the consideration of how deserved punishments can operate fairly in a world of social inequality.

It may be that evenhandedness in punishment should not be measured only in terms of rough equivalence of suffering, whether of pain or of degrees of loss of autonomy, but also in the functions to be fulfilled by a sentencing system. This is the typical lawyer's attachment, and a proper attachment it is, to equality of process. Within rough equivalences of impact on each offender, the just punishment must be imposed pursuant to an evenhanded weighing in every case of the functions to be performed by a criminal sentence.

Equivalence in function thus plays an essential role in the sentencing calculus, guiding or giving sentencing choices within the bounds of not undeserved punishments. If in an individual case the governing purposes at sentencing are retributive and deterrent, a short period of incarceration or a substantial fine may equally well achieve those functional purposes at sentencing. Similarly, if the retributive and incapacitative functions of punishment seem most apposite at sentencing of a drug-using repetitive thief, confinement or house arrest subject to electronic monitoring and frequent unannounced drug testing may be equivalent.

Thus within the bounds set by recognition of rough equivalency in pain or autonomy, we believe that judges at sentencing can appropriately take into account equivalencies in function to be served by different punishments.

For us, the high value we attach to parsimony, the value of avoiding unnecessary suffering, or as others have called it, a policy preference for the least restrictive alternative, urges that the least intrusive punishment be imposed that will within the bounds of not undeserved punishment satisfy the functional purposes primarily to be served at sentencing.

A THEORY OF INTERCHANGEABILITY

When we say a punishment is deserved we rarely mean that it is precisely appropriate in the sense that a deterrent punishment might be in principle, were we to know enough about general deterrence. Rather we mean it is not *undeserved;* that it is neither too lenient nor too severe; that it neither sentimentally understates the wickedness or harmfulness of the crime nor inflicts excessive pain or deprivation on the criminal in relation to the wickedness or harmfulness of the crime. The concept of desert defines relationships between crimes and punishments on a continuum between the unduly lenient and the excessively punitive within which the just sentence may on other grounds be determined, but it cannot do more.

Complexities of social relationships and the dialectic of human thoughts and actions determine over time the values that set these minima and maxima of deserved punishments for diverse crimes. What is determinative is that these values exist and underlie concepts of "desert" which set the limits of acceptable intervals on a spectrum of just punishment.

Desert considerations do not, and cannot, define the specific punishment warranted in any given case, but they can give guidance as to limits. The concept of "just desert" sets the maximum and minimum of the sentence that may be imposed for any offense and helps to define the punishment relationships between offenses; it does not give any more fine-tuning to the appropriate sentence than that. Nor should it. Experience shows that too often decisions about punishment policies are made with the most villainous of offenders in mind. Because of this, there is a long tradition in our jurisprudence of urging that many offenders receive punishments less severe than the most that could be justified. Thus Bentham called for parsimony. The clergy call for mercy. The *Model Penal Code* and the American Bar Association call for the "least restrictive alternative."

Professor Hart suggests in *Punishment and Responsibility* that "there is, for modern minds, something obscure and difficult in the idea that we should think in choosing punishment of some intrinsic relationship which it must bear to the wickedness of the criminal's act, rather than the effect of the punishment on society and on him."

Matching punishments to desert cannot create an even marginally acceptable system of punishments; there can be no system of just deserts if like cases are to be treated alike. A punishment scheme that sought only desert plus equality would be intolerably severe. If all criminals are to be punished equally according to the harm they have knowingly achieved, Solzhenitsyn's gulag would seem like a country club. If intentional and legally unprovoked killings attract their deserved punishment, a punishment matching the harm encompassed, then we would have approximately 10,000 executions a year in the United States (a country which has never executed 200 in any year). Likewise, white-collar criminals who have intentionally polluted the rivers and streams and atmosphere, or risked the lungs of their workers, would never properly be released from prison. The point is obvious: under a pure and equally applied system of just deserts, who escapes whipping?

So desert plus equality must be modulated if excessive severity is to be avoided. The first necessary modulation is that of proportionality. Larger harms in general must be punished more, lesser harms less. So a graded system of "deserved" and "equal" punishments must be created by which armed robbery risking life must be punished, in the normal case, more than armed robbery not risking life. In the main, crimes against the person attract more punishment than crimes against property. This becomes not a system of justly deserved and equal punishments but a system of less-than-could-be-deserved punishments, ranked by harms achieved and intended, and ranked in terms of moral fault.

But even that system, which might be represented as desert plus equality plus proportionality, would be excessively severe, and for a reason that can easily be stated. Rankings of harms and of moral faults can be done only by rough groupings, unless a system of single instances is to be created, which will lead to gross disparity of punishments. What defines the punishment in each group or in each cell in a sentencing guidelines grid is the "worst case." A legislature or a sentencing commission looking at any such grouping will strongly incline to define the punishment within each cell in utilitarian and punitive terms suited to the most threatening and most wicked criminal within that cell. Hence if a workable system of reasonable fairness is to be developed, we must abandon the idea of equality as an inflexible principle within those cells and move to a system that is parsimonious in the use of punishment within the concepts of desert, equality, and proportionality.

We set aside the modulation of capital punishment as an impossible and intolerable exercise, though the U.S. Supreme Court and many legislatures believe it can be done. How is a prison term to be modulated in a rational sentencing system? First: the groupings or boxes should provide a range. Congress directed that the ranges for prison sentences in the federal sentencing guidelines not exceed 25 percent to cover the diversity within any single imprisonment guideline. That is the first modulation. Second: though a case falls within a guideline range, there may be an unusual mitigating or aggravating factor in this case which merits a reasoned "departure," itself a modulation. Third: there is very great diversity where and how a prison sentence will be served; parsimony and economizing with scarce prison resources will justify a very different level of adversity between one criminal sentenced to prison and another. Anyone acquainted with American prisons knows that they vary from the most brutal and terror-ridden challenges to survival to safe and educative institutions, with family visits, furloughs, work release, graduated release procedures, halfway houses called prisons, and so on. In short, there is ample and proper room for treating individuals sentenced to similar terms within such a system differently on grounds of social protection and humane identification.

All punishments imposed within the roughly equivalent range will be subject to, and properly subject to, amelioration in imposition—not expungement due to inefficiency or overload, as is the current situation of the fine and of probation, but controlled amelioration. For imprisonment, amelioration may come through easier prisons, open institutions, working out, furloughs, graduated release, placement in community treatment centers, and so on. For fines, reduction or more time to pay on cause shown, serious efforts having been made. For probation with condition of being drug free, since addiction is a relapsing disease, judgment must be used in relation to positive urine tests and revocation. For intensive probation, successful adjustment, passage of time, and so on.

The following scheme summarizes these propositions about desert, equality, proportionality, parsimony, and punishment:

desert + equality = grossly excessive severity

desert + equality + proportionality = excessive severity

desert + modulated equality + proportionality + parsimony =

a reasonably fair and workable punishment system

Punishments should be imposed under the ceilings, the maxima roughly defined by concepts of what is not undeserved and what is not too unequal between similar criminals; they are then fine-tuned by ideas of social protection, economizing with scarce pun-

PART II

Having made the case for a greatly expanded use of intermediate punishments, in which they fill out the middle range of punishments for crime and occupy a principled place in a comprehensive punishment system, we now turn to examine the main intermediate punishments themselves and draw lessons for future development from current practice.

Their grouping is as follows: in Chapter 5 the surprising story of America's failure to develop the fine as an effective sanction against other than minor crimes is discussed and suggestions are offered for its incorporation into a comprehensive punishment system, both as an independent punishment and as an adjunct to other punishments.

In Chapter 6 the community service order is discussed and its proper role suggested. Like the fine, the community service order is primarily a retributive sanction, though the expiation that both provide may also have rehabilitative effects—at least on some criminals.

Chapter 7 begins the task of incorporating treatment purposes into intermediate sanctions, effecting the blend of retribution and crime prevention that we suggested necessarily characterizes a comprehensive punishment system. Its title, "Control and Treatment in the Community," suggests the range of topics examined, ranging from house arrest, halfway houses, intensive probation with conditions of treatment (particularly treatment for drug and alcohol addiction), and the challenging problems of effective enforcement that such sentences present. We address the evidence concerning the "success rates" of these intermediate community-based sentences and include an analysis of the part that electronic and telephonic monitoring systems can play in such sentences.

The last chapter confronts the political, financial, and other obstacles that impede the development of intermediate punishments. They are substantial but, in our view, can be surmounted, and they will have to be if our punishment policy and practice is not to continue to oscillate randomly, as it now does, between unprincipled severity and unprincipled leniency.

5

Fines

Why fines first? Why not probation and its more recent intensive and restrictive forms allied to electronic developments? Why not community service orders and their promise of more effective punishment to the advantage of victim, offender, and community alike? They would certainly be more usual choices; but in our view the choice of the fine as the lead intermediate punishment, within our definition of that phrase, takes us swiftly to the heart of the problem of such punishments in the sentencing systems of this country.

It is paradoxical that a society that relies so heavily on the financial incentive in its social philosophy and economic practice should be so reluctant to use the financial disincentive as a punishment of crime. One need only recall the overheated economy in December 1986—when consumers bought cars at record rates, in order to be able for the last time to take a full tax deduction for their sales tax payments, and when investors sold real estate and securities in record volume, in order to benefit from soon-to-be unavailable capital gains rates—to recognize how powerfully financial incentives drive our behavior. We all know that about ourselves and, perhaps with less sympathy, about others. Yet for some reason our sentencing practices seem premised on the belief that financial disincentives will not have comparable effects on offenders.

Theory

Whether one thinks of punishments in deterrent terms, with the economists, or in retributive terms, with the philosophers, there can in principle be no reason why the fine cannot serve as a credible punishment for nontrivial, indeed serious crimes. And no one can doubt that financial penalties can be devised that are draconic to a point where they ultimately constitute financial capital punishment. There is, on this issue, an alliance in principle between the conservative economists of the now-fashionable, right-wing, free-market, Adam Smithian school of economists and penal reformers—surely strange bedfellows. Both wish for an extension of the application of the fine to a larger number of criminal offenders and both advocate a substantial increase in the quantum of the fines imposed.

We are, of course, concentrating on fines imposed on individuals, not those imposed on corporations. Since corporations clearly commit crime, and equally clearly have no bodies to be whipped or imprisoned, the fine is the sole applicable punishment. But the time may have come, if minimum ethical practices are to be restored to some businesses, to consider the introduction of capital punishment against some corporations who plunder the marketplace or destroy the environment—capital punishment by enforced suspension of the corporation and the prohibition of its senior officers later engaging in any form of corporate management or directorship.

Returning then to the use of fines against individual offenders, and for the moment forgetting what we think we know about the extent of the use of fines as punishments in the United States, let us consider the possibility that the fine might be the punishment of choice for all but a few criminals—the punishment first considered, the punishment to which all the rest are "alternatives."

First, for minor crimes where there is greater willingness to accept the fine as the punishment of choice, there is a strange belief in this country that it cannot be applied to the poor. This is surely wrong. At the lower levels of severity of crime, the case for a greatly increased use of the fine seems obvious. A common scene in an English Magistrate's Court first led us to a particular interest in the fine as a criminal sanction: the shoplifter, unemployed, on welfare, with a record of minor property offenses, is being fined. If he is to be committed to prison, it will be for two or three months, but the alternative of a fine is being considered. The question is whether he will be able to pay two pounds a week for two years or whether four pounds a week for a year is within his reach. Such considerations are rare in American courts; they should not be. In these cases we too often impose a substantial penalty on ourselves, collectively as taxpayers, a penalty in excess of $1000 per month, so that we may imprison the shoplifter for a few months rather than punish him by the fine and, if he refuses to pay for no good reason, then move to a more restrictive punishment if that be necessary. It is hard to understand why this is not both good economy and good sense.

The planning group for an experimental day-fines project in Richmond County (Staten Island), New York, found that poor people can and do pay fines and other judicially imposed financial obligations. Among restitution orders imposed in Richmond County in 1986, for example, one-third of those so ordered were unemployed or students. The amounts they were ordered to pay and their payment records were fully comparable to those of others ordered to make restitution.

There are, after all, at least three sources of funds on which many poor people can draw: undisclosed income or assets, the assets of family or friends, and illicit sources of income. Of these, only the last presents problems. There can be no reason why offenders who are participants in the off-the-books underground economy, as many lower-income occasional workers are, should not be expected to apply that income to payment of criminal fines. Similarly, we see no objection—indeed some beneficial side effects—to having poor offenders pay fines from funds provided by parents, spouses, siblings, other relatives, or friends. Especially for minor offenses or newly active offenders, there may be salubrious side effects from fines paid with others' money. The offender's need to seek help may bring his troubles to the attention of those most likely to be concerned and supportive and, whether from altruism or self-interest in being repaid, his financial backer may take greater interest in his life, and may provide psychological support and social reinforcement that otherwise might not be available. Thus, ironically, imposition of fines on at least some impecunious offenders may serve preventive ends by catalyzing family and social support.

No doubt some offenders will commit more crimes to pay their fines. If that be a serious risk, then there is merit to adding controls in the community for a period greatly to reduce the risk of that criminality. The technology to that end is at hand.

But it is not only as a punishment for minor crimes that the fine has a role, either alone or together with another intermediate punishment. It holds promise of a much wider swath. Here are some characteristics of fines that should make them the punishment of choice for most crimes:

- Although in current practice fines are generally set in amounts too modest to be calibrated meaningfully in relation to serious crime, in principle fines can vary from small change to economic capital punishment.
- Although in current practice fines are too often haphazardly administered and collected, in principle fines can be collected with the same vigor and ruthlessness that characterize our friendly neighborhood finance companies.
- Although in current practice fines seem likely to be unfair to the poor and unduly lenient to the rich, in principle fine amounts can be tailored to each offender's assets and income so as to constitute roughly comparable financial burdens.

If the leading purposes of sentencing are deterrence and retribution, the amount of the fine imposed on any offender can be made sufficiently burdensome for these purposes, influencing both him and those who are criminally like-minded and economically like-situated, provided that collection of the fine is ensured—and it can be—or an equally deterrent and retributive sanction can then be substituted.

If to these properties of variable severity, retributive force, and deterrent capacity one adds adjustability in relation to the offenders' means and collectibility, the stark difference between the mean cost of imprisonment ($10,000–20,000 per offender per year, not counting capital costs) and the cost of a serious system of fines (very low), the case would seem to be made: the fine should be the hands-down favorite for punishment of many serious crimes.

Why isn't it? Why, as we shall see, is American practice so very different? There is no answer to this question that precludes movement in the direction we suggest when a greatly extended, rational, and fair use of the fine is within reach.

Legislation can be changed—and in some jurisdictions has been—to increase authorized fine amounts to levels high enough to have punitive credibility. Systems can be devised to assure that fines are collected just as well as the finance company collects its loans—perhaps by having the finance companies do some of it. The European day-fine systems provide the model and the experience for development of a system of means-based fines that treat the poor and the not-so-poor in justly comparable ways. And if these problems of credible amounts, effective collection and enforcement, and the taint of class-based unfairness can be overcome, there should be no reason why judges and others should be unwilling to use the fine as a serious sanction in many more cases than now occurs. Indeed as we write, a day-fine system is being established in Richmond County, New York, and serious consideration is being given to establishment of such systems in Phoenix, Minneapolis, Portland (Oregon), and elsewhere. In the pages that follow we try to show how and why fines can be used as punishments for serious crimes, but first one moral objection to the fine as a punishment for wide application to more serious crimes must be considered and dismissed.

Some argue that the fine is not an appropriate punishment for other than minor crime because its use would blur the distinction between discharge of moral and social obligations and discharge of economic obligations as a matter of economic convenience. We all have debts to pay, debts that can be enforced against us by the law if we fail to pay; to put the criminal offender in the same situation in respect of his crime, it is argued, is to blunt a central moral distinction. Crime will come to be seen as a business, just like any other business in which bankruptcy is a risk, a business in which discharge of moral responsibility for crime can be bought.

We doubt this. If this pattern of thought exists, it exists with our present range of punishments, attended as they all are by the formalities of charging, pleading, and guilt-finding. A much increased use of the fine may actually increase the deterrent effects of punishment at the lower end of gravity of crime, since the fine will be realistic and may well be coupled to other controls over the offender. At the deeper end of punishment the deterrent effect is unlikely to be attenuated—after all, it is the judge and not the offender who selects the fiscal penalty, with or without other elements of punishment and social control. Moral condemnation resides not only in the punishment; it is a product of the criminal process and the punishment.

At all events, the fine is used in the United States much less frequently than it is used in Western Europe. In 1979, for example, 82.4 percent of all sentenced criminals in the Federal Republic of Germany were ordered to pay a fine; these included 66 percent of offenders convicted of crimes against persons. Three out of four offenders are fined in the case of "ordinary" criminal offenses. Approximately 95 percent of all traffic offenders are fined.

But West Germany is not the only country that uses fines extensively. In Sweden, fines alone constituted 90.8 percent of all sentences in 1979. In England, in 1980, fines were imposed as sentences in 47 percent of convictions for indictable offenses (excluding motoring offenses). Lest readers assume that these high percentages of convicted offenders receiving fines are a statistical trick that results from mixing masses of minor crimes, such as motor vehicle offenses, with smaller numbers of serious crimes, consider this: in 1980, of persons convicted of summary offenses in England, roughly equivalent to American misdemeanors, 89 percent received fines, and this excludes motoring offenses. Of persons convicted of indictable offenses, roughly equivalent to American felonies, 45 percent of those convicted of sex offenses received fines, as did 24 percent of those convicted of burglary and 50 percent of those convicted of assault and other nonsexual offenses against persons.

Whatever the overseas experience, however, there is great resistance in the United States to use of the fine as the only, or the primary, punishment for persons convicted of other than trifling offenses. No sentencing guidelines system of which we are aware contains a provision for use of fines in place of incarceration. Several jurisdictions, including Pennsylvania, and the federal guidelines, expressly limit the fine to a supplemental role, something to be imposed in addition to the real sentence.

Judicial and prosecutorial opinions reflect this scant usage. Too many of the functionaries of the criminal justice system, particularly among prosecutors and judges, see the fine as inapplicable to the poor, useless against the rich, and inappropriate, certainly alone, as a punishment for all but minor first-time offenses. A recent national survey of judges' views about fines, conducted by George F. Cole and his colleagues, confirms these assertions. Most regarded fines as a weak punishment. More than half considered fines to have little impact on the affluent. A quarter of general jurisdiction court judges believed fines have a perverse impact on the poor—"to pay the fine in time, commit more crime." In the broad, the ground for planting fines in American sentencing is not fertile, but we believe the effort should be made.

One does not have to look outside our boundaries to make this case, though data from overseas certainly buttress it. Such is the diversity of fining practice between jurisdictions and even within jurisdictions in this country that our natural laboratory, even cursorily studied, reveals that fines can be fashioned sufficiently and properly to punish the poor and the wealthy and can be used for a broad swath of offenders, certainly not only for minor offenders and first-timers.

Practice in this country has been extensively studied by a team of researchers, headed by Sally Hillsman, at the Vera Institute of Justice, and practice further studied and judicial attitudes surveyed by researchers at the National Center for State Courts, headed by George F. Cole. The literature of practice and theory from England and Western Europe, particularly the United Kingdom, Sweden, and West Germany, is substantial. And all of this evidence points in broadly the same direction.

Fines in America, except in the case of federal securities, antitrust, and similar laws, have traditionally been limited to amounts so low that they cannot seriously be viewed as even roughly equivalent to a term of imprisonment. For example, under federal law before 1984, the maximum authorized fines were at such low levels that it was hard to argue that a fine could have much impact, actual or potential, on many offenders. The federal limits for individuals at the time of writing, however, in broad terms were

$250,000 for a felony, $25,000 for a misdemeanor, and $1000 for an infraction. Multiple-count convictions can, of course, greatly inflate these already substantial figures.

Maximum limits like these permit the imposition of fines that are fully as punitive or as deterrent as incarceration. And in those cases where the governing purposes at sentencing are deterrent or retributive, there is neither wisdom nor economy in having the state pay for imprisonment of offenders who could instead be fined.

Consider, for example, the case of a postal worker who is convicted of a serious case of postal theft. Exactly at what point the average employed working-class defendant will willingly accept prison for six months rather than pay a fine is a matter for speculation, but there must be such a point. Is it the point at which his car must be sold, his house remortgaged or sold? We don't know, and we don't urge that the law lightly choose to destroy the fabric of an offender's life and that of his family. Imprisonment, however, often does these things and fines could also if that punitive result were our purpose. And, in any event, we don't believe that the offender should be given the choice—a matter to which we shall return.

From an economic perspective, then, the case for fines is powerful for offenders whose sentences are primarily deterrent or retributive in purpose. Of course, for those whose sentences are shaped by incapacitative considerations, and for those cases in which the seriousness of the offender's behavior will be unduly depreciated by a fine, some other punishment is in order. Nonetheless, in the main, for most offenses and for many offenders, a fine should serve as well as prison. In dollars, it costs enormously less to administer. In human terms, it allows the offender to continue to earn a living and support a family (albeit in diminished circumstances) and it spares the offender (and his family, if he has one) the experience of prison.

In West Germany increased use of fines results from the conscious policy decision to minimize short-term imprisonment, the belief being that prison sentences of six months or under should be avoided, for they are destructive to those who serve them and seldom achieve any penal purpose not equally well attained by the fine. The First Criminal Law Reform Act of June 25, 1969 in West Germany directs courts to impose prison sentences of less than six months "only when special circumstances, present in the act or in the personality of the offender, make the imposition of the sentence indispensable for effecting an impression on the offender or defending the legal order." A recent report of the National Swedish Council for Crime Prevention likewise notes that short-term imprisonment is generally disapproved as a sanction in Sweden.

We suggest, then, as a working hypothesis that there are many prisoners in the "shallow end" of severity of crime and criminal record of those in prison who would, for our and their sakes, be better punished by a fine, allied where appropriate to another intermediate punishment. Moreover, there are many convicted offenders in the potentially "deep end" of severity of crime and criminal record of those on probation, now nominally supervised by probation officers with excessive caseloads, who would be better punished by a fine, allied where appropriate to another intermediate punishment. The problem, like so many others in the criminal justice system, becomes one of rational, effective, and fair sentencing, of the selection by prosecutors and judges of those who might better serve intermediate punishments than experience our present excesses of both leniency and severity.

Let us return to our assumption of the primacy of the fine as a punishment for the purpose of trying to define its proper role. Suppose then that in this country the basic sanction, the sanction to which all others are "alternative," is not the prison cell but the fine. Assume that upon conviction of any felony or misdemeanor the sentencing cast of mind turns immediately to the question: "What is the appropriate fine?"

In what cases should a fine *not* be imposed? When could an appropriate fine, together with other community controls, *not* be fashioned and imposed? When would a fine, no matter its size, be inadequate? When would it be excessive?

The answer to these questions cannot be given in terms of substantive categories of crime. We find it hard to think of a murder conviction appropriately punished by a fine, though, of course, there is long-established doctrine that the murderer and the murderer's estate cannot profit from the homicide by taking under a will; but there are certainly murders that should not be punished by a prison term. Instances of mercy killings by loving spouses unable further to tolerate the pleas of their partners for a surcease of suffering from terminal and painful illnesses are to be found in most jurisdictions and are met, unless they become sensational causes célèbres, either by an absence of prosecution or by a sentence of probation upon conviction. But a fine would be a most unlikely response. So, perhaps, treason, murder, incest, rape, and bank robbery apart, it is not too difficult to invent cases of conviction of all other crimes appropriately punished by a fine, and certainly by a fine combined with another intermediate punishment.

Only to a limited extent, then, at the high end of severity of crime, is the fine an insufficient and inappropriate sentence. There remains a wide range of serious felonies, including much of the street crime that fills our prisons, to which the fine could well be the sentence of choice were it properly sized and effectively enforced.

It is the combination of severity of crime and extent of criminal record that conditions most people's views of the appropriate severity of punishment, so that to write of certain types of crimes as being properly punishable by a fine somewhat avoids the issue. Thus for a very few crimes, whatever the virtue of the offender's past behavior and the total absence of a criminal record, a fine would depreciate the gravity of the offense. But for most types of crime it is only a combination of crime and criminal record that should properly exclude the fine from consideration.

For example, consider burglary: a fine, allied with an enforced condition of residence, confining the burglar electronically to his home if he has one or to a probation hostel if he does not, for the evening hours of every day, may well be the best way to prevent his future involvement in burglary without risking causing those who were of like-minded burglarious intent more diligently to practice their profession. The enforcement of the fine, attuned to the offender's capacity to pay, limiting his freedom in the community for a fixed time and certainly until the fine was paid, and the prison term if he willfully fails to fulfill these conditions, seems sound policy, though now standing far removed from the conventional wisdom of punishment.

A similar exercise can be pursued to a similar result for almost all crimes, subject of course to the recognition that past failure of such punishments to interrupt the criminal careers may push the punishment level beyond that which the fine and other intermediate punishments alone can achieve.

At the other end of the continuum of criminality, are there crimes for which, and criminal records for which, the fine cannot be imposed because of the offender's indigency and the length of his criminal record? Consider shoplifting as an example. The offender has taken goods worth $20 from a store and has an arm's-length record of similar behavior. How should he be punished in a system in which the fine is the primary sanction? Can the fine be combined with other social controls and other compelled assistance to him, and control of him, in such a fashion that he is enabled to make restitution to the store and pay a suitable fine to the state without relying on shoplifting to find the funds for these beneficent purposes? Is it worth the effort? We think so. The present failure adequately to enforce the law against shoplifting is a serious burden on many businesses. Part of that failure flows from our present lack of enforced middle-range punishments.

That this is so is shown by the experience that prosecutors from Huntsville, Alabama, to Ventura County, California, have had with "bad-check bureaus." Payment of the bounced check is demanded, together with a processing fee that increases in amount with each successive demand; the percentage of payments elicited by even the first demand is startlingly high and becomes higher with reiterated demands.

The bad-check bureaus, so long as their services are available only in cases in which probable cause exists to believe that the checks involved have been negotiated with knowledge that the maker's bank account lacks sufficient funds to pay them, are one of those rare institutions that seem to benefit everyone. The merchant is made whole; the prosecutor's office provides a public service, recoups its costs, and sometimes makes a profit; the writer of the check is spared formal prosecution but is firmly reminded that passing bad checks is unlawful and can have legal consequences.

It may well be necessary and wise to link the fine to opportunities to pay it by community service orders, employment training, and employment assistance. For all but the most alienated, hostile, handicapped, or incompetent it should be possible (or if we wished firmly enough to do so, we could make it possible) for the offender to pay his fine unless he lapses into deliberate noncooperation with the sentencing authorities—in which case an incarcerative punishment or other intermediate punishment may become appropriate, not for the original offense, but for the deliberate contempt and the original offense combined.

What are the disadvantages of such a determined approach? It would take effort and be costly, but not as costly as our present jailing and imprisoning practices. It would, of course, by giving training or assistance, give advantages to the convicted offender that his unconvicted brother, not a shoplifter but alike in all other respects, would lack. This is the problem of "lesser eligibility" that must not be allowed to preclude a rational sanctioning policy. This notion—that offenders, the unworthy, should not be given opportunities or resources not provided the worthy, noncriminal poor—has frustrated penal programs for a century. Prison industries and work release programs are beginning to break that notion's hold on correctional practice and we see no reason why an attempt should not be made here also. It was a mean-spirited philosophy with little to commend it. Equality of opportunity should not be achieved by a leveling down.

In sum, there are advantages in seeing the fine as the primary punishment behind which stand the prison and the jail for crimes and criminals whose criminality would be depreciated by anything less than an incarcerative punishment and for those from whom, because of their immediate danger of violence, the community is entitled to a temporary and complete respite.

In this penological utopia, there would also be a range of controls and supports and treatments in the community which give further social protection and rehabilitative promise to the fine as the basic sanction for rich and poor alike, for the serious crime and for the crime which is only a nuisance to the community but which should not be ignored. All, of course, depends on effective enforcement.

As a matter of theory, then, what are the preconditions to the use of the fine as a penal sanction? We attempt a formal reply, and add some commentary:

A. As for any punishment, one indispensable constitutional precondition to the imposition of a fine for a criminal offense is conviction by a jury or bench trial, or by an acceptable plea of guilty, for an offense for which a fine is a legislatively authorized punishment.

B. Other preconditions to a fine *alone,* that is, not accompanied by any other intermediate sanction:

   (i) the imposition of a fine at the maximum authorized by statute would not unduly depreciate the seriousness of the crime or crimes committed,

  (ii) the offender is not a continuing danger to the physical safety of a member or members of the community,

 (iii) the offender is not otherwise in need of control or treatment in the community to lessen the likelihood of his continued involvement in criminal activities.

It must be stressed that these "preconditions" refer to the fine as the sole sanction. If the fine be combined with one or another means of community control, then all three subentries in proposition B will vary considerably. To that variance we return in the recommendations at the end of this chapter.

If the fine were the basic coin of punishment, in which all calculations of interchangeability were to be made, how would the exchange rates be set? Three sets of considerations must be taken into account: the gravity of the crime, the resources of the offender, and the governing purposes at sentencing.

In Chapters 2 and 3 we argued that 24 months' real time in prison should normally be the outer bound of interchangeability. Heinous crimes or crimes involving substantial or gratuitous violence are likely in most jurisdictions to result in prison terms in excess of two years. Twenty-four months' presumptive incarceration is generally a reasonable proxy measure for identification of those criminal cases in which imposition of any punishment other than imprisonment would unduly depreciate the seriousness of the offender's crime. We believe that prison should be used sparingly and that punishments can be fashioned that are roughly equivalent to two years' incarceration in their punitive and deterrent effects.

The offender's resources, assuming he has any, can be taken into account, as we will demonstrate, by relating fine amounts to offenders' ability to pay. For those offenders who lack resources to pay a fine but seem otherwise eligible for a sentence not requiring incarceration, the answer here is a community service order, sometimes called "a fine on time," so that those without employment and income can pay their penalty in labor.

As to the governing purposes *at* sentencing, these will shape the nature of the punishment imposed but not necessarily the calculations of equivalence.

As we earlier suggested, purposes of sentencing and purposes at sentencing may differ drastically, and it is the latter that shape the nature of the punishment imposed, but not necessarily the calculation of rough equivalences of punishment between "like" offenders. It is not a rough equivalence of pain for the offender that defines the justly deserved punishment at sentence, but also a rough equivalence in punitive functions.

For example, if in a given case the primary governing purposes at sentencing are retributive or deterrent, and incapacitative purposes are not a major consideration, fines (and community service for the indigent) should be the punishments of preference. If, in such a case, incapacitative considerations loom larger, then the equivalence calculations come into play and the judge must consider whether house arrest or periodic drug testing or intermittent confinement or other community-based punishment can provide adequate levels of restraint; only if they cannot should an incarcerative sentence be imposed or added to a fine.

With these three notions, the fine as the preferred sanction in all cases where a prison sentence of two years or less is to be imposed, the distinction between purposes of sentencing and purposes at sentencing, and the distinction between equivalency in pain and equivalency in function, the path is clear to a comprehensive system of sentencing that incorporates all crimes and all punishments.

For the fine to play its appointed role as the basic medium of punishment, two preconditions must be met: there must exist principled means for adjusting the amount of the fine both to the offender's culpability and to his resources, and there must exist efficient and reliable systems of enforcement and collection to assure that fines imposed will in fact be paid.

Practice

With these theoretical propositions behind us, let us turn to the practical realities that currently restrict the use of the fine, with a view to fashioning some precise recommendations for their greatly extended application. More than elsewhere in this book our task is that of summarization of sound policy recommendations made by others, though there are some issues of difficulty we confront beyond the well established. The sequence of our consideration of the role of the fine in sentencing policy is as follows:

1. present use of fiscal penalties;
2. reasons for their widespread neglect;
3. desert, fairness, and equality in fining;
4. recommendations.

Present Use of Fiscal Penalties

Fiscal penalties are increasingly applied under the pressure of judicial and correctional budgetary constraints, but there is little evidence that this is true of the fine as punishment for nontrivial crimes, certainly of the fine standing alone. Distinctions among fiscal penalties have to be made. Restitution to the victim by the criminal is often appropriate and is increasingly being awarded, as is payment by the criminal to the victims' compensation fund in the federal system and in that increasing number of states where such schemes exist. Current federal law, for example, presumes the appropriateness of restitution orders in every case and requires judges to provide reasons for ordering partial restitution, or none at all, in any given case [18 U.S.C. 3663(a)(2)]. The first $100,000,000 in federal fines collected each year is paid into the Federal Victims Compensation Fund. Further, there is a surge in the requirement by criminal courts that the convicted offender should pay a fee for probation services, for any treatments ordered as a condition of probation, and in some cases a fee toward the costs of his jailing or imprisoning. And, of course, court costs may be awarded against the convicted criminal, and this practice too grows in our criminal justice systems. Further, it is becoming increasingly common for courts to add a fine to other punishments imposed on those who have profited financially from their crimes. Finally, the complexities of law enforcement aimed at drug trafficking and organized crime have led to increased use of forfeiture of assets used or gained in illegal activity. Forfeiture, however, is a special case, partly aimed at removing offenders' financial capacity to continue their criminous ways, partly aimed at economic *in terrorem* effect. We shall not discuss it further.

All these fiscal penalties stand on a different footing from the fine alone as a punishment for crime. They are compensatory to the victim or to the state, meeting expenses that the criminal has imposed on the victim or on the state, or relieving him of his ill-gotten gains; they should not be regarded as a punishment in the sense that we have defined that term, a response to the criminal by the state, justified by and at its maximum limited by the criminal's desert.

There is, of course, this closer link between fines and most other fiscal penalties: the quantum of those penalties can be made to relate directly to the offender's capacity to pay, whereas it will not relate to his capacity to go to prison or to dance on the end of a rope. Hence we discuss restitution, fees, costs, payments to compensation funds, and forfeiture only in relation to assessing the amount of a fine; otherwise they bear no more on intermediate punishments than on all other punishments.

Yet it is interesting that whereas these attendant fiscal penalties have grown in popularity with courts of general and limited jurisdiction, the same is not true of the fine. The evidence is that use of the fine, alone or allied to other punishments, has remained relatively stable in its diverse usage in this country.

What is known of that usage? A series of studies by the Vera Institute of Justice is the best source of data on the use of the fine by courts of limited and general jurisdiction. No clear patterns emerge, which is not a criticism of that body of work but reflects the lamentable state of record keeping by criminal courts. Surveying the extraordinary diversity of practice in these courts, all that the 1984 final report of the various Vera studies, written by Hillsman, Sichel, and Mahoney, could produce were general propositions like these:

Fine use in the United States is not confined simply to traffic offenses and minor ordinance violations. On the contrary, it is clear
that many courts depend quite heavily on fines, alone or as the principal component of a sentence in which the fine is combined with
another sanction, in sentencing criminal defendants for a wide variety of offenses including some generally considered serious. Other
courts, however, use fines only for a narrow range of relatively
minor offenses.

The Vera research did reveal, however, that some courts, for
example, several in New York City, make extensive use of fines
for misdemeanors, including many misdemeanors that were originally arrests for felonies such as some drug offenses, lesser assaults, and thefts:

> Forty-seven percent of the misdemeanor convictions that resulted in
> a fine in Bronx County had originally entered the court as a felony
> charge (after initial screening by the District Attorney's Office), as
> had 51 percent of the misdemeanor convictions in King's County
> and 13 percent in New York County.

A 1987 survey of judges' attitudes toward fines and their beliefs
about fine usage built on the Vera studies and came to a similar
conclusion. George Cole and his colleagues observed that "fines
are used extensively in U.S. courts, they are most commonly used
in combination with other sanctions. At present, judges do not
regard the fine alone as a meaningful alternative to incarceration
or probation." And, like the Vera studies, this study found very
substantial differences among jurisdictions and an appreciable
number of courts, both of general and limited jurisdiction, in
which occasional use is made of the fine, standing alone, as a
punishment for serious crime.

Patterns of use vary widely between jurisdictions and within
jurisdictions. Fines are by no means confined to traffic offenses
and minor offenses; some courts make limited use of the fine
as a principal penalty for felonies. Other courts see the fine as
appropriate only to minor property crimes and to such crimes by
first offenders, or at least those without a record of prior convictions. In practice and in judicial attitude, the fine standing alone
as a punishment for a felony is relatively rare; it is less rare as a

part of a larger package of nonincarcerative punishments such as a fine together with a condition of restricted movement or residence or compelled treatment in the community. This is not true of all courts, but it is true of some.

The diversity has been laid bare, but the consequences of different practices are unknown. Studies have not revealed the effect of more rather than less fining on subsequent rates of criminality; there are no studies of differential deterrent effects. There are no studies in this country of the later conduct of those fined, with or without other sanctions also being imposed, as contrasted with a matched group who were jailed or imprisoned. Economists and econometricians including Gary Becker, Robert Gillespie, and Richard Posner have, of course, speculated on these matters and constructed mathematical models to test their hypotheses, but there are no studies of the deterrent or crime prevention effects of different uses of fines in practice. We are thrust back to opinion, attitudes, and that most frail reed, untested reflection.

In an odd sense, such is the diversity of practice with fining in American criminal courts, such the lack of information on usage and collection, such the lack of scholarly analysis of the fine as a criminal sanction, that it is easier to know where we should be going than where we are. We should be heading toward a much greater use of the fine as a punishment for crime, fines matching the gravity of the crime, fines which are collected or, if not paid, lead to other punishments. What are the obstacles? The main reasons offered for the restricted use of the fine are that fines are not seen as a credible punishment and that they are seen as unfair to the poor.

The heart of the matter is that for a variety of reasons the fine is widely disregarded as a punishment for all but traffic offenses, minor misdemeanors, and ordinance violations. It is not taken seriously. This is partly a question of judicial, legislative, and prosecutorial attitudes; partly a function of insufficient information about the financial situations of many offenders; partly a result of lack of effective collection mechanisms; and partly a sense that the fine works injustice between the wealthy and the indigent. These realities must be confronted if the fine is to take a larger place in our armamentarium of criminal sanctions.

Reasons for the Widespread Neglect of the Fine

Attitudes often govern practice, and so it is here. The recent study of judicial attitudes toward fines reveals that judges of both limited and general criminal jurisdictions are much more favorably inclined toward the fine as a punishment in theory than in practice. They wish to use it more than they do. What, then, are the impediments? They believe the fine cannot be set high enough to constitute a credible punishment in the eyes of the public; they believe too many fines are uncollected for it to be as effective a punishment as they would wish; and they believe it discriminates against the indigent. There is some truth in all these beliefs, but none is inexorable, each can be overcome.

When legislators thought of fines as applicable only to minor crimes, the ceilings of fines were set low. Recently, many legislatures, particularly under the pressure of increased attention to white-collar crime, have raised those ceilings. For example, the maximum fine for a federal felony has now been raised to $250,000 per offense for an individual; with such a ceiling credible fines can clearly be fashioned. It is obvious that if the fine is to be made an effective punishment, legislatures must give the courts the power to set fines high enough to have substantial punitive effect.

There is another paradox in public and judicial attitudes to the fine. It is thought unfair by a fine to take a man's home, car, and accumulated assets. It seems too severe, particularly in its impact on his family. Hence judges hesitate to impose what would be financial disasters on convicted offenders and their dependents. Those same judges have less hesitation in imposing a substantial prison term that sometimes has at least as severe an impact on the prisoner's family and financial expectations as does the confiscatory fine. There is little argument one can offer on this; it is patently a class-biased paradox.

If we are serious about the use of fines, there can be no good reason why, sometimes, they should not be made very substantial indeed. Think for example of a worker in an automobile factory in rural Wisconsin who earns $35,000 a year, including overtime, enough to be buying his home and to own a cottage on a lake, a motor boat, a snowmobile, an ATV, perhaps a horse. Imagine that when he drinks he becomes quarrelsome and disrespectful of other people's property. He has several times been convicted of minor assaults and now he has willfully broken the plate glass window in front of a Kenosha bar and violently resisted the owner's attempts to persuade him to leave. After prior convictions and sentences to probation and suspended sentences, he has qualified himself for consideration for a 12-month prison sentence.

Might he instead be fined the equivalent of a year's after-tax pay? This might be $25,000 and, assuming he has not been good at deferring gratifications and saving money for a stormy day, may require that he dispose of many of those assets that make his, and his family's, life a pleasure. He may have to remortgage his house or perhaps sell it and move into much less adequate rental accommodations.

Cruelly punitive, you say? Perhaps, but no more so than would be a year's imprisonment. From both the offender's and the state's perspective, this financial calamity may be better than imprisonment. A substantial penalty has been imposed that sends clear deterrent signals and is unarguably punitive. The offender, his employer willing, may be able to keep his job. The likelihood that his family will survive as a cohesive unit is greater than if he were imprisoned. And, no small matter, he is spared the devastating effects of spending a year in prison. The state, of course, saves the direct cost of his imprisonment and the probable indirect cost of supporting his family, and it collects the fine money to boot. Assuming the fine order directed application of proceeds first to restitution to the victim, then to court costs, then to a victim compensation fund, all of these collateral fiscal objectives will be served. This is the very opposite of a zero-sum game; everyone wins.

Within the limits set by a sense of a justly deserved punishment, the fine should not be eschewed on grounds of its infliction of excessive pain, and most certainly it should be set at a level to achieve legitimate social purposes of deterrence under that deserved ceiling.

But there are other impediments to the full flowering of the fine as a punishment. It must be credible in another sense; if imposed, it must be collected, unless supervening circumstances preclude its collection. The law must keep its promises here too.

And we face the reality of widespread failure of collection. The 1985 General Accounting Office study of enforcement of fines in the federal system, and all other studies of fines in this country, have revealed widespread failure to collect fines. For example, of five federal district courts studied in 1982, only 34 percent of the money owed by convicted felons and misdemeanants was paid.

That study, by the General Accounting Office, of federal practices before the Criminal Fine Enforcement Act of 1984 took effect, describes a system in which no single office or official had an interest in fine collection, with authority dispersed among a number of agencies. At the national level, the Department of Justice then had primary responsibility for monitoring and accounting for fines. At the local level, three agencies were involved. Responsibility for accounting for payments was split between U.S. attorneys and court clerks. The probation office and U.S. attorneys were responsible for monitoring fines, and U.S. attorneys were responsible for taking legal steps to enforce fines in default. As a result, minimum procedures were not in place to determine the defendant's ability to pay or to assure that information required for enforcement went to the appropriate office.

The GAO study estimated that probation officers did not obtain information to support a conclusion about the offender's financial ability for 55 percent of felony fines and 43 percent of misdemeanor fines sampled in 1979 and 1982. Even when court records contained financial information, the GAO found that the courts did not routinely provide it to the U.S. attorneys' offices. When GAO examiners compared U.S. attorneys' records with those of the probation offices, they found that the U.S. attorneys' offices had no record of 40 percent of the fines imposed. And when U.S. attorneys' records were compared with those of the clerks' offices, it was found that the two sets of records of unpaid balances did not agree for about 60 percent of the cases sampled. Even within the U.S. attorneys' offices, the GAO found that the specialist fine collection units could not rely on other U.S. attorney personnel to send judgment orders to them consistently.

Given this lack of system and integration, it should come as no surprise that many federal fines went unpaid. Although many enforcement techniques were available, including demand letters,

court-ordered appearances, seizure of property, and imprisonment
for contempt for willful nonpayment, most were rarely used. Justice Department rules required that demand letters for full payment be sent within two to ten days after every judgment that
orders payment of a fine. In the sample of cases the GAO examined, such letters were sent in only 17 percent of cases and
these letters were sent, on average, 143 days after judgment. In
a similar vein, the GAO found that garnishment procedures were
never used in the cases examined, and other procedures were
used infrequently.

The reasons why the federal system was so haphazard and
ill-organized are clear. No agency benefited from collection of
fines—before the 1984 Act, payments went to the Treasury; after-
ward, to the Federal Victims Compensation Fund and to the
Treasury—and most of the agencies involved had little interest
in the work. Moreover, no agency much wanted to do it. The
GAO noted that U.S. attorneys' fine collection efforts suffered
from "staffing problems" (mostly that assistant U.S. attorneys
would rather be doing other things) and that many probation
officers viewed "bill collection" as inconsistent with their rehabilitative mission. A U.S. Sentencing Commission staff report prepared in 1987 by David Tevelin stressed that neither the Justice
Department nor the Administrative Office of the U.S. Courts wants
responsibility for receiving fines "because of the many ancillary
administrative burdens attendant to the receipt of money."

Readers will be relieved to know that we will not summarize
other major fine collection studies in comparable detail; their
descriptions of inefficiencies, disjointed procedures, and failure
to use available remedies are similar (e.g., for the United States,
see the 1984 report by Hillsman, Sichel, and Mahoney; for England, see the 1981 analysis by Messrs. Morgan and Bowles).
Even the details of the fine collection stories are similar. Silvia
Casale and Sally Hillsman noted in 1986 that English probation
officers, like their federal American brethren, are "concerned that
fine enforcement duties will strain their relationships with offenders."

What is most striking about these seeming intractable problems
of fine collection and enforcement is how eminently and swiftly
soluble they are. The survey research on fines has shown, amidst

the confusion and failures, jurisdictions that *do* collect fines efficiently, and much has been learned about how this is done. The lessons are not startling:

- Insist whenever possible on immediate payment.
- If there are to be installment payments, keep the payment schedule short.
- Don't impose fine amounts which, taken together with court costs, restitution, probation fees, and other charges, are impossible for the offender to meet.
- On the first signs of delay or default, send stern admonitory notices of the consequences of nonpayment.
- On further delay or default, step up the intensity of demand and institute garnishment or contempt proceedings.

None of this would surprise anyone involved in consumer credit or consumer debt collection. All that is needed are well-planned, well-managed procedures. That this is possible is shown by the fact that in some jurisdictions it is done. The bad-check bureaus operated by prosecutors' offices that we mentioned earlier, for example, are remarkably effective. But even were that not true, experience with other criminal justice management systems shows that system, efficiency, and accountability can be achieved where once they were absent. In 1969, in his now-classic book *Discretionary Justice,* Kenneth Culp Davis pointed out that parole boards and prosecutors' offices, agencies dealing with interests as substantial as liberty itself, operated haphazardly and with few or no management controls. Today, most well-run parole boards and prosecutors' offices have systems of guidelines in place to govern these decisions, backed up by management controls and procedures. If system and order can be brought to paroling and to plea bargaining, they can certainly be brought to fine enforcement.

Recent experience with probation offers another lesson. The way to motivate people, including public officials, is to give them incentives. Probation departments across the country, by the most recent counts in more than 35 states, have begun to charge fees to their probationers; many departments have been allowed to use the fees collected to support departmental programs. Georgia's much-heralded intensive supervision probation program, for example, is supported by revenue from fees charged all Georgia probationers. The prospect of more money for expansion of programs and improvement of services is likely to be a powerful incentive to probation executives and, through the departmental ethos, to their employees.

Before we move on to discussion of the principles we believe should govern fining, we offer a few observations concerning the information about offender's finances that is crucial if means-based fines are to be set, and about the potential for involvement of the private sector in fine collection.

A precondition to a rational and effective fining system is that the judge must be informed of the capacity of the offender to pay a fine; too often judges inclined to impose a fine lack sufficient information to that end. They know the offender's crime and his criminal record, they hear what counsel and sometimes witnesses say about his character; but if a credible, fair, and payable fine is to be imposed, they need to know precise facts about his capacity to pay. Strangely, on this there is often a dearth of reliable information.

This is a society properly protective of the individual's independence and of his right to preserve as private what is private information; but here we go too far. It seems obvious to us that there is ample authority for the judge to say to the convicted offender, in effect, "If you wish me to consider the imposition of a fine as a punishment for your offense, let me have the following precise details of your financial circumstances before the sentencing hearing which I now set down for. . . . Of course, if you wish to preserve secrecy in such matters and I do decide to impose a fine I shall impose it on the assumption that you will have no difficulty in paying."

There are many variations on such a statement, suited to different cases, but surely the thought of a tender care for the convicted offender's right to conceal his financial situation, including his tax returns, from the sentencing judge is an absurd sensitivity. Yet the fact remains that a major reason for the relatively rare use of the fine, certainly alone as a sanction for other than trivial offenses, is this lack of information about the offender's finances. It is not an intractable problem; in the last resort the judiciary is responsible for the implementation of their sentences, and it is far from outside their competence to arrange for the availability of such information; they have no insuperable difficulty in obtaining it in important matters such as litigation about the quantum of damages in a civil suit.

We thus come to the largest obstacle to the development of an efficient system of fining: the widespread lack of responsibility for the collection of fines leading to extensive defaults. In many jurisdictions, there is no agency whose primary responsibility is the collection of fines; there is no clear accountability for non-collection. It is distasteful work. The judge leaves it to others; court administrators leave it to probation officers; probation officers do not consider fine collection a high-priority aspect of their work—no one is accountable. This is a remediable situation, and we will offer some suggestions to its cure. But to launch the discussion let us merely assert the obvious: if the fine is to be a credible punishment, it must not only be imposed, but it must be collected. It should be borne in mind, however, that this obvious proposition is extensively honored in the breach and to no small extent accounts for a serious deficiency in our armamentarium of punishments.

Just as hospital administration cannot be left to practicing doctors, so over the past two decades it has come to be recognized that court administration should not be left to the judiciary. It is to the rapidly emerging group of court administrators that we must look to bring accountability and efficiency to the collection of fines. Of course, much will depend on the size of the jurisdiction. One can find small rural and suburban courts where each judge's probation officer can also be responsible for the collection of the fines the judge has imposed; but in busier courts where the pressures of presentence reports and probation case management already overburden the probation department, adding responsibility for the collection of fines leads to the common result of widespread default.

Another functionary of the court, the clerk of court, is in some jurisdictions responsible for the collection of fines; but again it is a duty extraneous to that official's central functions.

Hence it seems to us that in most jurisdictions, certainly in the larger and busier courts, a single official or group of officials under the control of the court administrator should be charged with the tasks of aiding the judge in the acquisition of information on the financial situation of the convicted offender on whom the judge is contemplating imposing a fine, keeping records of all fines imposed and monitoring payments, promptly pursuing all payments in arrears, advising the judge of persistent defaults, having discretion in appropriate cases (in consultation with the judge if that be required) of varying the terms for payment of fines, and having the discretion to return the fined offender to the judge for resentencing if the fine is in default—generally, to monitor and assume accountability for the system of fines. The chief judge should know on a weekly basis the status of all fines imposed in his jurisdiction; each judge should know on a weekly basis the status of all fines he has imposed. All this seems obvious enough; yet at present it is rarely in place.

Georgia's experience with probation fees shows that a motivated bureaucracy with an institutional self-interest—for example, that the court may use some or all of the collected monies for discretionary purposes—works excellently. However, when the institutional self-interest in government cannot be created, or even if it can, there may be wisdom in harnessing the private sector to collect some or all fines and giving them market incentives to do it.

We do not have in mind the specialized firms that contract with cities to collect traffic fines. More than 125 cities have delegated all or a portion of parking fine collection to private corporations. More than 80 cities, including Detroit, Philadelphia, and New Orleans, have contracted with Datacom Systems Corporation, a subsidiary of Lockheed Aircraft. Corruption allegations and scandals have broken out in a number of cities. On March 31, 1986, New York City terminated its contracts with 11 different collection agencies.

The experience in some cities with privatization of traffic fine collection is discouraging but not, we think, highly relevant to collection of fines imposed for misdemeanors and felonies. Unfortunately, petty corruption has long characterized many traffic court operations. The low-amount, high-volume business and its relation to essentially regulatory rather than criminal fines are important differences. In addition, there are no probation officers in traffic courts and the role of prosecuting and defense counsel is much less than in criminal courts, making relations between the collectors and the fined all but invisible.

Privatization plays an increasingly useful role in corrections, not in our view in running penal institutions, which we see as an unwise and ultimately economically and socially damaging delegation of state responsibility, but in providing many ancillary services to correctional agencies, institutional and community-based, and doing them better and cheaper than those agencies. Examples include food, medical, and educational services to prisons and alcohol and drug treatment programs in and out of institutions. The private sector could play an important and appropriate role in the collection of fines.

Let us outline a modest proposal, using an imaginary "Debt-Collect" as our contractor.

Major banks and finance companies like DebtCollect are efficient in their pursuit of debts in arrears on credit cards; to that we can testify. Since the courts have larger threats to bring to bear on the delinquent payer, they should be at least as efficient. As we have seen, the defect in this argument is that debt collection is only a minor part of the work of the courts, and not a particularly attractive part. At all events, it is clear that it is not a function that American courts have performed well.

Private sector involvement in collection of criminal fines could be structured in a variety of ways. At simplest, unpaid fines could be referred to collection agencies on a commission basis: for every dollar collected, the collection agency might keep 30 percent. The court would bear all risk of nonpayment and would receive only what is collected by the collection agency less its commission. In more complex arrangements, the unpaid fines could be sold to a finance company, which would pay for them at the time of purchase, probably at a discount from their face amount, and would assume all risk of nonpayment; much financing of automobile and appliance purchases is handled in this way. In effect, the finance company would be making speculative purchases of debt instruments, much as finance companies purchase residential mortgages or automobile loans. Because criminal fines would not be backed by collateral like real estate or automobiles, they would be much riskier investments for finance companies and the purchase discounts would reflect this, unless there were arrangements that debts uncollected by their ordinary means of collections would be repurchased by the courts—after all, there are interests beyond the financial here and the court may well wish to pursue the matter further and exercise its contempt powers.

We won't pursue further how more complex arrangements might be structured. Instead we describe a relatively simple understanding between a court and a finance company in order to discuss some of the issues of policy and practice that are raised.

Suppose the court administrator contracts with DebtCollect, a corporation with substantial experience in the collection of civil debts, to collect some fines. The proposal is that DebtCollect agrees to collect all fines, between $100 and $10,000, that are not paid within a week of imposition of the sentence, on terms that DebtCollect remits to the court three-quarters of such amounts as it collects. From the perspective of the court, this 25 percent discount is justified both by the saving of administrative costs associated with the administration of the collection of fines and by the probably increased rates of successful collection.

DebtCollect agrees to use no methods of debt collection for these fines that it does not ordinarily use for the collection of other debts; in other words, DebtCollect is not invested with the extra threats associated with nonpayment of criminal fines as compared with other debts. At the same time, DebtCollect may treat the fines like any other debt referred to it for collection and, accordingly, may attach the offender's property, garnish his wages, and take any other legal action used in civil debt collection. While these measures are in theory available to court personnel, in practice they are virtually never employed.

Resort to private collection agencies does not, of course, mean that all fines would be paid. There are a number of different ways to look at the residual unpaid fines.

From one perspective, the preferred course is to let the private market work. Often for cost/benefit analysis reasons, commercial creditors and collection agencies write off some debts as uncollectible, either because the amounts are too small to justify the cost of collecting them or because the debtor is judgment-proof and lacks sufficient assets or income to pay the debt. From this perspective, the preferred course is to defer to the collection agency's judgment and let the matter rest. After all, many fines now go uncollected; if a collection agency operating with financial incentives is unable to collect the debt, it is unlikely that probation officers or other judicial branch employees will be any more successful.

From another perspective, it is important that the law keep its promises; it is important that these unpaid fines be pursued vigorously with the full power of the court. DebtCollect should refer back to the court all fines not actually collected, informing the court of the procedures already followed in relation to fines remaining unpaid in whole or part. The court will regain responsibility for the collection of fines that do not respond to ordinary debt collection methods; here the contumacious must not escape punishment; the matter moves from possible financial inefficiency to contempt of court.

It is of first importance that all imposed fines should be collected or transmuted into other punishments if credible systems of fine imposition are to come to this country, and the fines returned from DebtCollect to the court merit the close attention of the court administrator, the police, and the court.

The hypothetical contract between DebtCollect and the court administrator seems to us a sound enlistment of the private sector to the work of the courts, making use of their established staffs and skills and ongoing practices, and it should be a wise investment for DebtCollect since the commission should provide appreciable profit. From the perspective of the criminal court it also seems sound practice.

The court will retain responsibility for small fines (under $100), which should be immediately or promptly paid. If they be imposed on the indigent or near-indigent, such fines will require the services of the court's probation staff overseeing a community service order, or time payment arrangements, or some other special arrangement for justification. The court might also retain responsibility for larger fines over $10,000 where the expenditure of state funds and the efforts of state personnel are financially justified by the size of the fine.

There is another reason why this engagement of the private sector makes sense: most research on the payment and nonpayment of fines reveals that the single most important step in en-

suring the payment of fines is the prompt notification to the debtor
if his payment or payments fall even briefly into arrears. Thus,
as Hillsman, Sichel, and Mahoney noted, in 1984, there is
evidence

> from courts in England and West Germany as well as the U.S., that
> notification to an offender that fine payments are in arrears . . .
> has positive results. In two English courts studied by Vera, almost
> a third of those "reminded" paid in full after receiving such a letter,
> and in the German town studied by Albrecht almost half responded
> to reminder letters with full payment. . . . A brief experiment
> with telephone notifications by the Englewood, Colorado, Municipal
> Court, indicated that use of telephone "reminders" produced a re-
> sponse in 53% of cases in which a warrant would otherwise have
> been issued.

These types of "reminders" are exactly what DebtCollect does
best and are likely to be much less well done by the courts or by
their probation departments.

Desert, Fairness, and Equality in Fining

So much for the collection of fines; but the larger task may be
that of adjusting the fine to the offender's means. At present an
important impediment to the use of the fine is the belief that it
works injustice between the poor and the less poor, between the
less poor and the wealthy—that the fine is inapplicable to the
indigent and lacks impact on the rich, and, more broadly, has
unequal impact on equally undeserving offenders.

Although neither American legal practice nor thought has been
hospitable to fines as felony sentences, leading American economists like Gary Becker in 1968 and Richard Posner in 1977 have
long urged increased use of fines. A survey of major proposals
for sentencing reform confirms what short shrift even the reform-
ist lawyers have given to the fine.

Sections 702(1)–(2) of the American Law Institute's *Model
Penal Code* authorizes imposition of a fine for felonies if the
offender gained money or property through his crime but permits
the imposition of a fine in any case if the fine will suffice for public protection. In general, however, the *Model Penal Code*'s com-

mentary makes it clear that the use of fines is to be discouraged. Section 7.02(1) provides that "the court shall not sentence a defendant only to pay a fine, when any other disposition is authorized by law, unless . . . it is of the opinion that the fine alone suffices for protection of the public." To like effect, the National Commission on Reform of Federal Criminal Law observed in 1971 "fines are to be discouraged . . . unless some affirmative reason indicates that a fine is peculiarly appropriate."

The American Bar Association also urges only limited use of fines as punishments. Section 2–7(a) of the 1980 American Bar Association Standards on Sentencing Alternatives and Procedures directs that "the legislature should not authorize the imposition of a fine for a felony unless the defendant has gained money or property through the commission of the offense." The commentary explains that there "is no positive advantage to punishment in the form of a fine. In the very few cases where imprisonment would be too severe and probation not severe enough, restitution [will suffice]."

We disagree with these approaches; they are too restrictive of fining. In particular, the ABA approach reflects the traditional prison-or-probation dualism that has impeded development in this country of intermediate punishments. Fines in credible amounts that are enforced by effective procedures can serve as adequate and appropriate punishments for many felonies. In this last section, we attempt to show how development of the day fine can meet American sentencing needs and we then set out principles that we believe should govern the use of fines.

For us it is axiomatic that a just fine must be calculated in relation to the offender's means, earning capacity, and financial obligations to dependents. This presents no great problem for the wealthy, for the indigent, or for the rest of us in between.

For the wealthy, if the fine imposed satisfies general deterrent and sufficiently retributive purposes, taking into account their wealth, there is no problem provided the statutory maximum of the fine is set sufficiently high to achieve these purposes. There may be, of course, questions of fairness between offenders alike other than in their financial means—and to these problems we will soon turn.

If the convicted person's wealth is such that a fine within the statutory maximum is insufficient to make a punitive dint in his resources, then other sanctions must be added; but it is our experience that such cases are not the common stock of the criminal courts.

At the other end of the economic stratum, as well as those questions of fairness between offenders, there is the blunt difficulty of capacity to pay a fine sufficient for general deterrence without depreciating the seriousness of the offense. Assume that a fine of at least $5000 is necessary to meet those purposes, and assume further that $5000 is far beyond the means and current earning capacity of this convicted offender. Is the fine necessarily excluded as an appropriate punishment? We think not, if it be added to community service or to punitive restrictions like house arrest or intensive supervision. A commitment to community service combined with a stated fine, the fine being paid off in part in the coinage of hours of community service, would seem to us often to meet the needs of deterrence, and should not be seen as unduly depreciating the seriousness of the offense.

What this comes to is that indigency *per se* should not be regarded as a bar to fining, particularly to the imposition of a fine combined with a condition of treatment, or a condition of residence, or a condition of community service.

But the problem remains of fairness between "like" offenders— "like" other than in the depth or shallowness of their pockets. Most sentencing systems seek to adjust the fine to the offender's capacity to pay, unless mandatory fines are prescribed for certain traffic offenses, minor misdemeanors, and ordinance violations. It is not generally seen as unfair to impose a fine of $50 on one offender and $100 on another, though their crimes and criminal records are identical. Although this appears obvious, it merits note that it is less easily accepted for other types of sentences. Take, for example, a prison term. For the very old it is not unusual to reduce the term imposed and the term served; and for the offender under the jurisdiction of the juvenile court it is at least believed that less severe sentences are imposed. Little other adjustment is made in the term of imprisonment imposed or served for the "bite" or pain of that imprisonment. Yet the range of pain in a year's or month's imprisonment is very great, as all who know about American prisons will agree. The year or month can be served in a terrifying, brutal, out-of-control big-city prison, a center of rape and violence, or in a safe, clean, untesting environment with considerable educational and recreational opportunities. Yet a year is a year is a year, though the "bite" is profoundly different for one convicted offender and another, and for the family of one and the family of the other, if he has one.

We are, of course, not suggesting that terms of imprisonment should be adjusted to the severity of the prison environment in which the prisoner will be placed; we are merely noting that a similar adjustment is, in effect, by unfettered judicial discretion now done for the fine.

And for the fine, other countries have gone further toward a more principled and predictable gradation of fines matched to the offender's capacity to pay. The key conceptual overseas development is the day fine, which, in our view, merits adoption here.

Finland introduced a day-fine system in 1921; Sweden in 1931; Denmark in 1939. In 1975, on ideas drawn from the Scandinavian legislation, West Germany introduced a far-reaching day-fine system. An experiment with the day fine is now being launched in the courts in Richmond County, New York, by collaboration among the district attorney, the criminal court judges, and the Vera Institute of Justice. Similar efforts at earlier stages are now under way in Phoenix, Minneapolis, and Portland (Oregon). We move slowly but we will get there.

The Swedish and West German approaches to day fines differ in many details, but their broad thrust is the same. The number of day-fine units must be decided first by the sentencing court without regard to the means of the offender; the value of each day-fine unit is then calculated. In practice, the West German and Swedish systems are quite different. In Sweden, the day fine is 1/1000 of the offender's annual income less reduction for taxes, dependents, and significant debts; it is increased based on the offender's net worth. The Swedish system is in effect a system for depriving offenders of the pleasures of life, those expenditures that are made after basic living expenses are met.

The German day fine is calculated as, in effect, the cost of a day of freedom. The day fine is, in theory, the offender's net income for a day without deduction for family maintenance. The daily net income the offender would have forfeited had he been imprisoned is the amount he must pay. In practice, the fine is often adjusted to reflect the offender's individual circumstances.

The National Swedish Council for Crime Prevention reports the extension of this system of fining in Sweden over the years since its introduction to more and more serious offenses, offenses that were previously punished by imprisonment. "Formerly fining was regarded as a sanction to be used when no other sanction was available and then only for comparatively small offenses. Nowadays the preventive function of fines is regarded as good." The Council concludes: "In Sweden short-term imprisonment is nowadays generally considered to be an inappropriate sanction from the social, ethical and economic points of view. We wish to find other sanctions which have the same preventive effects as prison. Fining in the form of day-fines is regarded as a good alternative."

Many thousands of offenders each year are punished by day fines in Sweden. Their enforcement mechanism is such that only about 40 persons per year are imprisoned for recalcitrant and willful nonpayment.

One interesting aspect of Swedish practice is that prosecutors routinely invite those they propose to charge with an offense to accept a fine calculated on day-fine principles. As a result, nearly 70 percent of fines imposed in Sweden are determined in this way.

To dispel any notion that the Swedish day-fine system is confined to petty offenders, here are some 1979 data that Silvia Casale's 1981 monograph has provided on crimes for which such a punishment was imposed: offenses against life and health, including assault and some homicides, 1966 cases; sexual offenses, 128 cases; larceny and allied offenses, 10,186 cases; robbery, 2 cases; embezzlement, 328 cases; forgery, 133 cases; perjury and false statements, 149 cases; narcotics offenses, 734 cases.

The West German day-fine system, report George Cole and his colleagues in their 1987 report, uses "a guideline approach that establishes maximum and minimum day-fine units for particular offense groups . . . fine use has been high, fine amounts have been increasing (especially in cases involving affluent offenders), and there has been a significant decrease in the utilization of short-term incarceration as a criminal sanction." West German practice in setting the monetary values of the units of punishment is more flexible than that in Sweden, relying less on police inquiries and more on information obtained from the offender (on pain of further punishment for mendacity).

There is little doubt that the German reliance on fines has worked a substantial reduction of short-term imprisonment. In 1968, the year before the passage of legislation to encourage increased use of fines as criminal sanctions, over 113,273 sentences to imprisonment of less than six months were imposed by West German courts, which was 20 percent of all prison terms imposed in that year. By 1976 this number had dropped to 10,704, which was 1.8 percent of all prison terms imposed. During the same period, according to Robert Gillespie (1980), the proportion of fine sentences rose from 63 percent to 83 percent of all sentences.

Consideration is currently being given in England and Wales to the introduction of a day-fine system. As part of that consideration data have been collected to assess, as best one can, what effect the Scandinavian and West German systems have had on the later incidence of crime. Does such a system reduce the deterrent effect of the criminal law and thus increase criminality? The elusiveness of such a question to serious scholarship is well known. Little is available to improve on Silvia Casale's 1981 analysis of West German and English data on the later behavior of convicted offenders, which suggests lower reconviction rates for those fined than for similar offenders placed on probation or for similar offenders imprisoned for three months or less. The problem with such findings, as she readily suggests, is that comparability of the control group is extraordinarily hard to achieve. This, however, can be said: though no statistically significant reduction of later criminality by those fined has been demonstrated, as contrasted to similar groups on probation or subjected to short-term imprisonment, the data tend in that direction.

A recent survey of American judges investigated attitudes toward introduction in this country of a day-fine system. There was considerable ambivalence but the conclusion of George Cole and his colleagues in 1987 was that "[a]lthough some judges expressed reservations about the feasibility of such a system in their courts, a majority felt that it could work and many of them indicated a willingness to explore its application."

Regrettably, though the U.S. Sentencing Commission had before it preparatory materials and much information on the day-fine system, the sentencing guidelines set out in the April 13, 1987 Report to Congress do not incorporate such an approach to fining, nor have any of the subsequent revisions of the federal guidelines. The guidelines do lay out broad directions to the sentencing judge to take into consideration in imposing a fine: "the ability of the defendant to pay the fine (including the ability to pay over a period of time) in light of his earning capacity and financial resources; the burden that the fine places on the defendant and his dependents relative to alternative punishments"; and other considerations akin to those included in a day-fine system. But the Commission has done nothing, it seems to us, to encourage a wider use of the fine as a criminal sanction in this country or to bring the calculation of fines onto a fairer basis. There seems to be no provision in the guidelines for the fine to be imposed alone except for trifling crimes. Considering the range of federal crimes, felonies, misdemeanors, violations, and breaches of regulations, this is an absurd result, and one that the Congress can hardly have intended in adopting the Sentencing Reform Act of 1984.

Setting aside restitution wherever it is statutorily permitted and special assessments under the Victims of Crime Act of 1984, for both of which the proposed guidelines merely track the enabling statutes, the Commission provides that, subject to only one exception, "the court shall impose a fine in all cases," but never as an independent punishment. Requiring fines in all cases trivializes the use of fines as punishments.

Though the Commission considered staff memoranda on the day-fine system and on interchangeability between the fine and other punishments, none of these ideas found their way into their April 1987 report to Congress or into the guidelines. An early interest in the fine as a model punishment waned, leaving a pale reflection of what already exists: the court, in determining the quantum of a fine within the recommended range, is directed to consider the ability of the defendant to pay the fine and a variety of similar long-established considerations that have not at all reduced the gross disparity in fining springing from different judges and different views of the function of the fine and the evenhanded means of its assessment.

Nor does this conclude the story of fiscal penalties under the sentencing guidelines developed by the U.S. Sentencing Commission. Quite apart from the fine imposed as above, but subject to ability-to-pay considerations, "[T]he court shall impose an additional fine amount that is at least sufficient to pay the costs to the government of any imprisonment, probation, or supervised release ordered" [Section 5E4.2(i)]. These costs will, of course, vary from time to time, and from prison to prison, and from one community treatment facility or organization to another, but a conservative present estimate would be $18,000 per year for federal imprisonment and between $600 and $3600 for community-based punishments (a few would be higher). These seem to us the ideas of those who can but rarely have visited a larger prison, federal or state.

The day fine is much to be preferred to this complex and unreal hodgepodge of ill-considered fiscal penalties. It is very much to be hoped that the experiments that the Vera Institute will study on Staten Island, New York, and in Phoenix, Arizona, will energize American legislatures to emulate this sensible system.

The fine can and should be greatly increased in its application, alone or with other intermediate punishments, so that it becomes the modal sanction for a wide range of criminal offenses. This can be achieved without decreasing social protection, fairly, and at lower cost than our present neglect of the fine inflicts on all of us.

Recommendations

The following few paragraphs sketch what one would hope for as a newly appointed judge of general jurisdiction facing the task of sentencing those tried and convicted before him, and wishing to use the fine as a fair and effective punishment.

The legislature must have provided for adequate fines to be imposed and allowed for time to pay fines.

Whatever the structure of court administration, there must be in place systems for collecting fines, for tracing late payments promptly and pursuing them immediately, and for bringing back to the sentencing judge any cases of clear delinquency in payment. The judge must have the power to vary collection arrangements, to extend time for payment in appropriate cases, and to impose an alternative punishment in contumacious cases of nonpayment. There must be in place, either through the court administration or by other means, a fine collection accountability system, accountable on a regular and detailed basis to the sentencing judge.

Those fining powers and collecting arrangements presuppose a fair and principled assessment of when a fine is an appropriate punishment, alone or in conjunction with other punishments, and the quantum of the fine. For this, knowledge of the convicted offender's personal financial circumstances is essential: his net worth, his income, his obligations to dependents. The judge who is determined about the matter already has the power to have such facts found as a precursor to a sentencing hearing; all that is necessary is a sufficient supporting court staff, either probation officers or others, concentrating on such inquiries, to gather this information from the offender under the clear threat that assumptions will be made of the sufficiency of his funds to meet any fine within the statutory maximum if he is noncooperative in revealing his income and assets from legitimate and illegal sources alike. Giving access to his past tax returns need not be compelled but should be one of the options open to the convicted offender. Banks, finance companies, and colleges' financial aid offices routinely require provision of income tax returns as a precondition to considering an application; surely the courts can do the same. It should be made clear to him also that both on suspicion and on a random basis such revelations of assets and income may be carefully audited, the sanctions for mendacity being severe and within the contempt power of the court.

But the problem of fairness remains. Even though the substantial fine the judge has in mind may be a not undeserved punishment, appropriately meeting the deterrent purposes of the criminal law, it is still highly desirable that it be broadly congruent with sentences imposed on other similar offenders convicted of similar crimes. In our chapters on sentencing, we have shown how this might be done.

A final requirement for fair assessment and imposition of the fine, alone or combined with other punishment, is that something like the European day fine be in place. Once it is agreed that the fine should be adjusted to the financial circumstances of the offender, and this does not seem to be in dispute, some exchange rate between punishment and dollars must be broadly agreed between the judges imposing sentences in any jurisdiction; the day fine is a promising technique for achieving that congruence. But the day fine is, of course, by no means the only technique, as the preparatory work for the U.S. Sentencing Commission demonstrated. It is possible and, we think, sensible to build such an exchange rate directly into a general system of sentencing guidelines; the means to this end were discussed in our sentencing chapters.

Thus guided, thus legislatively and administratively supported, the fine can become a fair and efficient sanction. There will remain difficulties of decision. When does community protection require a period of imprisonment? When are residential restrictions appropriate? When should the fine be combined with other restrictive or treatment-oriented conditions?

To these and other issues we turn in the remainder of this book.

▦▦▦▦▦ 6

Community Service Orders

The prison is a punishment exacted against freedom of movement and association; the fine is a punishment exacted against money and what money can buy; the community service order is a punishment exacted against time and energy. Some see the community service order as a fine on time.

The Thirteenth Amendment to the Constitution provides, in Section 1: "Neither slavery nor involuntary servitude, except as a punishment for crime whereof the party shall have been duly convicted, shall exist within the United States." Not until 1966 was the invitation embedded in the exception clause of this amendment given any force. In that year, in Alameda County, California, the judges of the municipal court instituted a program of punishing certain traffic offenders by sentencing them to periods of unpaid labor as "community service."

This Californian idea took hold and swiftly. It attained its largest acceptance in the United Kingdom, community service orders in 1987 being imposed on about 8 percent of offenders sentenced for serious crimes in England and Wales; but in one or another form such sentences are now to be found in all American jurisdictions,

150

in Australia, Canada, New Zealand, Scotland, Sri Lanka, Greece, Yugoslavia, West Germany, and Poland—to list only countries whose community service programs have been the subjects of published studies.

The community service order can be an intermediate punishment in itself or it can be part of a more complex punishment. In the United Kingdom it is more frequently used as a stand-alone sentence; in this country it is more frequently a part of a larger punitive package.

The modern resurgence of community service as a punishment has, of course, several punitive antecedents. The community service order is involuntary servitude. It is a successor of impressment: the convicted offender makes recompense to the society he has wronged by serving it unpaid over time in ways and for periods determined as a criminal sentence. It is also a successor of transportation, more particularly of the "ticket of leave" that the transportee could be given if he agreed to be indentured to a free settler. It is framed as volunteering for service, as an alternative to some other punishment; but when that other punishment is the prison or jail it is no more volunteering than were most of those impressed from the English courts into the English navy, or those wishing to escape the miseries of the Australian convict prisons by risking servitude to a free settler.

Queen Elizabeth I captured the euphoric spirit often to be found in advocates of the introduction of community service orders in her appointment of a Commission in 1602 to arrange that "except when convicted of wilful murder, rape and burglary" a criminal might be spared other punishment and impressed to the navy "wherein, as in all things, our desire is that justice may be tempered with clemency, and mercy . . . our good and quiet subjects protected and preserved, the wicked and evil-disposed restrained and terrified and the offenders to be in such sort corrected and punished that even in their punishment they may yield some profitable service to the Commonwealth." The prescient queen, whose foresight is memorialized in a 1914 book by Ives, already perceived the diversity of purposes behind such involuntary servitude, as, we suppose, did the Romans when they spared their criminals for a brief marriage to the oars of their galleys.

The ideas behind the community service order thus have a

long and bloody inheritance, but in its modern resurgence this punishment is one of the more promising intermediate punishments in a rational punishment system.

In two recent comprehensive studies of community service orders, by Ken Pease in *Crime and Justice* in 1985 and by Douglas McDonald in *Punishment Without Walls,* an important book published in 1986, the American Bar Association's definition of a community service program is accepted (as reported in a 1980 ABA monograph by Harris):

> A community service program is a program through which convicted offenders are placed in unpaid positions with non-profit or tax-supported agencies to serve a specified number of hours performing work or service within a given time limit as a sentencing option or condition.

Only slight commentary on this definition is necessary. We do not consider similar programs for those awaiting trial as a condition of bail, though they exist. We shall not consider programs by which convicted offenders are placed in *paid* employment and as a condition of probation must meet fiscal obligations by way of restitution or compensation to their victims, or fines owing to the state, though such programs draw close to community service programs and help to illumine some of the difficulties in their administration.

The modern story of community service orders begins in Alameda County in 1966 as a punishment for traffic offenders. It spread, usually imposed as a condition of probation, to a wide diversity of white-collar offenders in many American jurisdictions. Convicted doctors are ordered to give defined hours of their services to those who otherwise lack medical attention; traffic offenders are ordered to serve in hospital emergency rooms to learn the injuries they risk imposing on others and to assist others who have been injured; drug offenders who are prominent sportsmen are ordered to lecture in high schools on the perils of drugs; and so on.

The list is limited only by the imagination of the sentencing judge and the availability of some supervision to ensure that the offender fulfills the terms of the sentence. The list is not currently limited by any absence of need for community service: the hospitals of America depend heavily on volunteers; this new type of "volunteer" is needed. The mental hospitals, the homes for the aged, many of our social services, and many of the parks, roads, bridges, and communal resources of our country stand in need of such voluntary assistance. In particular, the destroyed and dilapidated inner-city neighborhoods, with their ill-planned and poorly maintained public housing, are sponges to absorb such assistance.

These types of sentences attracted a great deal of press attention, mostly favorable. Particularly for white-collar offenders for whom it was not thought necessary to impose prison or jail sentences, the community service order was welcomed by judges, prosecutors, defense counsel, by those so sentenced and in public commentary. But in this country and still today, this broad consensus has not been fashioned into a principled, institutionalized sentencing system, except to a degree in New York City; by contrast, in England and Wales it has been formally blended into the criminal justice system.

In 1970 a subcommittee of the Advisory Council on the Penal System chaired by Baroness Barbara Wootton recommended legislation to incorporate community service orders into the United Kingdom system of punishing criminal offenders. In 1972 Parliament accepted that recommendation. In 1973 six probation areas were designated as "experimental" areas and community service programs were introduced in each. These programs were carefully studied by Home Office research teams directed by Ken Pease; a number of reports and evaluations were published. Thereafter, in 1975 community service orders were extended to other probation areas; they are now available and imposed throughout the United Kingdom.

To be sentenced to community service in the United Kingdom, the offender must be over 16 years of age and must have been convicted of an offense "punishable by imprisonment." The sentencing court must consider a social inquiry report by a probation officer before imposing such a sentence, to ensure that the offender is suitable and that work is available. The extent of the work obligation must be between 40 and 240 hours, to be fulfilled within one year. There are arrangements for supervision and revocation for breach with consequent resentencing.

In excess of 38,000 offenders were sentenced to community service orders in England and Wales in 1982; in that year, and in most recent years, this sentence accounted for about 8 percent of offenders sentenced for more serious crimes. We consider later what judgments can be made as to the success of this development.

The American experience is less institutionalized, much more diverse. Community service orders are to be found in virtually all jurisdictions, but no clear pattern has emerged except perhaps that they tend to flourish among white-collar offenders, in juvenile courts, and for minor offenses; they have less frequently been applied in this country to the poor and to those convicted of repeated though less serious offenses against property—and rarely to those convicted of crimes of violence. Some states make surprisingly extensive use of community service orders; for example, in Washington State that sentence is currently imposed in a third of all felony convictions. Imposition does not, of course, ensure enforcement, or that the work order is performed. Nevertheless, by the late 1970s there was legislative acceptance of community service programs in about a third of the states and well over a hundred projects had been started to introduce and evaluate such programs. Douglas McDonald, America's leading scholar of community service, reports in *Punishment Without Walls,* "surveys conducted in 1977 and 1978 counted fifty-eight organized community service programs for adult criminal offenders and another seventy for juveniles." The largest initiative came from the Federal Office of Juvenile Justice and Delinquency Prevention: starting in 1978, in three years that office contributed $30 million to establish community service programs for juvenile offenders in 85 jurisdictions.

The subsequent retrenchment in federal funds for these and kindred purposes, reports McDonald, has destroyed more than half of the programs for juveniles and has led to a considerable reduction of those for adults; the exact census is not known. But a general overview leads to the broad conclusion that in most states there is both experience with these programs for juvenile and adult offenders and general, though skeptical, satisfaction with their operation.

The most ambitious initiative has been that of the Vera Institute of Justice in collaboration with the courts of New York City. The story of this development is well told in McDonald's *Punishment*

Without Walls; summary will suffice here. The Vera Institute, in collaboration with New York City governmental authorities and private foundations, launched the New York City Community Sentencing Project in the Bronx County courthouse early in 1979. By the end of 1981 it was firmly established in the Bronx, Brooklyn, and Manhattan. Currently about 1200 convicted offenders are each year sentenced to 70 hours of community service in New York. Much is distinctive about this project, but its most significant demonstration is that it applies the community service sentence to the untrained, ill-educated, chronic, and persistent property offenders who crowd our city jails.

To extend the community service order to repeat offenders, many of whom would otherwise have served jail time, the Vera Institute placed full-time court representatives in the sentencing courts to assist prosecutors, defense counsel, and judges in the selection of offenders for this sentence, provided tough "foremen" to ensure that those so sentenced did indeed perform the services they were required to perform, and also provided insightful caseworkers to assist them in the many problems that confront the shiftless and often addicted who made up the "work crews" of offenders. It was and is an expensive and far-reaching intermediate punishment, by no means a "walk." Later we discuss the costs of such a sentence and its benefits; for the time being all that is claimed is that it has been clearly demonstrated that the community service order can be extended to a wider swath of offenders than had previously been considered suitable, and in that extension can meet with acceptance by the courts and by governmental authorities.

Selection for CSOs

The criteria by which the community service order should be evaluated are these:

- as advantages:
    —the value of the services it provides,
    —the jail and prison costs saved,
    —the improved sentencing capacity of the courts,

—giving the offender a sense of self-worth, of self-confidence
in his working and earning capacity;
• as disadvantages:
—the cost of the program itself,
—the crimes that would have been prevented by sentences that
otherwise would have been imposed,
—the displacement of free labor,
—the possibly excessive widening of the net of social control;
• debit or credit in doubt:
—the recidivism rate.

Most of these elements of the relevant cost/benefit analysis are
still speculative; accepting that, how can one strike a tentative
balance as a guide to sentencing policy?

Value of Services Provided

There are now reports on community service projects from many
jurisdictions in many countries, the most detailed being those from
the United Kingdom and New York City. All agree that the services performed by those sentenced in this way are welcomed by
the recipients of those services and that the sentenced offenders
prove to be more diligent workers than had been anticipated. It
seems not at all unreal to value, for example, the 70 hours of
work performed by the current 1200 in New York each year at,
say, $5 per hour, or a total contribution of $420,000 per year.
Rand Corporation researcher Joan Petersilia, in her 1987 book,
Expanding Options for Criminal Sentencing, calculates that the
work of the nearly 7500 offenders sentenced to community service
in New York through the end of 1988 would exceed $2,500,000
in value.

The New York program, because of its structure and control,
can be assessed in this way. The value of the services provided by
many other community service programs is more elusive, particularly those which provide services that are needed but otherwise
would not have been done—services to those in hospitals and institutions, reforestation and land and river reclamation services,
and similar contributions to the decencies of life and to the economic infrastructure. But it can be said that there seems to be

appreciable value in the services performed under community service orders and that the work done tends to be greatly appreciated by those who are its beneficiaries.

Jail and Prison Costs Saved

This proves harder to measure than the protagonists of the community service order usually allow. Astonishingly, the present cost of jailing in New York is about $40,000 per prisoner year and this takes no account of construction costs for jails or amortization of capital costs. Elsewhere, of course, costs are much lower, but they remain high. Hence advocates of alternative sentences often suggest that jail costs per year far exceed the costs of alternative punishments per year and that the difference is a clear saving. But this is not the whole truth. It fails to take into account that such savings accrue only when the alternative sanction reaches a threshold of sufficient usage to allow systems changes in the costs of jailing or imprisoning. The marginal costs of a few new prisoners or jail inmates is nothing like the $40,000 per year often claimed. One more cell is double or triple inhabited, extra food costs are negligible, other extra costs are marginal, no new guards are hired, the whole system comes under greater pressure from each increment of overcrowding, but the increased costs in money terms are not great.

In financial terms, it is only when substantial systems of community service orders cut into jail and prison costs sufficiently to preclude the opening of new wings in jails or prisons, or ideally to preclude the perceived need to build new jails or prisons, that the financial savings are measurable and substantial. This is not an argument against recognizing the potential financial advantages of such sentences; it is only a cautionary word about the accuracy of claims commonly made.

This does not, however, dispose of the question of whether community service orders save governmental funds; a further difficulty remains, the problem of "net widening." Many alternative punishments, including the community service order, are supported by the argument that they will be imposed on those who otherwise would receive a jail or prison term. This claim proves exceedingly difficult to measure, and there is a considerable record of the pool of offenders sentenced to the "alternative" being drawn not from those who otherwise would have gone to jail or prison but from those who otherwise would have been sentenced to a less restrictive punishment—to probation or to a suspended sentence. Again, though no one of the many studies of community service gives a compelling answer to this question, the thrust of all of them (with one exception) is so similar that reasonably confident statements can be made about the extent of net widening by community service orders. In particular, the English studies and the New York experience suggest that in practice no more than half of those sentenced to community service would otherwise have been incarcerated, even when diversion of offenders from incarceration is the program's stated purpose, and this finding seems to be confirmed by a large number of more speculative assessments.

The English legislation explicitly aimed at reducing short-term imprisonment, but it achieved this in about half the cases so sentenced. The New York project aimed at this effect in half the cases so sentenced and, after early failure to achieve this level in the Bronx and Brooklyn, managed to achieve this 50 percent level in those counties and in Manhattan, by changing the approach of the court representatives to case selection and by influencing the attitudes of the district attorneys.

Unless sentencing power be redistributed so that the selection of those given community service orders is made after they have been judicially sentenced to jail or prison (and this is politically unlikely—though it is the basis of the one exception noted above to the net-widening effect), or unless binding and effective sentencing guidelines can better channel and influence judicial and prosecutorial discretion, this half-and-half selection of cases for community service orders is probably about what will occur, half being drawn from those who otherwise would have been incarcerated, half from those who would have been more leniently treated.

This is sometimes phrased as a criticism of community service orders and other alternative punishments; this, we submit, may often be an error. In the continuum of control from very little to complete denial of freedom, which should make up the continuum of sentencing options, it may be entirely proper that a sentence like the community service order should draw both from those who previously were more controlled and those who were less controlled. American sentencing has long suffered, and continues to suffer, from limited imagination and an unwillingness to recognize as meaningful those punishments that fall between nominal probation and severe incarceration. When community service orders, or any other intermediate punishments, are devised to fill in the center gap in a bipolar, bimodal punishment system, it should come as no surprise that those sentenced to the newly available punishment come from both sides of the scale. Just as there may be persons imprisoned who should appropriately and could safely be subjected to a less intrusive and less destructive punishment, so there may be persons probationed who should appropriately be subjected to more intrusive and more constructive punishment. The question concerning rightness of fit between a punishment and its subjects should always be "Are these the kinds of offenders for whom this is an appropriate sanction?" It should seldom be "From whence do they come?" For those who see "alternatives" or intermediate punishments as primarily a means for removing people from prison, net widening is *prima facie* a program failure. For those, like us, who see intermediate punishments as a desirable midrange of punishments between prison and probation, the issues are more complex.

The idea of saving jail and prison costs has another aspect: given limited existing cell space, the limits often set by judicial orders pursuant to the Eighth Amendment, there is a great deal to be said for saving that space for the more threatening offenders and for those offense–offender relationships for which the larger threat of incarceration should be reserved. This argument rests both on deterrent and incapacitative purposes. There is thus a further "saving" by the use of intermediate punishments, including community service orders, in that they help to reserve a scarce resource for use where it is thought to be most needed. This theme leads appropriately to the next claimed advantage of the community service order.

Better Scaled Sentencing

Because we do not know the answers now does not mean that they will not in time be learned. It is entirely proper that the judge should have available a sentence that is more punitive than the typical probation order and less punitive than a prison or jail term; it is entirely appropriate that some offenders should make social reparation by free service to the community they have wronged. These propositions need no research support; they are grounded in concepts of proportionality of punishment, punishment proportional to the severity of the crime taking into account the criminal's record, punishment that it is hoped will be deterrent and yet allow room for self-direction to a law-abiding life if that is the criminal's wish. In these terms, the introduction of community service orders as part of the sentencing repertoire of the courts makes good sense; thereafter one hopes that critical evalution of the consequences of such sentences will clarify the categories of offenders to whom they are best applied.

Cost of the Program

This cost turns entirely on what is provided, on how a community service order is served and supervised. As a condition of probation with the service to be performed for a governmental or tax-free entity which supervises the fulfillment of the order, the cost is slight. By contrast, when work crews are formed of more entrenched offenders selected for community service orders and closely supervised, as is done in the New York City project, costs escalate; costs of that program in 1983 were $916 per offender.

The community service sentence can thus be fashioned to a variety of costs; it all depends on the level of intensity and enforcement of the program, as well as on the range of supportive services provided to select those suited to different types of community service and to control and support them in their assigned work.

There is a further aspect of costs to be considered here. The closer the supervision provided, the less likely those so sentenced are to be involved in other crimes during the currency of the program. In New York City, the foreman's eye is constantly on those performing their service, which, of course, does not minimize their likelihood of committing crime while not at work or traveling to and from work. In fact, the Vera Institute evaluators concluded that the recorded criminality of community service order offenders in the 90 days following conviction was for all practical purposes equivalent to that of a matched comparison group of jailed offenders during their first 90 days of freedom. But this can be minimized if a community service order is blended with a condition of residence in the community.

Hence all one can say about the costs of such programs is that they will vary with the intensity of supervision and support provided, as well as whatever costs go into the selection of candidates for this sentence. But, all in all, it is often likely to be less than jail or prison.

Unprevented Crimes

If the offender is in jail or prison, he will not, during the period of his incarceration, commit crimes against anyone other than fellow inmates and guards. There are exceptions to this: some prisoners manage to continue to be involved in criminal enterprises from behind the walls, but they are not the types of offenders likely to be sentenced to community service. Hence to some extent this alternative punishment must cost the community and individual victims in terms of crimes committed which would not have been committed had this sentence not taken the place of an incarcerative sentence.

Suppose it is true that half of those who are sentenced to community service would otherwise have done some time. It is clear that there is a real cost to these sentences, but it is not a cost that is at all easy to measure. Some of those sentenced to community service will commit new crimes in the community while in the program and these crimes would not have occurred if those offenders had been incarcerated for the period of community service. For example, Ken Pease reports that for the years 1979 through 1982 there was a reconviction rate for a new offense in England and Wales of 10 percent of those serving community service orders. Moreover, that cost in additional crimes cannot be reduced unless all who are at risk are incarcerated for the maximum period deserved by their offense and their criminal record, that is, unless from the mass of offenders considered for a community service sentence we had the skill to predict the likely high levels of criminality of a few who would therefore be denied this sentence. The sad truth is that these predictions are beyond our present capacities except in fairly obvious cases. And in those fairly obvious cases it is customary not to risk community service as a punishment: those with heavy drug or alcohol addiction related to their criminality are unsuitable candidates for this sentence and are generally excluded; those with records of personal violence are normally excluded. The New York project, for example, screens out all defendants charged with crimes against a person and all defendants whose criminal records indicated past crimes of violence. In addition, defendants without verified addresses or with severe drug, alcohol, mental, or emotional problems were excluded. And most programs explicitly exclude those convicted of sexual offenses.

The problem of crimes committed while serving a community service sentence is a conundrum. In New York, for example, the repetitive property offenders targeted for the program were, by definition, at high risk of further offending. The evaluation showed that their pattern of criminality on receipt of the community service sentence was neither better nor worse than that of comparable offenders who were jailed. It is not financially realistic to jail all repetitive property offenders for extended terms, nor is it pleasing to report to the public or press that we must accept that 15 of every 100 community service offenders (this was McDonald's 1986 estimate for New York City) are likely to commit offenses that would have been averted had they been jailed. We are inclined to accept the truth that all human activity has foreseeable but preferably avoided costs—the predictable but unavoidable traffic fatalities that we accept as a price of the convenience of the motor car or the equally predictable and unavoidable loss of life associated with building tall buildings—and to weigh the choices in terms of the level and nature of foreseeable criminality. McDonald observes on this point, in *Punishment Without Walls:*

Should the public spend five thousand to ten thousand dollars to incapacitate offenders who are averted from stealing items costing a few hundred dollars? Would not a better policy be to extract punishment in a financially less expensive manner (such as by ordering community service) and perhaps even expand the ability of victims to cover part of their losses by drawing from a crime victims' compensation fund?

Clearly, reasonable people can differ about the appropriate level of state response to repetitive minor property offending. For those jurisdictions—and there are some—that share McDonald's view, community service seems an appropriate intermediate punishment for use in such cases.

Displacement of Labor and Private Enterprise

The final disadvantage of the community service order—the extent to which such sentences unfairly conflict with the labor of those who have not been convicted of crime and with private enterprise—is different from those so far considered, and it also differs from other intermediate punishments. The definition of community service we offered stressed that the service was to be performed for nonprofit or tax-supported agencies. But that does not ensure, of course, that this indentured unpaid labor will not supplant or avoid the necessity to employ free and paid labor and those who organize such labor as private enterprise. In a situation other than full employment, such conflict is not easy to avoid.

In an era of tightened purse strings in most Western countries, and in most American jurisdictions, the attraction to public officials of a program that provides public service at no cost or nominal cost must be very great. It seems clear that in England those performing community service for substantial numbers of hours, up to 240 per offender, in governmental and tax-exempt agencies do in fact often save those agencies from the employment of free labor. Even in New York City where there is an effort to use the Vera work crews on building rehabilitation work and similar work that would otherwise not be done, it soon becomes apparent that much of it would indeed have had to be done and paid for by the city housing authorities.

Some community service—in homes for the aged, in mental hospitals, typically work otherwise done by volunteers—is not competitive with the market, but much is. How, then, does one estimate the importance of this objection to community service orders?

In a sense, if our processes of assessing and enforcing fines were well developed, and if the government were the employer of last resort, there would be little room for community service orders; but in the world as it is, with so much to be done by way of improvement of the environment and reclamation of natural resources as well as assistance to the deprived, the sick, and the aged, there would seem to be ample and proper room for sufficiently noncompetitive community service orders that this objection of unfair competition ceases to be of much significance. Much more often than not the choice is not likely to be whether to provide the service by use of paid or compelled services, but whether government will provide the service at all.

Weighing Costs and Benefits

One obvious cost or benefit of programs of community service is not included in the preceding balance sheet, because it remains unclear on which side of the ledger it should be posted. In terms of later criminality by convicted and sentenced offenders, does the community service order diminish or increase crime? The honest social scientist must admit to uncertainty: the answer is unclear. Studies have failed to demonstrate a result of criminality reduced among those sentenced to community service compared with comparison groups not so sentenced.

It will be remembered that, for programs like Britain's and New York City's, the comparison group will likely have been sentenced half to jail and half to probation or suspended sentence. With the exception of McDonald's work and that of Pease and his colleagues in the United Kingdom, there have been only a handful of subsequent offending follow-ups of community service, notably a 1983 report by the British Home Office Research Unit and a Tasmanian report in 1978 by Rook. Both Pease and McDonald conclude that there seems to be little difference in subsequent criminality when the treatment group is compared to the two comparison groups.

This is an all-too-common conclusion of critically pursued recidivism studies. A large part of the reason, as the 1979 and 1981 reports of the Panel on Rehabilitative Techniques of the National Academy of Sciences suggested, is that absent a true experimental research design (which no community service study has had) it is peculiarly difficult to demonstrate any such result in terms of recidivism as an outcome of the sentence being studied. And there has been great reluctance throughout all countries where the community service sentence has been introduced to allow a true experimental design to test it. It is our view that the ethical considerations supposed to preclude such experimentation are misguided; but there is no doubt that they exist and insulate us from any convincing claims of the effects, good or ill, of community service orders on the later criminal behavior of those so sentenced.

Lacking that important measure of the wisdom of such a sentence, or, probably more accurately, lacking knowledge of which categories of offenders respond to such sentences by reduced criminality and which by increased criminality, how does one strike the balance of assessment of this sentence? A cautious optimism seems appropriate, particularly in the present situation of severely overstrained incarcerative punishment resources. There would seem to be wisdom in extending the range of offenders sentenced to community service to include a wider array of offenders than the traffic offenders, juveniles, and less serious white-collar offenders who made up the original grist of the mill of this punishment. The Vera Institute and the New York City courts demonstrated the likely advantages of extending community service orders to persistent thieves and minority underclass offenders. Further extensions should be tested.

Such extensions might test a rather different approach to one type of community service order. Currently, famous sports figures who are convicted of using prohibited drugs are being required to lecture youths on the evils of drugs; it might have greater impact to use indigent drug addicts for this purpose; their appearance, mannerisms, speech patterns, and wider experience might have greater impact. Surely this possibility is worth testing.

A tentative conclusion seems safe: there is need for experimentation with the community service order combined with other nonincarcerative punishments such as conditions of residence and fines. For example, for the unemployed offender placed on probation, a community service order might well be a wise sentence to be used as a precursor to opportunities of paid employment that might be found.

If, as we hope, the widespread though scattered support for this sentence hardens into formalized and measured sentencing systems, there are a few key issues that merit particular attention: the purposes to be served by this sentence; problems in its enforcement and revocation; and the severity ranking of the community service order in the hierarchy of punishments of a rational sentencing system.

Purposes

Too much is often claimed for any new penal sanction; the community service order is no exception. It is to be a punitive, retributive sanction; compulsory unpaid work is obviously punitive and that punishment is justified by the crime committed. Also, it is to be a deterrent to the offender and to those who are like-minded. Further, it is to be reparative: the convicted offender makes reparation to the society he has wronged—the community a symbolic victim to be restored, just as the actual victim, if there was one, is to be compensated. And yet further, it is to be rehabilitative, teaching the convicted offender good work habits and the value of service to others, so that he will turn away from crime. It is wonderful what claims are made for penal sanctions when one considers the sad history of their general lack of impact on criminal behavior, either of the criminal or of those who might emulate his crime. The community service order seems greatly to attract such claims.

Another frequently advanced purpose of the community service order claims less and is certainly part of the reason for the spread of this sentence. There is widespread dissatisfaction with short-term imprisonment and jailing: it seems to be an ineffective deterrent, it is disruptive rather than rehabilitative in its effects on the criminal, and it is expensive. When jail and prison cells are in demand, it seems sensible to reduce that demand by other punishments that should do less harm and at least as much good as short-term incarceration.

The Advisory Council on the Penal System, which in 1970

recommended establishment of community service as a sentence in the United Kingdom, and those who passed the legislation which gave it force, made mention of all these justifications for the community service order: it was to be retributive, punitive, deterrent, reparative, and rehabilitative all at the same time, as well as reducing the number of offenders incarcerated. Baroness Wootton, who chaired the Advisory Council on the Penal System that produced the 1970 report, *Non-Custodial and Semi-Custodial Penalties,* which led to the spread of this sentence throughout England and Wales, in 1978 commented wryly on this conflation of purposes: "We did include a paragraph in the report of which I have always been slightly ashamed, as an undisguised attempt to curry favor with everybody."

Does this confusion of purposes matter? To an extent it does. Thus those who planned the New York City Community Service Sentencing Project defined their objectives in predominantly punitive terms. The work was to be hard, attendance and performance would be energetically enforced, and it was to be limited to 70 hours to be performed over two consecutive weeks. The courts were not to try to adjust the duration of the punishment to the gravity of the offense or the record of the offender; if a community service sentence was thought appropriate, then it would be for 70 hours, no more and. no less, and this primarily for reasons of administrative convenience and effective control.

Of course, to define a punishment in those terms does not at all preclude the pursuit of other rehabilitative and reparative aims, and the New York project demonstrated this. But the justifying purpose was punitive and to provide an alternative to jailing which the judges and the community would accept.

The first offender sentenced under the New York project provides an excellent model of this proper combination of purposes within an overriding policy of jail delivery. "Warren," as Douglas McDonald describes him in *Punishment Without Walls,* was an unlikely candidate for this type of sentence. Aged 31, he pleaded guilty to shoplifting, to stealing a pair of pants worth $20 from a department store. He had been previously arrested on 23 occasions, mostly for shoplifting and possession of drugs, but there had also been four burglary convictions and one conviction for robbery and assault. The last had earned him a five-year prison term. For 15 years he had been addicted to drugs and was, when arrested for stealing the pants, enrolled in a methadone clinic. His wife was also a drug addict. He claimed he had stolen the pants to sell to help maintain their child.

Warren was sentenced to 70 hours of community service in the Bronx. His recognition of the likelihood of a jail sentence led him to plead guilty to the charge, to accept the community service sentence, and to agree to report to the Vera project the next morning.

A preview of things to come: the next morning, a Friday, Warren did not appear at the work site. For two days project staff searched for him. On Monday morning they found him at the methadone clinic. His explanation: "I never thought you'd come looking for me. I just didn't think it mattered." Warren, like many other petty criminals in New York and, indeed, in most of the larger cities of this country, has been conditioned to the view that the only enforced punishment is prison or jail, the rest is largely symbolism not to be taken too seriously—a "walk."

This sentence was, however, to be enforced. Threatened with jail, as he realized, Warren reported for work and completed his 70 hours of work cleaning up a senior citizen's center. But project staff had to provide a great deal of social assistance to him as well as supervising his work. He was destitute and needed and was given an emergency loan; his home life was chaotic, his drug addiction a constant threat.

What the Warren case demonstrates is that for some offenders a community service sentence is an entirely appropriate blend of retributive punishment and social assistance; for others such efforts are unnecessary; for most they will be unavailable. We are surely used to multipurposive systems, and the community service order is no exception.

Difficulties remain, however: if a duration of community service is to be at all proportional to the gravity of the crime and the length of the offender's criminal record, there will be severe limitations on its use as a punishment, standing alone.

As we shall see, the key to the efficiency of such sentences lies in their enforcement. It has proved unwise to inflate periods of community service beyond 240 hours, which is the maximum term that can be imposed in the United Kingdom, and there is a general sense among those reporting on these sentences that a much lesser period, something around 100 hours, is a sensible maximum. After that, laxity in enforcement too often sets in. Hence if the community service order is to be extended to a greater range of crimes, and to more serious crimes and to those with longer records, it will have to be combined with other nonincarcerative punishments. This development seems to us both likely and sensible; it is a theme to which we return at the end of this chapter.

Enforcement

"Warren's" original understanding of his sentence to community service must not be reinforced; it is fundamental to the development of this sentence that it be diligently and determinedly enforced. This is, of course, true of all criminal sentences; but the deplorable history of nonenforcement of conditions of probation due to excessive caseloads, noncollection of fines, and even nonenforcement of arrest warrants, particularly in the cities of this country, makes it essential to stress the obvious.

Perhaps an anecdotal aside may be allowed to underline the need for the law here too to keep its promises. It was the breach of this obligation that led one of us to the interest in noncustodial sentences that was the genesis of this book: observing Night Court in Manhattan, the arrangements for bail and detention, the appalling conditions of overcrowding and unseemliness that characterized "Central Booking," one of us heard a report by a court official to a judge that a named alleged offender had failed to appear for trial. The request for an arrest warrant followed. The warrant was made out and handed to a police officer in the court. The observer accompanied the police officer back to Central Booking. The police officer entered the fact of the arrest warrant in the appropriate computerized file on the alleged offender, and then threw the document itself into a drawer. Then followed this dialogue:

"Are you not going to try to find him and arrest him?" "No. Don't worry. He'll turn up. And if he doesn't, that's good, isn't it?"

These attitudes—some would say these inescapable realities—characterize too much of the enforcement mechanisms of the criminal justice system in cases that are not of a very high level of gravity or political interest. These attitudes and these realities flourish in noncustodial sentences. They go a large way to explain the failure in this country to develop and rely on punishment systems other than imprisonment and probation.

Enforcement of community service orders raises genuine difficulties. If it is left to already overburdened probation departments and probation officers, the result is not hard to predict. If the actual supervision is left to the governmental or tax-exempt agency for which the offender is to work, there will be great unevenness in supervision—some will be closely and well supervised and controlled, some will be ignored or laxly observed.

A rough classification of types of community service customarily ordered may assist in analyzing their quite different enforcement and supervision needs. Arbitrarily, let us classify community service orders as using either the particular skills of the convicted offender, or his inspirational/confessional capacities, or as directing him to service in public facilities.

The professional skills of the convicted doctor or nurse or business executive or accountant can easily be directed to serving governmental or tax-exempt agencies. Not much supervision is required. Provided the agency served has the need for these skills—and agencies often do—that same agency can be made responsible to account to the sentencing court that the order is being obeyed or has been fulfilled. The probation service will be put under no great extra burden as the liaison between the court and the agency being served and the offender. The offender will need no support services. Thus enforcement of community service orders on this category of offenders presents no problem; but this category does not cover many criminals and certainly not the ordinary flow of criminals in the city courts.

The inspirational/confessional category is similarly restricted. The drug-using sports hero can lecture to Boys' Clubs of the past evil of his ways and the bright future that awaits them if they avoid those paths. The notorious insider trader or antitrust law offender can, in addition to any other punishment imposed, be required to bare his erstwhile greedy soul to businessmen's lunches. Again neither supervision nor enforcement is required; a responsibility of an accounting suffices, and again this group does not cover the grist of the mill of the criminal courts.

It is the third group—the "Warrens" of persistent property

crime, who lack skills and education, whose social setting is disrupted, who clutter the city courts of first instance—who present the largest challenge to the community service order. The lessons of such sentences in many jurisdictions, but particularly in the United Kingdom and in the New York City courts, is that their supervision and control is a considerable and an expensive burden if it is to be done at all efficiently.

Whether work crews be formed for such offenders, as in New York City, or in major programs in Detroit and Charleston (South Carolina), or whether their labor is farmed out over their leisure hours to public agencies, as in England, it is of the first importance that their regular attendance be confirmed and that supervision be maintained over the quality of their work and over their good behavior while at work. What is needed for the work crew is not at all the insights of the probation-officer-social-worker; what is needed is the tough directness of a work crew or factory foreman who will not tolerate tardiness, slackness, or misbehavior. The same type of supervision is needed when the convicted offender's labor is spread individually among agencies, but it is then very much harder to provide; all that can be done, it is suggested, is to have a supervisor of the community service program whose task is precisely such supervision and who maintains regular and close as possible contact with the agencies where offenders are placed.

Yet close supervision to ensure appearance on time, fulfillment of work quotas, and good behavior on the job, though necessary, is not sufficient. This category of offenders on community service orders have a variety of social handicaps that impede their work and which must be addressed if only to ensure the proper completion of the community service order. Hence they need supervision of another type as well as supervision by the "foreman" or foreman substitute; the traditional skills of the social worker will be needed for support services. It is asking too much to expect the probation officer to combine these two skills, that of the job supervisor and the client supporter, yet both are necessary. Hence however community service orders are to be fulfilled, by work weeks, weekends, or evening work, enforcement in terms of supervision and in terms of support will prove essential.

The relationship between supervision and support raises the problem of revocation. Breach of the order empowers the sentencing court to impose any punishment it could have imposed at the time of original sentencing. This would seem to be the case whether the community service order was or was not the product of a plea bargain; the only exception would seem to be when the community service order was imposed as a condition of suspension of some other sentence, normally to jail or prison, in which case if there be revocation, that sentence is restored. Two issues must be considered: Should all breaches of a community service order lead to revocation? And should all breaches of a community service order be reported to the court? The answers will vary with the organization of the program, but reality compels the conclusion that some discretion must be given to the program supervisors, both the foreman and the social worker, not to report less significant breaches, and that thereafter there remains the typical judicial discretion whether to revoke or not on which general advance guidelines are unlikely to be helpful.

A final cautionary theme must be developed if community service programs are to take a larger place in the repertoire of sentences in American courts: it is essential to supply the infrastructure of supervision and enforcement of these orders before any large-scale program is launched. Such programs should grow on a strong base of seriousness of enforcement purpose allied to existing capacities to provide supervision; if they are loaded onto already overburdened probation departments or onto individual probation officers, they will not be strongly enforced and will soon become what "Warren" first thought the community service order was, a "walk."

Imposing a CSO

The next issue we must address is the place of community service in a comprehensive system of interchangeable punishments. For some offenses and offenders, community service can be a stand-alone sentence. For others, especially those of lowest or no income, it may be a substitute for the fine. For others, especially those who present apparent threats to public safety, the community service order may be but part of a package of punishments.

First, the exchange rate. Because of the logistical limits to the feasible duration of a community service order—240 hours is often seen as the outer bound—there are natural limits to equivalences between community service and other penalties. Washington State sentencing guidelines permit substitution of community service for prison days at the rate of eight hours of work for one day in prison, with a limit of 30 days. In New York City, the Vera project apparently regarded 70 hours as the punitive equivalent of a month's jail. The English Court of Appeal (*R. V. Lawrence,* [1982] Crim. L. Repts. 377) held that an order of 190 hours is equivalent to one year's imprisonment. Recommendations have been offered in England by Ken Pease for a "two-tier" approach to community service: orders of 100 hours' work, or less, are seen as substitutes for nonincarcerative sentences; orders from 100 to 240 hours are seen as substitutes for incarcerative sentences up to a year in length.

While acknowledging the probable wisdom of the 240-hour upper boundary, we would argue for equivalences more generous than Washington State's and more like the English. Whether a community service order is appropriate in a given case will depend in large part on the appropriate purposes of punishment raised by that case at sentencing. For crimes of violence or offenders with histories of violence, a 6- or 12-month jail sentence might be appropriate in a case in which the nonviolent but comparably culpable offender might receive as much as 240 hours of community service.

We mention six months advisedly because of interaction among the roles of short incarceration, fines, and community service. In Western European countries that use the day fine, one overriding purpose—underscored in West Germany by statutory presumption—has been to diminish use of prison sentences of six months or shorter duration. If, say, a fine assessed as 20-day units can be comparable to 6 months' incarceration, it would appear *prima facie* appropriate that the judge be able to impose 20 days' community service on the insolvent or unemployed.

This leads inexorably to an issue that has stirred heated debate in England: whether community service should be authorized as a substitute for a fine when the offender is unemployed. This seems a debate almost scholastic in tone, and perhaps is explained in England by the greater ideological overtones of public issues relating to employment or social welfare programs. If 6 months' incarceration is deemed equivalent to a fine of 20 day-fine units or to 20 days' community service, and this is an offender who seems not to require the greater controls of incarceration or the lesser controls of close human or electronic monitoring, it can only be cruel sophistry to insist that the impecunious be jailed. If community service be a "fine on time," both equity and symmetry argue that the poor be allowed to pay in work what the less poor pay in money.

Perhaps in a society that lacks gross economic inequalities and possesses a well-developed system of fines, the community service order would be redundant. Sweden rejected use of community service as a sanction for precisely these reasons. A 1978 report of the National Swedish Council for Crime Prevention observes: "[T]he group does not think that there is any need for alternative sanctions over and above these that already exist in the sanction system (fines, conditional sentences, probation, and intensive supervision). The purpose of other new forms of [punishment] is unclear." In the United States, in the foreseeable future, there do seem important purposes to be served by community service.

To summarize, we see the following roles for community service in a system of interchangeable intermediate punishments:

- for minor crimes that now receive unduly lenient nominal punishment;
- for more serious crimes, that might justify up to a 6- to 12-months' jail sentence, recognition as a stand-alone punishment or as an alternative for the impecunious to the fine;
- for more serious crimes or threatening offenders, as one component of a package of controls, conditions, and impositions that address the offender's needs and vulnerabilities, and the perceived need to provide greater assurances of community safety.

Thus far we have discussed those intermediate punishments, the fine and the community service order, that seem most appropriate when the purposes to be served at sentencing are primarily retributive and deterrent. We have repeatedly also noted that fines and community service may often be appropriately used as components of more complex intermediate punishments in which purposes of control and public safety loom larger. To these more incapacitative programs of residential controls and treatment conditions we now turn.

7

Control and Treatment
in the Community

There is a pernicious tendency to think of criminal sanctions as
either punishment or treatment, either pain or beneficent assistance, either the prison and the jail or the psychiatrist and the
social worker. Let us take a fresh look at the shopping list of current penal sanctions for adults and try to shake ourselves free of
this perspective.

The menu is not long; we are not imaginative in our punishment
of criminals. Current penal sanctions are:

Capital punishment
Prison and jail
Fines
House arrest
Probation
    Intensive supervision
    Residential conditions
    Treatment conditions
Community service orders
Intermittent imprisonment
Forfeiture

Restitution and compensation
Fees for service
Electronic monitoring

Let us set aside the stigmatizing effects of conviction and sentence for a criminal offense and consider all punishments on our menu as reductions of autonomy, with each dish being briefly described in terms of its effects on autonomy and the primary purposes in relation to autonomy it might plausibly serve. How would the menu read? We are not here concerned with retributive considerations and the limits they impose on the appropriateness of particular sentences in individual cases.

Capital Punishment

Total withdrawal of autonomy with general deterrent and incapacitative purposes.

Prison and Jail

Autonomy of association and movement greatly withdrawn, the primary purposes are deterrent and incapacitative; but for all who do not serve a sentence for the term of their natural lives there is also a purpose of specific deterrence, the hope that the experience of punishment will dissuade the offender from repeated criminality. (Actually there is no difference between specific deterrence and rehabilitation; they differ only in the means pursued to the end of avoiding future crime by the prisoner—to avoid carrying the emotional baggage that these two different means attract, let us call this single purpose "training for conformity." After all, negative conditioning by the threat of pain is also training.)

Fines

Autonomy in relation to property reduced or withdrawn; the primary purposes deterrent and training for conformity.

House Arrest

Autonomy of movement reduced or withdrawn; the primary purposes incapacitative and training for conformity.

Probation

Withdrawal of autonomy varying with the terms of the probation order; the primary purpose training for conformity. (A secondary purpose must be mentioned: if the conditions of the order are breached, there must be a threat of prison or jail for deterrence, general and specific.)

Intensive Supervision Probation

A more intensive withdrawal of autonomy than ordinary probation, for the same purposes, and with the same back-up purposes more imminently threatened.

Probation with Residential Conditions

Probation plus further withdrawal of autonomy of movement, for incapacitative purposes and training for conformity.

Probation with Treatment Conditions

Probation plus further withdrawal of autonomy of freedom for self-development, for incapacitation and training for conformity.

Community Service Orders

Withdrawal of vocational autonomy for deterrent purposes and training for conformity.

Intermittent Imprisonment

A lesser withdrawal of autonomy of association and movement than prison or jail, for the same purposes.

Forfeiture

Withdrawal of autonomy of property in ill-gotten gains.

Restitution and Compensation

Reduction or withdrawal of autonomy regarding finances to assist the victim of the crime; primary purposes to help the victim and train the criminal to conformity.

Fees for Service

It is doubtful whether these are penal sanctions at all. They can be so regarded or they can be thought of as achieving legislative decisions concerning the societal distribution of costs of the criminal justice system. They may be particularly important in meeting the costs of enforcing withdrawals of autonomy of those not incarcerated. It is too early to be sure what purposes they will in fact serve.

Electronic Monitoring

Apart from their incidental stigmatizing effects, these are not penal sanctions at all; they are means to the enforcement of nonincarcerative sanctions higher on this list. They can, of course, be used punitively, but that is not their primary purpose.

What utility is there in this perspective on punishment?

The intent is that it should facilitate recognition of the continuities of purpose and method over the entire range of punishments, continuities that are obscured by the bifurcation that defines prison as punishment, the rest as treatment. It should also give point to the need to develop a comprehensive sentencing system, better adjusted to the purposes and resources of the criminal justice system.

In such a system, community-based punishments would take their place in the present vacuum between ordinary probation and incarceration, being more reductive of autonomy than the former and less than the latter. Since in this book we have set aside the polarities of this continuum—capital punishment, imprisonment, and ordinary probation—and have already considered the fine and the community service order, what is left is:

Intensive probation and the role of the probation officer; the balance between control and treatment

Crime, drugs, and mental illness
Community-based drug treatment programs
Community-based alcohol treatment programs
Community-based psychological treatment conditions
Community-based sex offender treatment programs
House arrest and electronic monitoring
Intermittent imprisonment
Forfeiture, restitution, compensation, and fees for services

The overarching question we address concerning all these community-based punishments is the extent to which it is possible to combine control purposes, aiming at minimizing the threat the criminal presents to society, with treatment purposes, aiming to train the criminal for conformity. A subsidiary question is the extent to which these punishments are properly interchangeable in a rational sentencing system, with probation for those whose autonomy should be further reduced by an intermediate punishment and with incarceration for those for whom that degree of denial of autonomy is insufficient.

It is the central question of this book and merits restatement: To what extent can community-based punishments be combined with conditions of treatment to create punishments that both control and treat and are interchangeable with incarcerative sentences and with ordinary probation to create a comprehensive sentencing system?

Intensive Probation

In every state and in the federal system programs called "Intensive Probation" are to be found; their diversity is such that the term has almost ceased to have useful meaning. Their common feature, however, is that more control is to be exerted over the offender than that described as probation in that jurisdiction and that often these extra control mechanisms involve restrictions on liberty of movement, coercion into treatment programs, employment obligations, or all three.

One impetus behind such programs was to create the possibility for judges to avoid further crowding the prisons and jails by giving them "alternative" punishments that would be more acceptable to public opinion since they were sufficiently intrusive and demeaning to be perceived as punitive and they held promise of a closer supervision of the offender and therefore less likelihood of his continued depradations. Another impetus was the recognition by those running probation services that among those placed on probation there were offenders at higher risk of serious criminality than the rest, so that it was sensible disproportionately to allocate supervision and support resources to them. A further impetus was the failure of earlier experimentation with differential caseloads, the random allocation of those on probation, some to supervision by a probation officer carrying a small caseload, some to supervision by a probation officer carrying a much larger caseload, and the discovery that in the mass this made little difference. Hence selection of the higher risk group either by the judge or by the probation office for more intensive control.

Here is an outline description of three programs of intensive probation, in Georgia, New Jersey, and Massachusetts, that have served as models to other jurisdictions.

In Georgia, intensive probation is a judicially imposed sentence, the characteristics of which are small caseloads for team supervision, each team of two (a probation officer and a surveillance officer) normally supervising about 25 offenders, enforcing curfews, employment, and community service, with drug and alcohol monitoring, and at least five face-to-face contacts per week. Those on probation in Georgia pay fees for service of from $10 to $50 per month, the amount being set by the sentencing judge. The cost of intensive probation in Georgia in 1987 was about $985 per offender per year, as compared to the $7760 which was then the cost of a year's incarceration of an offender in Georgia, itself very much lower than the national average.

Erwin and Bennett in 1987 reported on their study of the Georgia program of intensive supervision that found a "failure" rate of 16 percent. Very few of these were arrested for serious felonies; most had absconded or had had probation revoked for breach of condition.

How does one evaluate such a program in the context of an overall punishment system? The Georgia claim is that their program has led to a 10 percent reduction in percentage of convicted offenders who are incarcerated. However, it appears that Georgia traditionally sends a higher proportion of convicted offenders to prison than do other states, so that the Georgia claim of reduced prison crowding may not be replicable by these means elsewhere. Moreover, precisely because Georgia has traditionally imprisoned a greater proportion of its convicted felons than have many other states, those less threatening felons diverted from prison may on average present less of a social threat than would persons diverted from prison elsewhere.

When the judiciary selects those who would otherwise be "prison bound" for intensive probation one cannot with confidence be sure that a net-widening effect is not taking place. But, in truth, though this is frequently the object of discussion concerning programs of intensive probation, it is not the central issue, since such punishments should properly draw both from the prison bound and the ordinary probation bound.

The New Jersey program of intensive probation seeks to avoid this net-widening effect; whether it does so in fact is speculative. The selection for intensive probation is made by having the offender who has been sentenced to prison apply to a resentencing panel for placement on intensive probation for a term of 18 months. Only certain defined categories of offenders may apply; for example, those convicted of violent offenses are excluded. The idea behind this procedure is that intensive probation will certainly reduce prison populations, but the idea presupposes that the judiciary take no notice of this possible resentencing procedure when they sentence to prison one who qualifies for a resentence application—and this is disingenuous.

Pearson studied the New Jersey program and reported an average frequency of probationer–probation officer contacts per month of 31 (including 12 face-to-face, 7 for curfew checks, and 4 for urinalysis checks), which is indeed an intensive level of supervision. Other features of the New Jersey program, as Pearson describes them, are the careful development of a life plan for each offender while on probation; his work, study, and community service obligations; the requirement that he be employed or in vocational training full-time; that he perform acts of community service; and the use of a community sponsor to assist each probationer and thus to extend the control and supportive reach of the probation officer.

The National Institute of Justice sponsored an evaluation of the New Jersey program by Pearson of Rutgers University. It costs more than the Georgia program, $13,693 per offender year (a prison year in New Jersey at that time was costed at more than $20,000), but like the Georgia program the results in terms of crimes committed by those on intensive probation seem favorable, with only 1 in 10 being arrested for a new crime (1 in 20 for a felony) and about a third of those whose applications for intensive probation are granted being returned to prison for violations of the probation order.

Massachusetts provides a third model of intensive probation. Here the probation department makes the decision of intensive probation after the offender has been sentenced to a term of probation. The decision is guided by a risk-assessment instrument based on the past experience of the probation department with similar offenders. The level of intensity of supervision is also set by the assessment of risk. As yet no critical study of this program has been published, though an evaluation conducted by James Byrne of the University of Lowell is nearing completion. It is mentioned here largely to give an influential example of a different approach to the problem from that in the earlier two models.

What emerges from this brief overview of patterns of intensive probation programs is that there are many ways to select a group of offenders whose risk to the community, provided they are closely supervised and vigorously assisted, is such that they are suitable for an intermediate punishment; that they will be drawn both from those who are otherwise prison bound and those who were otherwise likely to be very lightly supervised on probation; and that there is much promise in our gradually emerging knowledge of the costs and benefits of these programs and of the characteristics of the offenders to which they are suited.

A final general theme on intensive probation merits consideration before the problems of community-based drug treatment programs for addicts and for the psychologically disturbed are addressed: the problem of role conflict for the probation officer, a tension between his control function and his casework function, having to be both a policeman and a social worker.

This tension in the probation officer's role exists in all intensive probation situations because all such sentences (whether judicially ordered or, as in Massachusetts, administratively classified) necessarily involve this balance between control and treatment. If there is a condition of residence, it must be enforced, whether with or without the assistance of electronic technology; if there are payments to be made, they must be made; work ordered to be done under a community service order must be done; training courses ordered to be attended must be attended; limitations of autonomy that are imposed must be enforced. So the question arises whether this tension in the supervisory role of the probation officer is a serious and pervasive threat to the expansion of intermediate punishments we are seeking.

The tension is particularly sharp in relation to the supervision of drug treatment programs and will be discussed in that context; but the argument applies to all intensive probation arrangements.

Community-based supervision of the addict-criminal requires, in effect, police work; a determination by urine testing and other observations to ensure that he is remaining drug free and a willingness to report any breaches of this condition of the probation order. But addict-criminals usually also experience a wide diversity of personal, family, vocational, and community difficulties in which they need guidance and assistance if they are to avoid crime and struggle by in the community.

Such is the force of this conflict that many jurisdictions are experimenting with team supervision of those on intensive probation, duties being divided between two probation officers in relation to these often conflicting purposes. In relation to drug treatment as part of intensive probation, these role conflicts are particularly challenging since it is the universal testimony of those running such programs that drug addiction should be regarded as a relapsing condition, success being measured by the infrequency of relapse and the brevity of its duration until, in many cases, in the fullness of time, if he does not die, the addict-criminal becomes first an ex-criminal and then an ex-addict. Those readers who used to be addicted to nicotine will well understand that scenario.

Whatever the institutional arrangements, it is clear that community-based drug treatment programs, buttressed as they should be by urine testing programs, require of those supervising the addict-criminals a combination of the policeman and the social worker if the large contribution such criminals make to street crime is to be reduced.

There is no way in which effective, regular, but unpredictable urine testing to ensure that the convicted offender is drug free can be made other than as a police-type function; it is unlikely to be seen except by the most thoughtful offender as beneficent. In this situation it is hard to expect the agent of the state who has responsibility for that function also to be well-situated to assist the convicted offender with the many problems of employment and tangled social relationships that routinely surround the lives of the street criminal. Yet their need is great and it is in our interests, in terms of minimization of crime, to try to meet it.

Insightful assistance and forceful control can, in the view of many working in probation, be combined within the one probation officer. Some probation offices have gone further and have moved to different supervisory structures to minimize this role conflict.

One cost-effective structure is that of intensive team supervision. The caseload of the "social worker–probation officer" can be considerably higher than the caseload of the "policeman–probation officer." Their personalities will, of course, influence their roles, and there will be situations where the experience of the "policeman" with the convicted offender will richly infuse the decisional process, particularly when a test is positive after a long period of abstinence by the offender.

An alternative path to the same result is to arrange a closer liaison between the caseworker–probation officer and the police, undertaking roles suited to their other activities in relation to the supervised offender: seeing that he is not at large when he should not be, seeing that he is observing the conditions of his probation, and in particular arranging random urine testing. The police have the arrest power, they have the larger confidence of the community that they will not allow any sentimental regard for the offender to interfere with their supervisory duties, and unlike probation officers the police are on duty 24 hours a day and in particular at the times when the probation office is not open—which are also the favored times both for crime and for breaches of conditions of probation.

Yet another possibility is to establish a separate and distinct state agency for nonincarcerative punishments more severe than ordinary probation and less restrictive of liberty than prison or jail. There would be financial advantages in this: the saving of prison funds would be clear, as would the offsetting increase of cost of intensive supervision in the community. There would also be the clarity of function coming from the reality that there is little difference in the tasks of supervising the ex-prisoner on conditional release and the convicted criminal sentenced directly by the court to intensive supervision under defined conditions in the community—also conditional.

However this combination between casework support and "police" surveillance and enforcement of conditions is achieved, one way or another supervision of the convicted offender put on drug-free intensive supervision must ensure that the law keeps its promises, that close supervision is a reality, and that every relapse to the use of drugs will be taken most seriously not only by the supervising officer or supervising team, but also by the sentencing judge.

We now turn to some urgently needed intermediate punishments to address the problem of crimes committed by the addicted and the psychologically disturbed.

Crime, Drugs, and Mental Illness

Community-based intermediate punishments appear to be particularly attractive for the treatment and control of those whose criminality seems closely linked to addiction to drugs or alcohol or seems to be influenced by a pathological mental condition; there is widespread experimentation with such programs and they hold promise of playing an important role in a comprehensive punishment system. They offer the paradigm case of the effort to blend effective controls with effective treatment programs for two main reasons: the prison is such an inappropriate place for such programs and there is widespread understanding in the community of the need to provide treatment for the addicted and the mentally ill. Citizens may well object to a clinic for the ambulatory treatment of addicted or disturbed criminals being situated in their neighborhood, but they tend to agree that it is proper to have such clinics somewhere.

If the relations between drug or alcohol use or mental disorder or psychopathology and crime are clear and close, it may often be possible to couple treatment conditions with fines or intensive supervision probation or home detention in ways that offer preventive promises that those punishments alone cannot provide.

Alcohol, drugs, and mental illness are intimately related to crime. Does this mean more than that they are intimately related to a great deal of human behavior? The data suggest that it does. Worldwide arrest data and interview data reveal that a large proportion of criminals, particularly "street" criminals, had ingested substantial amounts of alcohol shortly before the commission of the crime for which they were arrested. Likewise, recent urine tests run on large numbers of felony arrestees in New York City, Washington, D.C., and many other cities, confirm what had long been suspected: many felons had used hard drugs shortly before the commission of their crimes. The confirmation exceeded the expectation; few had suspected the result that more than 50 percent of street felons—and in some cities 70 to 80 percent—fitted this category. In April 1986, some 67 percent of arrestees in the District of Columbia tested positive for recent drug use, not counting marijuana. In that same year, during September and October 86 percent of a random sample of persons arrested for nondrug felonies and booked at Manhattan Central Booking tested positive for cocaine, opiates, methadone, or PCP. More recent data from the National Institute of Justice's Drug Use Forecasting System, involving urinalysis of arrestees in 25 cities, shows that although drugs of choice vary from city to city, in most cities well over half the persons arrested for felony charges test positive for drugs.

That alcohol and other drugs figure frequently in the scenarios of crime, particularly street crime, is beyond doubt. But the leap to the equally frequently offered proposition that use of alcohol and other drugs *causes* crime lacks demonstration. Nor do we see our task here as probing that often impenetrable relationship beyond what is necessary for a rational and effective sentencing and punishing system. Our task is not etiological, except insofar as some understanding of etiology is necessary for punishment purposes.

Much the same is true of the relationship between mental illness and crime, though the correlation here is much lower than the correlation between drugs and crime. But here too our task is limited to an effort to understand these relationships sufficiently for punishment purposes.

Finally, and perhaps more obscurely, there is an etiological link between psychopathology and various forms of sexual offenses. Sexual offenders, especially those whose illegal acts occur within an ongoing family context, provoke polarized reactions: their acts are heinous and intolerably self-indulgent and they should be severely punished; their acts are also pathological, and the good of the offender, the family, and the victim requires that suitable community treatment be found.

The prison environment is far from a suitable setting for drug treatment programs or for psychological treatments, other than for the floridly psychotic who would in any event be held for treatment in a closed psychiatric hospital. A setting lacking the temptations of available drugs and alcohol, and lacking the rubs and pressures and temptations of ordinary social interrelationships, may be a good launch pad for drug and alcohol treatment programs and for psychiatric treatments, particularly psychotropic drug–supported treatment programs, but it can be no more than a launch pad. Prison administrators appreciate the need for such treatment programs, but they also appreciate that they are subsidiary to the punitive and incapacitative purposes served by the prison. These programs in prisons and jails may lay the foundations on which the prisoner so troubled may continue treatment and support in the community on release; they have value but they demonstrate the wisdom of the thesis developed by a serious scholar of the prison: "It is hard to train an aviator in a submarine."

Intermediate punishments with conditions of treatment would therefore seem particularly appropriate for addicted and mentally ill criminals, provided sufficient control of their behavior can be built into those programs to satisfy legitimate community anxieties. But there is a further proviso: there must be a sufficient nexus between the criminal's addiction or mental illness and his criminality to justify the provision of treatment services. Common sense suggests that there is, but common sense is often an unwise counselor and the question merits closer examination.

A visit to any large maximum security prison will confirm that it holds a disproportionate number of the disturbed and retarded—disproportionate in relation to the population at large, including that part of the population whose socioeconomic circumstances match those of the imprisoned. Similarly, if one visits a city court of first instance or a city jail, an even larger disproportion is to be observed. Correctional and judicial records confirm these observations. Can one then leap to causal statements tying crime to mental illness? The relationship is more complex than that; caution is needed.

Looked at it in the aggregate, convicted criminals and citizens diagnosed as mentally ill are two separate but overlapping groups. Most criminals are not mentally ill; most mentally ill are not criminal. But the overlap is large. The burdens and temptations of man do not hunt solitary; they come often in packs; and so it is with mental illness and a variety of pressures toward crime.

Sometimes the relationship is particularly close and deserves to be classed as a prime cause. There are some criminals whose criminal behavior is rooted deep in mental illness: the paranoid convinced of the persecution that must be resisted violently; the kleptomaniac; a few epileptics; and there are others. But equally there are mentally ill who would be criminal were they not psychologically disturbed or retarded; their mental illness and its treatment insulate them from criminality. In the aggregate, one cannot offer useful etiological propositions about mental illness or retardation in itself as a cause of crime.

Monahan and Steadman in 1983 in *Crime and Justice* carefully reviewed the literature on the aggregate relationship between crime and mental illness and concluded:

> While the unadjusted crime rate of the mentally ill is indeed higher than that of the general population, and the unadjusted rate of mental disorder among criminals is indeed higher than among the general population, both relations tend to disappear when the appropriate statistical adjustments are made for age, social class, and prior exposure to the mental health and criminal justice systems.

At the individual level these uncertainties tend to be swept away. More than cursory study of many criminal histories will reveal patterns of behavior influenced substantially by mental illness and retardation: cases in which inhibitions are clearly reduced; cases in which pressures toward crime are greatly increased; patterns of repetitive self-destructive behavior that fall outside the normal range of human irrationality. For these, the causal link sufficient to justify treatment programs which may reduce future criminality is clear.

There thus may well be policy justification for community-based psychiatric treatment programs for some convicted offenders, provided such programs are protective of society and cost effective. We will later discuss what that proviso means.

Turning to the alcohol–crime relationship, here common experience of crime throughout the world and the personal experience of all who regularly consume alcohol leads to a strong and simple consensus: alcohol is a powerful eliminator or reducer of inhibitions to undesirable and criminal behavior. To cite alcohol as a *cause* of crime is surely correct, provided "cause" is understood to mean the elimination or reduction of behavioral controls that otherwise would prevent crime.

Here again, if there are cost-effective community-based treatment programs that can reduce the dependence of criminals on alcohol, there would seem to be opportunity for more socially protective punishments than a jail or prison term can provide.

The relationship between other drugs and crime is more complex. We set aside the consumption, sale, distribution, and importation of illicit drugs as crimes in themselves and concentrate on the relationship between other crimes and the ingestion of drugs. And let us further exclude from consideration the milder drug of marijuana and focus on heroin and other opium derivatives, cocaine, the barbiturates, and the amphetamines. The relationship between use of these drugs and participation in street crime would seem to be extremely close.

We do not refer to the question of the "original cause," or which came first, the criminality or the ingestion of drugs, which for our purposes is an unhelpful question. The most careful analyses of this causal link, both quantitative, in 1988 by Douglas Anglin and George Speckart of UCLA, and qualitative, in 1986 by Eric Wish and Bruce Johnson of Narcotic and Drug Research, Inc., conclude that causal order cannot be shown and, in any case, the existence of a single causal relation between drug use and criminality is most unlikely. For some drug-using criminals, no doubt drug use leads to personal associations and financial needs that in turn lead to crime; for others, the sequence may be reversed; for yet others, there may be no causal links at all.

Rather than seek a single causal link, we refer here to three other links between the hard drugs and crime which Paul Goldstein has referred to as, respectively, "psychopharmacological," "economic–compulsive," and "systemic." The psychopharmacological link is the same as for alcohol, the creation of false confidence, the lowering of inhibitions. The economic–compulsive link is the pressure on some to commit crime to have the funds to sustain their drug addiction. The systemic link occurs where crime and violence are part of the pattern of drug trafficking in which offenders' involvement in drug taking has placed them.

In the language of the 1988 report of the National Academy of Sciences Working Group on Drugs and Crime (edited by Messrs. Roth, Tonry, and Morris):

> [R]esearch to date has established three empirical relationships rather definitively: (1) violent and property offenders who use drugs commit crimes at least twice the average rates for all such offenders; (2) individuals' frequencies of offending . . . increase with the regularity of their drug use—occasional, regular, daily; and (3) individuals' offending frequencies increase and decrease with variations over time in the intensity of their drug use.

Treatment programs in the community designed to reduce drug addiction among criminals thus hold promise of formidable payoffs in terms of crime reduction. Whether that promise can be realized is a different matter; but that the search is worthwhile is obvious from rapidly accumulating data on the close link between repetitive street crime and high levels of drug ingestion.

A treatment intervention may be effective even if the treatment does not deal with the "cause" of the behavior. To lift the burden of addiction or psychological disturbance from the shoulders of the criminal may assist him to deal with whatever else it was that "caused" his criminality. Knowledge of the etiological link is not necessary. Whether or not addiction and mental illness "cause" crime, in the aggregate or in the individual case, it is clear that there may be advantage to providing treatment for those conditions in criminals, and it is also clear that community-based programs hold more promise than those behind walls.

We use an idealized hypothetical situation as the foundation of our argument for the institutionalization of well-staffed community-based treatment programs for criminals whose criminality is closely associated with alcohol, drugs, mental illness, or a combination of all three. We take the "heroin addict–burglar" as a prototype since he is not usually thought of as a prime candidate for an intermediate punishment.

Our criminal, Sykes, has been convicted; the judge must impose sentence. He addresses Sykes as follows:

Here you are, William Sykes, again convicted of burglary. Admittedly you take pains to ensure that the houses you break into are empty, and have never confronted or threatened or injured anyone; but it is a serious crime and you are no novice—your record is lengthy and you seem to be able to survive in jail and prison, and to be willing to go back again. But this time we are going to surprise you: you need not serve time. You will be closely watched—have no doubt of that! but you won't be behind bars. And, you may be surprised to hear, we have decided that you will not inject heroin into yourself, nor use any other illicit drug. Understand, this is not because we care too much if you kill yourself that way, but we are tired of your persistent burglary and we see that when you are shooting yourself up you also do burglary. So, we are going to see that you are not on drugs for our sake, not yours. You will be put under intensive probation supervision. You will be under a 6 P.M. to 8 A.M. curfew, and if the probation office thinks it will help they can check up on you by one of those wrist or ankle electronic devices they now have. You will either be at work, if they can find a job for you, or you will be in training for a job. And, most important, for the next two months you will be a resident of the XYZ Drug Dependency Program and for several months thereafter you will have to attend that program on Saturdays and Sundays. We plan to take no risks with you. For the next two years we will quite frequently but irregularly check your urine; if you are "dirty," the probation office will report that fact to me and on their advice I will either bring you back and sentence you to prison for this burglary (not taking into account whatever time you have served of intensive probation) or take some other steps to keep you off drugs. In fairness I must add that if you do come back for resentencing, my inclination will be to keep you off the streets and away from burglary for as long as the law allows.

Taken seriously, implemented, is this not a rational punishment, a rational allocation of treatment resources?

What are its defects, and could a similar sentence be imposed on the alcoholic, on the psychologically disturbed criminal, on many sex offenders?

Many have suggested that treatment programs must be voluntary to be effective. In the prison setting that seems clear. The experiment with voluntary programming at the federal prison at Butner, North Carolina, now widely copied in many prisons, has established that there will be higher completion rates in prison treatment programs if participation is voluntary than if it is involuntary, and there will be no shortage of candidates for enrollment.

In community-based programs, the same advantage of voluntary over compulsory treatment programs seems to be true of programs like Alcoholics Anonymous and the "talking" psychiatric treatment programs, individual and group. For such programs it seems a prerequisite to success that the "patient" should see himself as having "hit bottom," as having nowhere else to go, as requiring help beyond his own capacities. There is, however, strong empirical data and a broad consensus among those running drug treatment programs that compulsory programs for treating drug addicts are as effective as those that are voluntary—indeed, more effective, since enforced participation tends to achieve the patient's longer retention in the program.

Duration of stay in the drug program proves to be the highest predictor of success, and this holds true between widely different programs—those that make use of substitute drugs like methadone and those than don't, those that follow philosophies similar to AA and those that don't, those that are residential and those that are outpatient.

It may thus be, particularly for those criminals whose spurts of crime are associated with spurts of use of hard drugs, that there now exist means of control that can better protect the community than our traditional custodial sentences followed by insufficient control in the community. A significant reason is that we now have at hand the means of monitoring conformity by nonintrusive testing for the absence of drugs in body fluids.

The sentence suggested for William Sykes may well achieve better protection of society than the 12 to 15 months he otherwise would have served. Nor is it any sentimental leniency of sentence that has been achieved; indeed its severity may be its central problem, for if too many so sentenced "fail" and are then imprisoned, there will be a substantial increment of punishment and a concomitant increase of correctional costs. The cost/benefit analysis of such sentences remains open for consideration.

Let us vary the hypothesis. Suppose now that our William Sykes was an alcoholic, his burglaries committed as an early part of drinking sprees. Do matters change? Can a similar sentence be imposed? It can, but experience so far suggests that the likelihood of successful completion of the program is not high unless—and it is hard to be sure—this Sykes has really come to the end of his tolerance of his own drinking behavior. If that be so, the cases seem on all fours, the only difference being in the greater ease of the alcoholic in self-deception and deception of his supervisors; there is no analogue of the urine test.

Yet a further variation: suppose our third William Sykes is seriously psychologically disturbed? Since there are few subjects, there is little empirical evidence on the success of psychiatric treatment programs on street criminals. For more privileged, wealthier criminals, the psychiatric clinic and outpatient department is often the path to avoid the prison or jail; but again satisfactory studies of the outcome of such treatments are lacking. All that one can properly affirm is that for some criminals the optimum control would be residential and psychiatric, followed by outpatient treatment. And insofar as the wards of state mental hospitals and the cells of the city jails house a group of minor offenders wandering from one to the other, there would seem to be room for a more extensive use of community-based psychiatric treatment as part of the punishment for some criminals.

All this by way of background to a closer consideration of the proper role of four community-based punishment–treatment modalities providing services to the addict, to the alcoholic, to the psychologically disturbed, and to certain sex offenders.

Community-Based Drug Treatment Programs

The "war on drugs" began with the passage of the Harrison Act in 1914 and the decision of the U.S. Supreme Court in the Behrman case, 258 U.S. 280 (1921), shifting the battle from the medical to the legal front. It has been a singularly unsuccessful war despite the continuing and frequent declarations of unwavering dedication to hostilities by federal administration after federal administration and by many firm-jawed U.S. attorneys in parades of publicity. The price of illicit drugs (corrected for inflation and adulteration) does not increase in response to law enforcement effort except occasionally for short periods—although it should if battles were being won, let alone the war. Nor have claims been made that the number of addicts decreases or that their depredations in terms of crimes committed have been reduced.

The only signs of success offered are those predictable photographs in the newspapers and on television news programs of the local U.S. attorney and sometimes a police chief or a representative of the Drug Enforcement Administration posing in front of a table loaded with wrapped packets of drugs, bundles of banknotes, and imposing exhibits of weaponry claiming that this last massive interception, brilliantly concluding a long-term undercover operation, has brought "Mr. Big" to his knees, and that the turning point has been reached—in Churchill's phrase, if not the beginning of the end of the war on drugs at least the end of the beginning. The only defect in this is that we have been observing that same photograph and reading that same news story at least once a month for many years. It reflects the truth of the Chinese proverb: "Much noise on stairs; nobody comes."

We offer no cure, no strategic plan for victory in this ill-chosen war. We are not suggesting that efforts to interdict the importation of heroin and its derivatives and of cocaine and its derivatives should be abandoned, though we doubt that that war can be won. Nor are we suggesting legalization of those drugs, whatever that turns out to mean in the mouths of its advocates. And we certainly raise no objection to the condign punishment of those who live by this destructive trade—though the punishment of the street addict–

pusher does raise difficult moral problems. We are, however, of
the view that this war is conducted too much at the national level
and too little at the local level; but that is not the subject of our
present concern.

Our present concern is much simpler, and comes to this: it is
well established that drug users account for a grossly disproportionate amount of street crime; it is well established that the intensity of their crime varies directly with the intensity of their use
of drugs; it is also well established that it is possible without excessive expense greatly to reduce the ingestion of drugs by addicts
and consequentially greatly to reduce their criminal depredations.
It is astonishing to us that this path is not well trodden.

It is an aggressive argument and it is therefore best to be careful
about its ambit. We set aside the detention of drug users prior to
trial for drug or other offenses; there is much to be said for urine
testing here as an aid to the bail decision, but that constitutionally
troublesome topic is not our present concern. We confine ourselves
to those who have been convicted of a crime or have pleaded guilty
to a crime, whether a crime of drug using or dealing or any other
crime, and focus on the question of discovering whether they are
active drug users and how to vary their sentences accordingly.

Perhaps the severity of this problem merits underlining. Data
from urine testing programs overseen by Eric Wish in Manhattan
(Wish, Brady, and Cuadrado 1986) and similar data from a
project in Washington, D.C., directed by Jay Carver (1986), combined with Rand Corporation self-reported data from California
and Michigan (Chaiken and Chaiken 1990), strongly suggest that
from 40 to 80 percent of felony arrestees in urban areas had ingested illicit drugs (other than marijuana) shortly before the commission of the crime for which they were arrested. Further, the
greater the usage, the more frequent the criminality. Moreover,
those who could be lured, drawn, controlled to either a cessation
of use or a reduction of use also greatly reduced their criminality.
The research data supporting these propositions are strong and
consistent, unchallenged within the drug research community.
Urine testing and self-reporting confirm these propositions, though
self-reporting consistently understates the linkage between drugs
and crime.

The opportunity is clear. Whatever the causal links, eliminate or reduce the ingestion of the drugs in the addict-criminal and you eliminate or reduce his criminality (in the mass, obviously not in every case). How, then, to pursue this opportunity? Keep him in prison or jail until, by effluxion of time or by drug treatment programs, he is no longer addicted; commit him civilly to the same end; put him in a methadone or other drug-based treatment program which may be segregative or residential and community-based; or put him in what is called an OPDF program, that is to say, an outpatient drug-free program. There is considerable literature on these competing treatment modalities; each has its strong advocates. But it is clear that no tested classificatory schemes have emerged to help the judge decide which treatments are best for which offenders. But what has emerged is not unhopeful.

It seems that all drug treatment programs have measurable and in many cases measured success in reducing the use of drugs by those committed to their care. None can validly claim success over the others, with the exception that while addict-criminals are in prison or in segregated civil commitment they do not commit crimes against other than those with whom they are compelled to live. But even this gives the judge little guidance, since the prisons and jails are full and are releasing addict-criminals as the time expires for which they can be justly held for what they have done.

There are two other points that must be made before our proposals for intensive supervision of addict-criminals in the community are advanced. First, those running all treatment programs in the community, whether based on methadone or on blocking agents, whether residential or OPDF, whether run by ex-addict-criminals or by medical and psychological professionals, all report that the longer the addict stays in the program the lower his posttreatment drug abuse and criminality. These results seem independent of whether he volunteered for the program.

Second, despite the 75 years of "war on drugs," despite the huge sums that have been thrown into interdiction of importation and capturing and punishing dealers, pushers, and users, there remain long waiting lists for admission to all types of drug treatment programs. Funds have flowed futilely for a "solution" to the problem on the supply side instead of sensibly to its amelioration.

We have to hand the mechanisms for that amelioration. If the addict-criminal is placed in a community-based, inpatient or outpatient, drug-free or drug-supported treatment program, we must provide and insist on regular and irregular urine testing. Testing positive must lead to some formal reaction, not necessarily revocation of probation, if the treatment program is part of the conditions of intensive probation as it often will be; but seriousness of purpose, a determination about noningestion of drugs, must be manifest and enforced.

We return to what is a leitmotif of this book. If this intermediate punishment is to "work," it must be enforced, and this requires the provision of sufficient resources to give it reality if it is to be more than a gesture. And the resources required are substantial.

Estimates of drug treatment costs vary. "In New York," wrote Doctors Wexler and Lipton in 1986, "the annual cost of drug treatment is $4,000 per treatment slot in 1986; methadone and outpatient drug-free programs cost somewhat less and residential programs more." New York, of course, has higher costs than elsewhere; but these costs are everywhere appreciable, particularly when one takes into account that they do not include the costs of the extensive urine testing we advocate as an essential part of any soundly based community treatment of addict-criminals. However, there are offsetting costs that merit consideration. In that same year in New York a jail "slot" cost $40,000 per year and a prison "slot" $24,000. A further offset, though harder to estimate, is the saving from the reduction in criminality by the addict-criminals who remain, and are forced to remain, in treatment. All in all, the cost/benefit analysis would seem powerfully to favor a very substantial expansion of community-based drug treatment programs.

We are, of course, not suggesting that addiction should immunize the criminal from prison. His crime and his criminal record may within any rationally graded system of punishment require a prison term. If it does, it would be wise sentencing to require his involvement in a drug treatment program as part of his release procedure, and the provision of such treatments in the prison as are appropriate to laying a foundation for such after-release drug treatment. But that is not our present concern.

Our present concern is to affirm that rational sentencing of the addict-criminal requires the sentencing judge to have available a diversity of enforceable community-based drug treatment modalities to be used as the punishment for crime or, more frequently, as *part* of the punishment for crime.

Community-Based Alcohol Treatment Programs

Much of our argument concerning drug treatment programs is applicable to the drug called alcohol, but there are differences relevant to the frequency of that drug's relationship to crime and to the treatment of those who ingest it and commit crime.

There is no effective way of measuring the role that alcohol plays in crime. Convicted offenders are swift to attribute their criminality to their drunken condition, police uniformly report this close association, and it is the experience of all who consume alcohol that it both lessens inhibitions and fuels anger. Few doubt that the relationship is close. In relation to one crime, drunken driving, the causal pattern is clear and accounts for the deaths of tens of thousands of Americans per year. In relation to sexual offenses, no one knows the figures but again few doubt either the correlation or the likely causal relationship.

Whereas we suggested that the prison and jail can provide only a launch pad for effective drug treatment programs, we think the case is different for alcohol treatment programs. Two of the main treatment modalities for alcoholics—AA and psychologically informed counseling—are entirely properly pursued, and protractedly pursued, behind prison walls. There is an amplitude of prisoners similarly afflicted to start the necessary individual and group work in prison or jail. Both programs will require follow-up in the community on the prisoner's release and his attachment to similar groups in the community; but more than the work of a launch pad to treatment should be provided in the prison.

Probation officers increasingly find themselves involved in the supervision of heavy drinkers whose crimes are precipitated by their drinking and by alcoholics whose crimes are inextricably linked with their disease. Two main treatment modalities are available, though each is subject to a myriad of variations, the same two that can first be pursued in prison: Alcoholics Anonymous and, now, a residential or outpatient psychological group treatment program. (We set aside psychiatric and psychoanalytic techniques as unavailable to the mass of offenders.)

Again, if the gravity of the crime or the particular danger of the offender does not require a prison sentence, economy and social protection combine to suggest a nonincarcerative punishment for the convicted alcoholic offender or for the criminal whose crimes are causally related to drinking. As with drug addicts, the heart of the matter is tough and determined enforcement of the sentence so that conditions of house arrest or residence in a treatment center, or community service, if ordered, are adhered to, and fiscal penalties by way of restitution, fines, and payment for treatment programs are met—and above all so that they do not drink.

It is harder to check on drinking than on the ingestion of hard drugs. The breathalyzer is less reliable than the urine test, and taking blood to test blood alcohol concentrations is more intrusive. Nevertheless, better probation practice now recommends frequent use of the breathalyzer by the probation officer and determined response to any positive finding.

Alcoholism, as distinct from persistent drunkenness, is, like drug addiction, a relapsing disease and should be so treated, so that effective treatment requires protracted surveillance. It is doubtful that such surveillance lies within the capacity of the probation or parole officer alone; some team support is essential. As with the drug addict, the team can be built within a probation office of a caseworker for, say, 25 under supervision and a surveillance officer for, say, half that number. Alternatively, as we earlier suggested, the police can be involved directly in the surveillance role. And there is a third pattern for such collaborative surveillance that has promise—the community team.

Writing in *Federal Probation,* an experienced federal probation officer, Edward Read, recommended a collaborative relationship between the probation officer and a member or members of the AA group with which the offender is affiliated, casting on the AA member much of the burden of supervision that the offender is indeed attending, and soberly attending, AA meetings, at a level, he suggests, of at least five a week.

Family, employer, minister, responsible friend can all be enlisted in appropriate cases to ensure that the sentence, whatever its precise conditions, is carried out. Their responsibilities can be made clear as a condition of the opportunity to avoid or to leave prison being given to the criminal—in some places the collaborators sign contracts precisely defining their roles. For many cases, this will be an equally effective and less expensive and intrusive way of extending the reach and the eyes and ears of the supervising probation officer.

A practical aside may not be inappropriate. For eight years one of us served on the Police Board of the Chicago Police, one of whose duties is the punishment of the more serious disciplinary offenses by members of that police force. A police force of 13,000 members produces a steady flow of serious disciplinary problems. The Board hears and determines all cases in which the superintendent seeks to dismiss a member of the force and also acts as an appeal board from all suspensions without pay of 30 days or less. The "alcoholic defense" is well recognized. Police whose disciplinary breaches—and they can be ornate and serious—are attributable to alcoholism or to excessive drinking often offer this defense knowing that in other than exceptionally serious cases the following sentence will be ordered: suspension without pay, usually for a year though sometimes for a shorter period, with the requirement that at the end of the period of suspension the officer reappear before the Board with witnesses to certify his completion of an AA or other alcohol treatment program and his having ceased entirely to consume alcohol. It seems to work well. It can work only once. The experience has been that the professional lives of many fine policemen and women have been preserved, for the public good and to the economic advantage of the Chicago Police and the citizens of Chicago. This experience inclines us to the view that there is a great deal to be said for similar sentences, appropriately modified, to be imposed by criminal courts.

What, then, are the data concerning the success of such community-based treatment programs of alcoholic offenders? Again, methodological adequacy is elusive. Those who run these programs, particularly AA, report well on them, claiming high rates of "success," but the definition of that term is often plastic and the means of its testing inadequate. Nevertheless, the congruence of methodologically unsatisfactory studies does point in a clear direction: such treatment programs when diligently pursued by the offender—and he can be prodded and pulled to the pursuit—seem to lessen, in the mass, his dependence on alcohol and hence his criminality. Where principles of deserved punishment do not preclude their use as part of a fair and adequate sentence, there is social sense in their increased use.

The increasing social acceptance of residential alcohol treatment centers, a movement led by a president's wife, by film stars, by those accepted as contributing citizens, has helped the courts use such centers as part of community service, fiscal, and other penalties for crimes for which other considerations do not dictate imposition of a prison sentence. But like other nonincarcerative punishments, they are used on a hit-or-miss, unevenly applied basis, the chance attitudes of the sentencing judge remaining of importance; they have not been institutionalized into a sentencing system.

And as one thinks about the contours of such a system, some further future likely developments merit mention, even if they are not current realities.

The drug Antabuse is just one of the alcohol-blocking agents that, if combined with alcohol, causes vomiting. The duration of the operative effect of such drugs is gradually being extended, and there is a further technical and pharmacological development on the horizon. For some life-saving drugs, and for some other drugs such as the antihistamines, slow-release methods are being developed—transdermal, intramuscular, and intravenous. With humans, such techniques for some drugs now permit a weekly application of a patch or a weekly consumption of a tablet, the drug being released in regular dosage over the week. In animal experimentation, one-month release periods have been achieved. We are thus on the brink of a technology that could have enormous importance for the treatment of the alcoholic. Soon we may be able to say to the alcoholic criminal "this at least we know, for the ensuing week you will not be drinking. So report here at the same time next week and we will ensure that this condition continues." With such a technology, if courts wish it, we have available the means greatly to reduce the incidence of crimes by those previously caught and convicted, and without the necessary use of the prison or jail.

One other imminent technological development that should be incorporated into sentencing policy merits mention. There is a report of the equivalent of the "morning-after" pill for drunkenness. The substance apparently has the effect, which coffee never had despite its use to that end, of rapidly and substantially sobering the drunk. One about to drive could now be in a position to avoid driving under the influence of alcohol by taking the pill and waiting a few minutes. One envisages all cars equipped with breathalyzers and a supply of such pills. Some science fiction dreamers have gone further and linked the breathalyzer to the ignition, precluding starting the car unless the person sitting in the driver's seat blows "clean" or presumably otherwise establishes fitness to drive in this respect.

These futuristic speculations apart, for those criminals convicted of drunken driving or driving under the influence of alcohol, community-based alcohol treatment programs will often be an appropriate part of their punishment. Again, and our drumbeat litany becomes incessant, it is of central importance that if this is ordered as part of their sentence, whether instead of or as well as other punishments, incarcerative, fiscal, or community-based, the order must be rigorously enforced. Misguided sympathy, the ease of identifying with the drinker's behavior, too often makes this an area of nonenforcement. The potential for saving lives of future victims is great; the potential of assisting such criminals and their families is also great; there is little to be said for relaxing enforcement efforts on the erroneous ground that "they are not really criminals."

Before we shift attention to treatment conditions addressed to mental disorders, we focus for a few pages on sentencing for drunk driving, a crime that provokes emotional and vigorous attention. The number of separate events of criminal drunk driving total in the millions per year at least, probably in the tens of millions. In the great majority of these cases, the drunken driver luckily makes it home safely, without injury to himself or to anyone else. In a small minority of tragic cases, random injury or death to an innocent is the result.

For the mass of cases, the offender is not apprehended and, when he is, the routine imposition of a severe punishment is simply impracticable. Even the most self-styled draconic mandatory sentencing laws for drunk drivers seldom call for more than brief incarceration and then generally not for a first conviction. But for the tragic case, the sentiment is strong and widespread that serious penal consequences should attach when drunk driving results in injury or death of another person. Thus although from one perspective drunk driving is not the kind of serious crime at which intermediate punishments are ordinarily targeted, in the notorious minority of cases, many people will settle for nothing less.

The results are not yet in on the efficacy of breathalyzer testing, roadblocks, license revocation as a result of refusal of a blood alcohol test, mandatory minimum punishments linked to given blood alcohol concentrations, motor manslaughter statutes, and similar efforts by criminal sanction to lessen the loss of life and the amount of injury flowing from drunken driving. Much is reported on all such efforts, and there seems promise in many, perhaps all of them. But there is also the tendency of each program to have early success followed by a regression to the mean.

If imprisonment is imposed as a punishment for drunk driving, amid much media attention, there does seem to be a reduction in the incidence of this offense in the early months of application of the new legislation, but this deterrent too begins to lose its threat under the pressures of custom and the avoidance of the penalty by increasingly sophisticated legal defenses. But this at least can be said: while the drunken driver is in jail he is not driving drunk, he is not risking the lives and safety of others or of himself.

This reality has led to a search for punishments alternative to imprisonment that may have the same or a better effect. Hence in some jurisdictions house arrest for drunken drivers enforced by electronic monitoring has become the modal use of the house arrest penalty. In terms of community protection it would seem that such punishments can be made adequately severe for other than cases where the driver has killed or seriously injured someone and can provide clearly better community protection than the relatively brief terms of imprisonment that are imposed when injury has not been done.

For the first offense of driving under the influence of alcohol, or for drunken driving, a fine may be appropriate—clearly there are such cases. It may be that a period of loss of license may achieve a sufficient and appropriate punishment—though there is a considerable record of those under such suspension continuing to drive, and sometimes unsoberly. But if it be thought appropriate to raise the penalty beyond these sanctions, either because of the offender's record or because of the gravity of the harm he risked or caused, or a combination of both, we seriously urge that the following form of house arrest be imposed. If the offender has employment, which is typically the case in those convicted of this offense, there seems no point in his losing it, which may well occur pursuant to a sentence of imprisonment. If he has a family, the argument for allowing him to continue to earn is reinforced.

So why not let him keep his job, continue to support his family, impose appreciable condign punishment, and better protect the community from the very real risks of his again driving under the influence of alcohol by imposing a term of 6 P.M. to 8 A.M. house arrest and house arrest from 6 P.M. Friday to 8 A.M. Monday? Let him keep his car and his license, but let us by electronically monitoring his movements ensure that he is not driving at all during those periods when all experience shows there is a risk of his combining drinking and driving. How long a period of monitored house arrest? That surely is the appropriate variable of time to match to the gravity of the offense corrected for the offender's prior record. Such a scheme would bypass the wearisome and unending argument between those who wish to solve this problem by increasingly applied and increasingly severe jail terms and those who realize the cost difficulties and doubtful efficacy of such solutions.

The scheme we propose is more socially protective and less costly than our present reliance on the jail or the prison for these middle-level drunken driving offenses; is it sufficiently punitive to achieve the community's expectations here, and hence sufficiently deterrent? It clearly can be made so if the duration of house arrest is substantial, if driving prohibitions and license revocations are added, and if—and this is centrally important—the sanction is firmly enforced and any breaches are treated with severity.

There are, of course, cases where the gravity or prior occurrence of the drunken driving behavior would render such a penalty inappropriately lenient or insufficiently deterrent, but for a mass of cases it would make better sense than what is now done.

Community-Based Psychological Treatment Conditions

A sharp distinction may be drawn in practice, though not of course in psychological reality, between the treatment of those criminals found to be insane in the sense that apart from their criminal conduct they could have been civilly committed as mentally ill and those criminals who though not so committable are nevertheless thought to be suffering such psychological problems related to their criminality as to attract psychological treatment, guidance, and counseling if these are available.

For the former—the clearly mentally ill—the policy issue is clear. They should receive, in or out of prison or jail, treatment services of quality and availability equal to those they would have received had they not been convicted of a crime. It may well be appropriate, in our view, to hold them accountable and therefore punishable (though subject to a humane understanding of the mitigating effect of their illness) for their crime, but the denial of treatment services because of that crime is both cruel and, if the crime be in any part a product of their mental illness, socially unwise and generative of crime.

It is with the less clear cases that difficulties arise. One way to test social policy is to inquire what one does for one's friends and relatives, those for whom one feels affection and responsibility. Careful inquiry along this line reveals the frequent use of the outpatient psychiatric or psychological clinic as a technique of avoiding the prison or jail, allowing the judge the appearance of responding responsibly and not weakly to the problem of rational sentencing of such a psychologically disturbed offender, and in many cases assisting the offender to restructure his life toward a larger conformity.

What is the evidence for this successful restructuring? There is very little. Indeed, there is scant methodologically satisfactory evidence that any of the "talking therapies," as distinct from the drug treatment therapies, have positive outcome—yet there is strong individual testimony to that effect, as there is strong individual testimony that religious conversion has that effect, and the personal test comes when one we happen to love or to care for gets into serious trouble. Then the services of the clinic and the therapists are swiftly pressed to assistance, often having the twin effects of avoiding imprisonment and allowing time and giving support for reshaping a threatened life.

Hence as judges at time of sentencing see both the possibility of such treatments and their availability, there is an increasing tendency for such treatment to be ordered as part of the sentence. It must be admitted that the frequency of such a sentencing response is higher in relating to other than underclass and particularly minority offenders. But this does not undermine the case for such sentences; rather it strengthens it.

Compulsory psychological treatment conditions, residential or outpatient, are particularly frequently ordered in relation to the less serious sexual offenses where otherwise the attitudes of the community and of the legislature have been pressing toward prolonged prison terms. We therefore separate this problem from the general issue of treatment conditions under intensive probationary supervision and deal with it as a special case in the following section.

Community-Based Sex Offender Treatment Programs

In the states of Maine, Minnesota, and Washington, the modal conviction of those in prison in recent years has been for a sexual offense. These are states that are seen as models of modest criminality and rational sentencing, yet in each there are more in prison convicted of sexual offenses than of any other category of offenses. This accumulation of sexual offenders results from the combined effects of increases in the number of persons imprisoned for sex offenses, especially those involving children, and substantial increases in the lengths of the sentences such people receive. This is analogous to the experience of determinate sentencing jurisdictions like California in which the absolute numbers of violent prisoners serving lengthy prison sentences is forcing populations higher as the accumulation grows larger and larger.

The National Institute of Corrections, a statutory agency of the federal government providing training to state and local correctional staffs, is besieged with requests from the field for training programs for prison, jail, and community-based correctional staffs to help them deal with those convicted of sexual offenses. They report that apart from the many problems created by the flood of such offenders, judge after judge in sentencing the sexual offender either to prison or to a noncustodial sentence has expressed the confident hope that he will be given help for his pathological condition—that he will be "cured."

We find it hard to believe that there has been any change in human sexual behavior or, for that matter, that changes in punishment policy are likely to have much effect on these forms of human behavior; the sexual instinct does not lack strength, even true believers not being inexorably deterred by the threat of an eternity of hellfire. But our task is not that of an etiological search, except insofar as causal understanding in the individual case and in categories of cases can guide us to rational and effective sentencing and punishment policies.

What then is happening to this increased flow of convicted sexual offenders? The answer varies from state to state but we think we perceive a general pattern. More are going to prison and for longer terms, much longer terms, but also more are being given nonincarcerative sentences subject to conditions of treatment and control. Washington State demonstrates the not untypical pattern. In a 1984 *Report to the Legislature,* the Washington State Sentencing Guidelines Commission captured the ambivalence that these offenses often provoke. First, because increasing awareness and concern for sexual offenses, especially against children, has led to calls for increased penalties, the Commission announced that it had raised the severity level, and thereby the presumptive guideline sentence, for every category of sex offense. Second, however, because "many victims and their families want to see the offender receive help rather than a prison sentence," and because "most legislators involved with the [guidelines] bill's passage believed treatment options for sex offenders should not be restricted," the guidelines actively encourage alternative treatment placements. As a result, in 1985, according to the Commission's 1986 *Report to the Legislature,* half (49.8 percent) of the persons convicted of sexual offenses received the presumptive prison or jail sentences, a third (35.9 percent) received Special Sexual Offender Sentencing Alternative (SSOSA) sentences, and 14.3 percent were sentenced to hospital treatment programs under conditional suspended sentences. An SSOSA allows suspension of the guideline sentence and imposition of conditions concerning inpatient and outpatient treatment programs. Under the hospital orders, the offender who completes the treatment program is released under a suspended sentence; those who fail are transferred to prison to serve the balance of the sentence. Thus there is a sharp bifurcation of punishments, either a substantial term of incarceration or none at all. It is not a pattern of graduated severity.

What are the reasons for these relatively recent developments of greatly increased numbers of offenders and then a bifurcated punishment system of incarcerative severity and of serious efforts at rehabilitation and self-restoration?

We doubt any change in the incidence of sexual crime. The more probable explanation is the obvious change in community attitudes toward such crimes, the greater openness of discussion and commentary, the increased willingness of victims and those close to them to report such crimes, the passage in most states of laws requiring doctors and other professionals to report suspected incidents of child abuse, the powerful influence of the women's liberation movement, and the widespread appreciation of the lasting and damaging effects of sexual violence and aggression, particularly on the child. All these combine to reveal more and more of the "dark figure" of sexual crime, to drive it into the open. All combine politically to crystallize public sentiment and drive up both the maxima and the norms of punishment at the legislative and judicial levels.

The pattern of punishment is of a "two-humped camel" rather than of an even gradation of severity of punishment; one hump is protracted imprisonment, the other is a variety of controls and treatment in the community. Why this distribution? We risk a speculative answer, not the product of close analysis: judges willingly accept the path of protracted incarceration as a punishment for such offenders unless they see it as an excessive reaction to the harm the offender has either encompassed or threatened. They rely on deterrent severity and prison time where there has been violence or the threat of violence, where there has been powerful coercion, where the offense has been frequently repeated, or where there has been a gross breach of trust—the presumptive punishment then is a long term of imprisonment, whether the victim be an adult or a child. But where these elements are lacking, where the offense is one of seduction of the underage, of affection and closeness moving to fondling and criminality, where it has been consensual, where the victim has not been placed by parents in the care and custody of the criminal—in such cases the judge will look to the language of psychology and the agencies of treatment for the sentencing response. The presumption changes toward non-incarcerative punishments, toward the other hump of the camel.

There is another factor, apart from the particular pattern of the crime, that is of obvious relevance to the sentence: the likelihood of future danger to the community or to a particular victim. The extreme contrast is between the repeated rapist and the father or stepfather who has been incestuously involved with his child. It may well be possible reasonably to ensure the future safety of the child in the family and not to need to break up the family, which in many cases increases the injury to the victim. In such cases, despite the grave and possibly lasting injury to the child from the sexual incident or incidents, it may well be the course of wisdom and of social protection to turn to community-based controls and treatment for the offender.

What then are the "treatments" appropriate to the sexual offender? For sexual violence, aging is a most effective cure. For such offenses the prison will work its silent cure. And, in fact, for serious sexual offenses which attract imprisonment as a punishment, the levels of recidivism are very low, despite the popular belief to the contrary. For minor sexual offenses—exhibitionism, voyeurism, and similar offenses of inadequacy—recidivist rates are high, and there is a tendency to conflate the serious and the very much less serious into a statement of the likely repetition of all sexual crimes, which is not the case.

Mercifully, our present task is not to discuss the prison treatment of sexual offenders, including those miserable special institutions for sexually dangerous persons or for so-called sexual psychopaths. Sufficient unto the day is the task of discussing the treatment of sexual offenders other than in prison or jail.

Donald West in 1983 offered in *Crime and Justice* a useful overview of treatment methods and their success. The difficulty of advocacy of any particular method of treatment for any particular category of offenders is the lack of reliable outcome evaluations.

Short-term evaluations, particularly by those responsible for the treatment administered, are often encouraging; longer term evaluations, particularly by others than those who administered the treatment, are often discouraging. The truth is that ignorance prevails and one is forced back to speculation. Nor is it easy to see how ethically acceptable, reliable long-term evaluations can soon be launched. The matched, untreated control group is ethically elusive; comparisons between different treatment modalities, particularly between the incapacitative and those that are community based, prove unhelpful for a variety of reasons.

There are four broad categories of nonincarcerative treatments: hormonal, behavior modification, outpatient mental health clinical treatment (in both individual and family therapy versions), and life skills training.

Hormonal modifications of libido can be achieved by castration, by doses of estrogen that can be administered in slow release forms to remain effective for months, by cyproterone acetate, which can be administered by regular oral doses or by a depot injection lasting 12 days—and other hormonal modifications are emerging. These treatments are clearly more appropriate to serious cases and to the situations of offenders who solicit such heroic treatments as part of their own desire to change their behavior. In this sense, some sexual offenders differ profoundly from those guilty of other types of crimes. More sexual offenders see themselves as "sick" and in need of cure—not the typical reaction of the burglar or the thief—and as a result more heroic interventions may well be justified.

Behavior modification techniques, either by aversive or positive reward conditioning, are appropriate for some sexual offenders and can be pursued on an outpatient basis.

The most common nonincarcerative treatment is, however, that modeled on the mental health clinic in which by group therapy supported by individual clinical interviews the sexual offender is given insight into his behavior, the precipitants of his criminality, and the psychological mechanisms he may mobilize for its control. Such therapies often involve the family of the offender, and this is particularly apposite to situations where a family member has been the victim of the offense, so that protection as well as assistance can be given.

Finally, training in life skills, counseling on the means of presenting and expressing the self in ways that avoid the rage and shame that often precipitate sexual offenses, is sometimes appropriate to lead the sexual offender to ways of sexual expression more satisfactory to him and less injurious to those with whom he associates.

Daniel Saunders and Sandra Azar (1989) recently completed, also for *Crime and Justice,* a careful survey of sex offender treatment programs. They lament the lack of methodologically sound evaluations of treatment interventions, particularly the difficulty of distinguishing the criminal sanction effects from other consequences of the discovery of the offense, reaching the only tentatively encouraging conclusion that treatment interventions seem to help a substantial number of sex offenders to avoid further such criminality but that no satisfactory treatment nosology has yet emerged.

Such is the complexity and the challenge of rational and fair sentencing of sexual offenders and their effective treatment that the judge and the prison administrator and the probation officer require clinically sophisticated advice on the selection of the punishment and the most appropriate treatment for the individual case. Specialized clinics have been established in many cities to provide these services, and in many cases to provide therapy on the mental health model, or behavior modification, or life skills training, or the control of hormonal treatments in collaboration with the probation officer responsible to the court to ensure the offender's adherence to the terms of his sentence. Such collaborations between those responsible for treatment and for control have much to recommend them for sexual offenders. Again, however, it can be seen that the probation officer is being called on to provide a difficult combination of services, casework support in collaboration with the clinic and "police" control. Again, either team probation or the involvement of the police may be appropriate.

House Arrest and Electronic Monitoring

Intermediate punishments provide the judge and probation administrator with a menu of choices capable of combination into a variety of dishes. House arrest may stand alone as a punishment, it may be a part of a program of intensive supervision, it may or may not be monitored electronically, and the fine and community service and obligations of attendance at treatment programs may all form part of the dish. But house arrest proves an increasingly popular additive.

House arrest programs have been established throughout the United States. Many are little more than curfews that restrict offenders' mobility by requiring that they be home at specified times; house arrest in this sense has probably existed since probation was invented in the nineteenth century. What is new are large, publicized programs that aim simultaneously to offer a community sentence that is seen as burdensome and intrusive, and therefore sufficiently punitive to be imposed on persons convicted of nontrivial crimes and, as a result, to reduce pressure on overcrowded prisons and jails. In the largest house arrest program, in Florida, many thousands of convicted offenders have been sentenced to house arrest. Florida authorities claim that most are people who otherwise would have been jailed or incarcerated. Like intensive supervision probation, in which there are "front-door" diversion programs like Georgia's and "back-door" prison release programs like New Jersey's, there are diversion and early release versions of house arrest. Florida's is the best-known front-door program. Oklahoma's is the best-known back-door program.

Though house arrest and electronic monitoring are often, as here, discussed together, it is clear that the former is the sanction and the latter merely one means of its enforcement. House arrest, after all, has a history as long as banishment, longer than the modern prison, but its earlier application was largely confined to political offenders; its modern application is intended to suit any convicted offender who need not be incarcerated and any arrested person who need not be held in jail but for whom reduced mobility in the community is desirable.

House arrest remains a popular sanction in some countries, for example, South Africa, for the politically suspect; Alan Paton, the author of *Cry, the Beloved Country,* spent many years prior to his death under house arrest. For us, house arrest has more mundane use.

House arrest is a most flexible punishment, in duration ranging from hours to years, and it can be applied at many stages of the processes of criminal justice—instead of jail, as a diversion from jail or prison, as a release mechanism from prison, as a condition of parole, as an intermediate punishment with or without other punishments. It can confine the offender to one site, his "home" (which raises problems of definition), or he can be required to be at home for precise periods of the evenings and weekends and at work or training programs for precise periods of each weekday.

The impetus to its modern growth has, of course, been the overcrowding of our jails and prisons and the hope of saving some of the expense of those institutions; but its potential is greater than that.

Most of the intermediate punishments we have considered, and this is certainly true of house arrest, are means whereby it is sought to achieve the crime prevention effect of the prison (in terms of incapacitation from crime in the community for the period of the punishment) with the rehabilitative opportunities of community-based training and self-developmental programs. Insofar as it is enforced, insofar as the burglar is in fact at work during the day and at home at night and weekends, he will not be a nocturnal burglar. The idea is clear, the enforcement mechanisms central.

As an enforcement mechanism, electronic monitoring has grown along with the recent increased interest in house arrest, and a considerable industry is rapidly developing to market monitoring devices. In our view, it is too early to write with confidence about the appropriate use of electronic monitoring, as distinct from personal (telephone or visiting) monitoring, of the offender's being where at any time he is supposed to be. There are defects in the technology, which are being eliminated, and the modern passion for electronic toys somewhat confuses the picture. But it is clear that the existence of such techniques makes house arrest a more acceptable punishment to the judiciary and to public opinion.

There are at present three main systems of electronic monitoring: active, passive, and tracking.

Active telecommunication systems consist of a small transmitter, strapped to the ankle or wrist of the offender, which emits a signal to a receiver-dialer unit connected by the offender's telephone to a centrally based computer. Provided the offender remains within a 150- to 200-foot radius of the receiver-dialer, no interruption in the signal occurs. If there is an interruption, the receiver-dialer conveys this fact to the central computer. Such a signal is also transmitted if the strap attaching the transmitter to the offender is interfered with. This system thus provides constant monitoring.

Passive systems also make use of the telephone and a centrally located computer, but instead of a transmitter and a receiver-dialer they depend on an encoder device and a verifier box. The encoder is strapped to the offender and the verifier box is connected to his telephone. Random or scheduled calls are made to the offender; he must make voice identification and also insert the encoder to verify his presence. If the telephone call does not go through, possibly because the offender's telephone line was engaged, or if he does not satisfactorily make verification, the computer reports this fact and the probation officer can check whether the offender is indeed other than where he should be and take whatever action seems appropriate.

Tracking systems are at an even earlier stage of development and are built on the technology that has been used to track wild and domestic animals. A transmitter worn by the offender emits a constant radio signal to a portable receiver in the monitoring offi- cer's car when he is sufficiently close to pick up the signal (at present, about a city block). The probation officer can then, at any time, without this fact being known to the offender, check where he is—or, more precisely, where he is not. This promises great flexibility for enforcing house arrest orders which are fash- ioned to allow the offender to leave his place of residence at spe- cific times for work or training purposes.

None of these systems is foolproof; each has produced its share of "bugs," false alarms, and unexpected costs; but these techno- logical problems will in due course be solved and it is best to con- sider the utility of such systems on the assumption that they will swiftly become reliable and affordable.

The claim made by the vendors of these devices is that they are cheaper than incarceration and that they facilitate the type of com- munity protection that can make community-based punishments politically and judicially acceptable. They are in their early years of application and firm conclusions on these issues and on the appropriate use of these enforcement devices cannot yet be reached. Let us briefly describe one such program to which an electronic monitoring technology is being added to give a sense of these developments and to isolate a few central issues for discussion.

One of the earlier house arrest programs was started by the Florida Department of Corrections and given legislative form in 1983. In 1987 the University of South Florida conducted a study of this program. The target for the first year's operation of this program, after its legislative acceptance, was that 1700 should be placed under "community control." They should be those convicted of nonforcible felonies and misdemeanors and selected for this program by the Department of Corrections from their inmate populations, as well as any offenders sentenced directly to this program by the judiciary. It was also thought an appropriate sanction for some who broke the conditions of their probation or parole.

Those under community control had to perform 150 to 200 hours of community service, make restitution to their victims, pay monthly supervision fees ranging from $30 to $50, be employed to support themselves and their dependents, keep a daily log of their activities, and comply with whatever restrictions on their freedom of movement were ordered. Surveillance officers carried a caseload of 20 or fewer and made at least 28 personal or collateral contacts per month with each offender under supervision.

The Florida program, until 1987, made no use of electronic monitoring. In February of that year the legislature allotted $418,000 to the Department of Corrections for lease or purchase of electronic monitors to provide continuous surveillance in cases selected for such control by the department or by the judiciary.

How can one evaluate the Florida program so far? It has exceeded its population goals. The first year's target of 1700 was exceeded, and by March 1987 a total of 17,952 offenders had been assigned to this program. It is hard to be sure how many of these would otherwise have been incarcerated had the "community control" program not been in place, but the 1987 study claims this figure to be around 67 percent. This is a substantial program.

At the time of 1987 studies by the Florida Department of Corrections and the Florida Mental Health Institute of the University of South Florida, 6430 of the 17,952 were still under supervision and 3698 had had their sentences revoked and were in prison.

Two-thirds of the revocations were for technical violations, one-third for misdemeanors or felonies.

The 1987 estimates show the cost of the program at $2.86 per day per offender, as contrasted with $31.50 per day for imprisonment. In this calculation, neither fees for service nor the value of the community service was taken into account.

It will be appreciated that these data are only the raw material on which, in time, critical evaluation will be pursued, but even at this stage it would seem that the Florida program has much to offer. It has received national attention, it is the largest such program, and it is being widely copied.

Recognizing that it is early to be commenting, several issues merit discussion. What is a "house" for purposes of house arrest? Are such programs inevitably class biased and therefore ethically and constitutionally vulnerable? Do they threaten an undue widening of the net of social control?

The Kentucky house arrest program started administratively in 1984 and was legislatively accepted in 1986. The enabling legislation defines a "home" for purposes of this act to include hospitals, hospices, nursing centers, halfway houses, group homes, and residential treatment centers; it did not include, however, a single property in which more than one family, other than the offender's, resided. This adds further flexibility to the concept of house arrest but it also highlights the issue of just how wide a range of living arrangements can constitute the electronic prison of the future. We offer no suggested answer to this question, being of the view that it is the type of question best solved by cautious experimentation and careful evaluation. In principle there would seem no limit to the types of living arrangements that could properly qualify for house arrest, but public and judicial opinion may not be so tolerant.

And this leads to the question of class bias. Not every offender has a private residence; most do not. Not every offender has a telephone; many do not. Not every offender is in a financial position to meet fees for service, particularly if those fees include the costs of intensive surveillance and substantial amortized costs for electronic equipment after restitution has been made to the victim and court costs have been met. There may well, therefore, be a tendency to apply house arrest and electronic monitoring to the more privileged and to deny it to the indigent. This tendency is already apparent in the increasing use of such programs for those convicted of driving under the influence of alcohol, a tendency resented by those victims groups, such as Mothers Against Drunk Driving, who see it as an insufficiently severe sanction and as a class-biased sanction. Again, all we do is point to the problem and look to experience for its solution—and that is not a weak expectation, for it is clear that the courts and correctional agencies of this country become increasingly willing to experiment with house arrest, with or without its little brother of electronic monitoring.

Finally on this topic, do house arrest and electronic monitoring, expanded to encompass the monitoring of all movement from residence to work to clinic to school, portend a future of an excessively widened net of social control? The very confidence we have in the expansion of programs of this type, of their attraction to the judiciary and to correctional administrators, means that they may well be increasingly and needlessly added to the punishment processes of the state. The cheaper they become, the more inclined will some be to add them to punishment after punishment. After all, if the cost is slight, why not make it harder for the offender to avoid his obligations by adding a "tracking" electronic monitor to every probation order, by adding to every punishment a requirement that the offender do something in the future, such as pay a fine on installments? Again we have no sage advice; all one can hope for is that the important desideratum of parsimony in punishment will restrain enthusiasms and respect autonomy.

We started by worrying whether these intermediate punishments could provide sufficient control of the offender; we end in anxiety that they may prove excessive.

Intermittent Imprisonment and Split Sentences

These two punishments are distinct, but they raise similar issues. Intermittent imprisonment is a method of allowing the offender to serve an incarcerative sentence without having to disrupt his employment and his family and community ties as does a longer single period of jail or prison.

The weekends of a year provide a longer period of incarceration than does a sentence to jail for three months; such a sentence may equally well express condemnation of the crime, impose retributive punishment seen as appropriate by the judge, and yet not have the criminogenic effects of a jail term, which often destroys those vocational, educational, family, and social relationships that help to insulate the offender from future criminality.

If something more than a nonincarcerative intermediate punishment is required for the just punishment of the offense, this is one way, and an increasingly popular way, to achieve that result. To our knowledge there are no methodologically satisfactory studies of the comparative advantages and disadvantages of intermittent imprisonment; in theory it makes sense and in practice it proves increasingly popular.

Split sentences prove even more popular. Here the judge can at once satisfy deterrent and retributive purposes by imposing a term of imprisonment but can reduce the term of imprisonment he would otherwise have ordered and add to the sentence either ordinary probation or any one of the intermediate punishments we have discussed.

In some states, split sentences become almost routine. In 1975 Maine abolished parole and has since made extensive use of the split sentence. The sentencing judge prescribes the period of imprisonment to be served, less time off for good behavior, and also the conditions of supervision, control, and treatment on release. In effect, judicial split sentences take the place of indeterminate sentencing and parole, the releasing decision and the terms of release being determined by the judge at time of sentence.

In states where the split sentence has not, in effect, absorbed the paroling decision, it functions as an added element in the judge's sentencing discretion, giving flexibility to the painful search for acceptability and effect, control and treatment, community acceptability without criminogenic effects, that makes up the sentencing decision.

Forfeiture, Restitution, Compensation, and Fees for Service

These fiscal penalties can be disposed of swiftly as part of a comprehensive system of intermediate punishments. They are adjuncts to rational sentences and not sentences in themselves; additions to, not substitutes for, other punishments. They will, of course, have impact on the sentencing decision, in particular on a fine, since the total punitive package, if fiscal penalties be involved, must be within the offender's realistic financial reach.

Whereas we have made a case for the privatization of the collection of a large proportion of fines, we make no such case in relation to these fiscal additives to other penalties. Their enforcement must be directly the court's business and there are sufficient governmental interests in their collection to support effective enforcement. This is clearly so in relation to fees for probation where, as we have seen, probation services can gain significant strength and initiative from these funds. Likewise, in relation to forfeiture of the assets of drug offenders the federal Department of Justice has demonstrated what a powerful and remunerative weapon this can be. But in the main these fiscal additives to penal sanctions apply over the field of punishment and do not raise problems specific to intermediate punishments.

So ends our survey of the roles of community-based intermediate punishments as components of comprehensive sentencing systems. To this point in this book we have explained why and how intermediate punishments should be built into comprehensive systems of sentencing and have described current experience and knowledge concerning the major sentencing options that are now available. In the final chapter we discuss the formidable impediments to change that confront efforts at innovation and that make major changes to the criminal justice system not impossible, but exceedingly difficult.

8

The Political Economy of Implementation

The impediments that confront reforms of the criminal justice system are daunting; they are especially challenging for innovative intermediate punishments. Constitutional, legal, political, organizational, bureaucratic, ideological, and financial complexities stand in the way.

- The constitutional complexities include the consequences of separation of powers notions that placed responsibility and accountability for various aspects of the criminal law and its enforcement in the three separate and independent branches of government and from the consequences of federalism, which created overlapping federal and state legal systems as well as separate state legal systems, today totaling 50.
- The legal complexities include the diverse criminal laws—both statutory and common law—in the various jurisdictions and the diverse statutory frameworks for operation of the agencies that enforce and administer the criminal law and its related institutional arrangements.
- The political complexities result directly from the status of many administrators as elected public officials accountable to different

constituencies; state governors (and generally the state attorneys general) are elected by a statewide constituency; state house and senate members are elected from different overlapping local electoral districts; prosecuting attorneys are generally elected from a county-wide jurisdiction, mayors and city council members from cities and districts of cities, elected local judges from districts that are often configured differently from any of the others; all of these officials shape the criminal justice system through their legislative, appointive, policymaking, and decision-making powers, and many of them have roles to play in carrying out any major criminal justice innovation.

- Organizational complexities result from the interplay of constitutional, legal, and political considerations; depending on the mix of elected and appointed judicial roles and state traditions, the judiciary may be centrally organized and administered or it may be fragmented; public prosecution is generally, though not always, organized on a county-wide basis, thereby making the implementation or enforcement of state-wide policies difficult and effectively subject to vetoes or circumvention in individual counties; some states have unitary correctional systems in which prisons, jails, and probation are centrally managed; in most states, however, prisons are managed by the state, jails by local authorities; the organization of adult and juvenile probation varies enormously.

- Bureaucratic complexities include those to which any bureaucracy is subject: people get set in their ways and often resist changes that repudiate or greatly depart from past practices; well-established bureaucracies, especially in the public sector, can be difficult to reorganize; labor unions often impede innovation.

- Ideological complexities include the mercurial nature of public opinion and media attention to crime stories, the too frequent pandering by politicians to public fears and stereotypes, the deeply held but divergent views that are present in our country about the causes of crime, the appropriate methods of responding to it, and the likely effects of criminal punishments.

- Financial complexities both confound and are caused by all of the preceding complexities; some criminal justice agencies are funded by the states, some by the cities, some by the counties, some by a combination of sources and, at each level, particular programs are funded as part of the budgets of separate agencies, which means inevitably that the question "Who pays?" takes pride of place among the questions "Is this new program a good idea?," "Would it be fairer or more predictable or more efficient?," and "Can we sell it politically?"

Perhaps more than in any other major area of public policy—certainly more than in education, or health, or most social service programs—the complex character of our criminal justice institutions provides bewilderingly complex problems to be solved before major new initiatives can be accomplished. The experience during the decades following the issuance of *The Challenge of Crime in a Free Society,* the 1967 report of the President's Commission on Law Enforcement and Administration of Justice, and the subsequent reports of the National Advisory Commission on Criminal Justice Standards and Goals (1973), demonstrates the problem. Both bodies offered numerous suggestions for improvements to the criminal justice system. Many of the proposed reforms were tried, and some took root, but most, despite the availability of billions of dollars from the Law Enforcement Assistance Administration, disappeared or shrank shortly after the federal funding ceased.

This litany of impediments does not mean that successful introduction and implementation of innovative programs is impossible, merely that it is often exceedingly difficult and requires well-thought-out strategies for dealing with complexities. While many major sentencing innovations failed, like the sentencing commissions in New York and elsewhere, or became dead letters soon after implementation, like mandatory sentencing laws and voluntary sentencing guidelines, others took root and survived. The most ambitious example to date is the establishment of presumptive sentencing guidelines in Minnesota and Washington, which radically altered the criminal justice systems of these states from plea bargaining through parole. The Minnesota innovation in large part succeeded because its proponents early developed and carried out strategies for dealing with the media and public opinion, the legislature, and most of the relevant professional constituencies.

Our purpose here, however, is not to write a treatise on program implementation but to identify some of the major impediments to change that proponents of new approaches to intermediate punishments must be prepared to address. Accordingly, in this chapter we consider some of the overriding obstacles to the achievement of a sentencing system that makes full and proper use of intermediate punishments. These obstacles, common to all the punishments discussed in detail in earlier chapters, are net widening, the separation of powers, budgetary constraints, and evaluation and accountability.

Net Widening

Fundamental to the thesis of this book is that intermediate punishments are not to be viewed as "alternatives to imprisonment"— they are independent sanctions required by the ideal of a graduated and comprehensive punishment system. If a just balance is to be struck between the needs of social protection and social control and the varying realities of wickedness of the offender and of the threat he poses, we must fashion a comprehensive system of punishments, not a binary system in which imprisonment is seen as punishment and everything else is an alternative, a letting off.

The time is ripe for such a perspective. A mindless severity is moving out of fashion. It is not only the soft-hearted academics who press for a broader and more effective range of social controls than the now overcrowded prisons and jails provide; judges, prosecutors, legislators, correctional administrators, sentencing commissioners, and political commentators increasingly advocate the expanded use of community-based punishments, and not merely to reduce prison and jail populations. A recent publication of the ultra-conservative Free Congress Research and Education Foundation, *Crime and Punishment in Modern America,* edited by McGuigan and Pascale, for example, contains a strong plea by conservative U.S. Senators William Armstrong and Sam Nunn for increased use of intermediate punishments.

Many who are now in prison or jail could better, in our view, be subject to community-based punishments; in earlier chapters we gave many examples of the types of offenders we have in mind. American criminal justice systems imprison too many and for too long, and we hope for sentencing systems that change this; but that view is not the basis on which the thesis of this book rests.

Nevertheless, since the alternatives movement has attracted substantial support, it is appropriate to consider one process that has impeded the achievement of the goals of that movement: the widening of the net of social control that follows most introductions of less severe alternative punishments.

The 1987 report of the Canadian Sentencing Commission offers a compelling explanation of net widening. The report submits that "a widening of the net of penal control is liable to occur when a new sanction is introduced with the intention that it should be used in lieu of another sanction, which is more severe." The report then precisely demonstrates how the new sanction tends to draw more from those previously treated with *less* severity than the new sanction rather than from those previously treated with *more* severity. And those previously not punished at all are then likely to be drawn into the net of social control to take the places vacated by those on whom the new sanction has been imposed. The report concludes: "The Commission is of the view that the widening of the net effect can only be contained by adoption of a policy which represents a fundamental shift in the perception of community sanctions."

The mechanism that operates to widen the net is obvious enough. When the only choices available to judges are prison and nominal probation, in situations of genuine choice between those two punishments, clemency and parsimony in punishment will often lead to the punishment of lesser severity being favored. By and large, judges do not wish to impose the more severe sanction when a lesser would in their view suffice. When an intermediate choice is offered it will tend to be filled more by those previously treated more leniently than by those previously treated more severely; if judges in effect have given the benefit of doubt, and a probationary sentence, to the offender for whom imprisonment seemed too severe and probation too lenient, the newly available intermediate punishment will be just what's wanted. And, regrettably, there seems to be an amplitude of convicted offenders to fill all these slots, hence "net widening."

The Canadian Sentencing Commission's analysis, the beliefs and experience of most practitioners, and the findings of numerous

program evaluations—including a thorough review of the literature by Jim Austin and Barry Krisberg—concur that net widening
commonly occurs.

Nevertheless, to reject alternatives to imprisonment as the justification for community-based punishments is not at all to reject
the concept that many who are now in prison could be better punished, for our sakes and for theirs, without incarceration. As the
Canadian Commission affirmed: "[T]here is no inconsistency in
maintaining that community sanctions should be considered as
sanctions in their own right and at the same time arguing that for
many offences they should also represent alternatives to incarceration."

To many people the growing use of intermediate punishments is
a source of deep concern. For some the concern is that the criminal justice system will become more punitive; if 30 percent of
convicted felons in a jurisdiction receive incarcerative sentences
and 70 percent receive nominal probation, creation of new punishments more punitive than simple probation necessarily means that
more offenders will experience relatively more punitive sanctions
than before. Alvin Bronstein, head of the ACLU's National Prison
Project, has said, "[I]f these programs are used as alternatives to
jail, then maybe there is no problem with them. If you're sending
the same people to jail, and putting people who otherwise would
be on probation on them, it's a misuse."

We find the notion of "intermediate punishments" liberating for
several reasons. First, although the state's punitive powers should
be used sparingly, credible alternatives to incarceration must be
available before a "least restrictive alternative" policy, like the
American Bar Association's, becomes realistic. The unimaginative
prison-or-nothing psychology of American sentencing has impeded
efforts to develop constructive nonincarcerative correctional programs. Other countries have managed to use fines or community
service as sanctions for serious crimes and greatly to diminish reliance on short prison and jail sentences; perhaps the United States
can also.

Second, concern for fairness compels concern for proportionality in punishment, both in the sense that punishments should in
some meaningful way be commensurate with the severity of the
offender's crime and in the sense that relatively more severe of-

fenses should in general receive relatively more severe punishments. Under current practice in many states, proportionality in either sense has been a possibility only for that minority of offenders who receive incarcerative sanctions. There has been little proportionality in punishment for those who are not bound for prison. When all of these people receive "mere probation," there is no feasible way to make punishments proportionate. Intermediate sanctions would provide the successive steps for a ladder of scaled punishments outside prison.

Third, the creation of intermediate punishments removes the arbitrariness and unfairnesses that occur when prison and probation are the only choices available to the judge. In such jurisdictions, offenders whom the judge regards as at the margin present serious difficulties and probably suffer serious injustices. Judges may genuinely feel that sentencing such offenders to traditional probation unduly depreciates the seriousness of their behavior but that sentencing them to incarceration is unduly harsh. Inevitably some offenders at the margin go to prison while others like-situated receive probation. A continuum of graded punishments can free judges from that forced choice and thereby avoid individual injustices.

Fourth, the notion of intermediate punishments refocuses and enriches thinking about net widening. Programs designed as alternatives to incarceration have been criticized severely because they are often applied to persons who otherwise would not have been incarcerated. For community service programs created as prison alternatives, for example, as Ken Pease in his 1985 *Crime and Justice* article and Douglas McDonald in *Punishment Without Walls* conclude, it has commonly been found in this country and elsewhere that as many as half of those sentenced to community service would otherwise have received probation. This is a powerful criticism of intermediate punishments if they are thought about in a criminal justice system in which prison and nonprison are the only punishment choices and intermediate punishments are conceived as "alternatives" intended only for the prison-bound. If a new correctional program is justified and funded to serve as an alternative to incarceration and is instead used for people who would otherwise not have been incarcerated, patently it has been misapplied.

However, once punishment choices are conceived as being made from a diversity of programs along a continuum of scaled control or punitiveness, the analysis of net widening changes. The question becomes not "Is this program being applied only to people who would otherwise have been imprisoned?" but "Is this program being applied for persons of the sort for whom it was intended?" If, for example, a highly intrusive and structured intensive supervision probation program has been designed for offenders who otherwise would be imprisoned, it can reasonably be said to have been misused if it is applied to offenders who otherwise would have received nominal probation.

Not all intermediate punishments, however, need to be designed to serve as alternatives to incarceration. Some may be designed as punishments for people whose crimes and criminal records make it inappropriate to do nothing to sanction their criminality and yet unduly harsh (or too disruptive of their lives or the lives of their families or dependents) to incarcerate them. The application of such a program, truly designed to fill the gap between prison and nominal probation, either to persons whose offenses warrant incarceration or to persons whose offenses warrant no more than nominal probation would be a misuse. The former case might be thought of as unwarranted "net narrowing"; the latter, unwarranted "net widening."

The notion of intermediate punishments does not resolve the net-widening problem, but it does give the analysis much greater specificity and clarifies differences between alternate viewpoints. Imposition of an intrusive intermediate punishment on persons deserving simple probation raises the policy issues usually associated with the net-widening critique. Use of such a punishment for a person for whom prison is the appropriate punishment is also a misuse, though net narrowing is not a banner behind which law reform groups are likely to march.

Thus the development of intermediate punishments redirects questions concerning the fit between punishment and punished and makes it easier to understand the decision processes that created net widening, in its pejorative sense, in the first place. For judges and prosecutors who must decide what punishments should be imposed on convicted offenders, the creation of a new program offering an alternative to incarceration may allow a judge to avoid doing nothing in cases in which, for whatever reason, incarceration seems too severe. In the mind of that judge, in that instance, sentencing an offender to the alternative program is not an inappropriate extension of state power over an offender who would otherwise not have been incarcerated; it is the imposition of a nontrivial punishment on a person for whom this is the appropriate punishment.

The Separation of Powers

Who should decide that an intermediate punishment is appropriate and who should enforce it? There are problems here on which many community-based programs founder.

Obviously enough, the legislature must in one way or another authorize community-based punishments if they are to be imposed by the judiciary. The legislature may give guidance to the types of cases that may attract such punishments, may make some mandatory, may preclude their imposition in some types of cases, or may (subject to constitutional constraints) set up a sentencing commission to guide judicial discretion in the imposition of such punishments. We are not concerned here with arrangements of this type; they present no obstacles in principle to the development of a comprehensive and graduated system of punishment. Our concern is the political realities of conflicts of power that pervade this field and their adverse consequences for community-based punishments.

Local communities, mostly counties, support most of the jails of America. The sheriff is the controlling functionary. Jail time for convicted misdemeanants is imposed by the courts and enforced by the sheriff. This division of responsibility is long-established and, subject to current exigencies of overcrowded jails and court-imposed caps on their populations, works well. The lines of authority, responsibility, and accountability are clear.

Much the same is true of imprisonment. The judge orders it; the director of the state department of corrections (or some like-named state administrator) is responsible for its implementation.

But with community-based punishments, obstacles of inadequate resources and uncertain lines of authority obtrude. The strongly prevailing tendency is to require the probation officer to be the supervisor and enforcer of the intermediate punishment. This is a role that may well in part conflict with the other roles of the probation officer. In Chapter 7 we discussed the conflict within the probation officer's role between supervisory or control functions and client-assisting functions, between the probation officer as police officer and as social caseworker. The tension we wish to discuss at present lies in the lines of authority to whom the probation officer is accountable, to whom he looks for promotion, and who therefore exercise a powerful influence on his priorities.

Adult probation is organized in the federal system and in some states under the control of the judiciary. In other states it is under the control of the executive either at the state or local level. These three organizational structures have implications for intermediate punishments.

When the probation office is a branch of the state or local judiciary, the duties of the probation officer are likely to be to assist the judge in imposing sentence by preparing a presentence report, to supervise those on probation, and to perform sundry other less burdensome duties. The probation officer's relationship with his administrative superior, the judge, revolves mainly around the presentence function and, if the caseloads for supervision are high—as they often are—there is a strong tendency for supervision to be neglected. If new duties of intensive probationary supervision are added—new duties relating to electronic control of the offender, ensuring attendance at drug treatment programs, confirming adherence to residential requirements—the burden on the probation office and on probation officers can become very great unless there is a reorganization of functions within the probation office. These might include a reduction or elimination of other duties for some probation officers so that they can concentrate on their new and more intensive supervisory functions, and generally an allocation of new resources to the probation office to allow these new duties to be efficiently performed.

When probation is judicially supervised, unless the particular judge is personally keenly interested in developing intermediate punishments, as is, for example, Judge Albert Kramer in Massachusetts, who has made this a major personal initiative, it is far from easy for the probation officer to find the time or energy or resources effectively to supervise community-based punishments. He is, in effect, too much "the judge's man" to take on these burdens, particularly when his closest working relationship with the judge centers on the sentencing function and not on supervision.

When probation is a local executive function, other than in the large cities or in large, prosperous counties, it is unlikely that sufficient probation resources will be diverted to the intensive supervision required if intermediate punishments are to be made effective. And in too many of our larger cities the sheer volume of offenders overwhelms resources; but there is at least the possibility, as in a state probation system, of setting aside specific staff for this task.

What it amounts to is that it is not at all easy to add intensive supervision of those on community-based punishments to the existing duties of probation offices and probation officers.

At a time of budgetary constraints, duties are often added without the necessary new resources being provided. Often, as a result, supervision becomes perfunctory and the newly introduced, community-based intermediate punishments become tokens, swiftly recognized as such. If there is one lesson that is driven home by a survey of community-based punishments, it is that unless they are vigorously enforced, they will fail.

Intermediate punishments demand close supervision; they are more demanding of the probation officer than those who launch them expect. Too often the new supervisory duties are tacked on to the existing duties of already overburdened probation officers. This reality explains one persistent phenomenon as one surveys intermediate punishments in this country and abroad: the phenomenon of early enthusiasm and success waning into routine and failure.

New initiatives in intermediate punishments are often launched by voluntary organizations, financially supported by federal or state funds. Examples include: the Vera Institute in New York, which provided the initiative, energy, and staff for experiments in community service orders and day fines; and the Safer Foundation in Chicago, which provided the initiative, energy, and staff for conditional supervision of those who otherwise would be in jail. Local reform organizations or individual judges or correctional agencies see the need for a new initiative, apply for funds to launch the experiment, and do so with enthusiasm. But the task of entrenching a new program is very different from that of launching a new program; it calls for a continuity of staffing and funding beyond that necessary at the beginning; it varies lines of authority; somebody's administrative turf will be invaded. And hence one observes a large number of what are properly described as successful experiments in intermediate punishments which, despite their "success," do not endure, do not become institutionalized.

Too frequently funding for new programs is provided on a short-term basis by the federal government or private foundations. Much too often, even when programs seem to be successes, state and local governments fail to step in when the short-term funds are gone.

Long-term funds are harder to find than funds for launching a new plan, but this is not a sufficient explanation of the phenomenon of discontinued successful programs. Much of the explanation lies in the administrative structures and conflicting lines of authority and range of duties to which we have pointed. But the budgetary constraints are certainly of importance.

Budgets for Intermediate Punishments

The conventional wisdom is that there is no difficulty here—intermediate punishments cost less than imprisonment. And, as usual, the conventional wisdom misses the point.

Because most nonincarcerative sentences are less expensive to administer than are prisons, many jurisdictions are attempting to save money by sentencing offenders to punitive nonprison sentences like intensive supervision probation or house arrest. Most of the evaluations of intensive supervision, house arrest, and electronic monitoring attempt to demonstrate that the per capita cost of administration is much lower than the per capita cost of incarcerating an offender and, as a result, that their jurisdictions are saving substantial amounts of money. For a variety of reasons, we suspect that often this is not true, but it is widely believed, and it is a frequent rationale for the establishment of new programs.

The cost savings claims are suspect for at least three reasons. First, comparisons of per capita costs are misleading. The marginal cost of one additional prisoner for a prison system is slight: a bit of food, some disposable supplies, some paperwork. Only when nonprison programs divert enough prison-bound offenders to permit the closing of an institution, or a section of an institution, or permit plans for new facilities to be scaled down, will nonprison programs realize substantial cost saving. In New York City, for example, as Douglas McDonald reported in *Punishment Without Walls,* a highly regarded community service program, though successful from many perspectives, in effect reduced demand for jail beds by 75 to 95 per year, a number so small relative to New York City's jail population and capacity as to be immaterial to total jail costs.

No doubt some nonprison programs have resulted in mothballing of plans for new construction; in Georgia, probation administrators and evaluators claim that the numbers of people diverted from prison to intensive supervision probation have eliminated a need to build two new prisons. In general, however, comparisons of the average cost per offender of administering an intensive supervision or house arrest program with the average cost per offender of imprisonment are seriously misleading.

Second, to be valid, comparisons must be based on something other than the annual average costs of operating nonprison and prison programs. For example, in calculating the costs and benefits of a 100-offender intensive supervision program, it is necessary to know how many of the probationers would otherwise have gone to prison and how many would otherwise have received probation. If, say, 50 offenders would otherwise have been sentenced to probation, the average cost of correctional programs for them will have increased and this will offset to some degree the savings, if any, realized by diverting the other 50 offenders from prison. Similarly, the prison costs for those later incarcerated following failure in the program, revocation, and resentencing, often a tenth to a third of those in the program, must be taken into account.

Third, cost/benefit assessments must be adjusted to take into account the time each offender is subject to control. If, and ignoring our earlier skepticism about comparisons of average per-person costs, the average cost per year per imprisoned offender is $12,000, and the average cost per year per intensive supervised offender is $4000, comparison of those average annual costs is inherently misleading. If the average intensive supervised client serves 12 months ($4000) but would otherwise have served 3 months in prison ($3000), the intensive supervision program is more, not less, expensive.

This isn't to say that nonprison programs cannot achieve cost savings, but merely that claimed cost savings must be scrutinized with care. In a large jurisdiction, diversion of 1000 prison-bound offenders for a year each may eliminate the need to build a new prison. In this case, there will be major cost savings (assuming that we *know* that those 1000 offenders really would otherwise have been imprisoned).

Our point here is simply that cost comparisons are complicated and that glib claims about cost savings associated with intermediate punishments often do not stand up to careful scrutiny. There are, however, other budgetary complexities raised by intermediate punishments and to these we now turn.

It may well be true that the convicted offender in prison or jail costs the hypothetical fisc more than if he is serving an intermediate punishment; but it is not the hypothetical fisc that pays the bill. The state department of corrections pays for imprisonment, the county sheriff's department pays for the jail; neither will meet the costs of an intermediate punishment unless probation falls under the control of the state department of corrections, as it does in some states. Generally, different budgets bear the burden of these different punishments.

The marginal savings of removing a few from prison may not be great; until a section or a wing of a prison can be emptied there will be no substantial savings. By contrast, the start-up costs of supervising intermediate punishments are substantial and each offender under the type of intensive supervision such punishments require is an immediately appreciable cost.

Transitional costs and different budgets bearing the different burdens do not at all facilitate either launching or institutionalizing intermediate punishments. And there are further budgetary obstacles. The most significant financial obstacle has already been discussed: net widening.

If a substantial number of those sentenced to intermediate punishments would otherwise have been placed on ordinary probation, with only a few being drawn from an otherwise incarcerated group, then quite apart from transitional costs and the question of who pays for different punishments, the total costs have increased, not decreased. Net widening is cost widening. This does not at all mean that there is no advantage in such a situation; indeed, it may well be to the advantage of society to expand the net of social control in this way, but it cannot be justified on the basis of cost savings.

A final problem related to the preceding three is this: those who order the intermediate punishment are normally not part of the administrative organizations that have to meet the costs of the intermediate punishments. For example, assume a court, and there are some, with an increasing number of judges interested in electronic monitoring of some convicted offenders. Unless they are sedulous in confining their orders for electronic monitoring to those who are a genuine risk of crime or flight, there will be increased total costs—this is the simple net-widening phenomenon. But there is more to it. The addition of electronic monitoring to a sentence, which may also involve intensive supervision and a substantial fine, makes the total punishment more politically acceptable and thus more appealing to the judge, even though he may well suspect that the electronic supplement adds little to the deterrent, control, or rehabilitative aspects of the sentence.

Those who impose such sentences may well have different purposes from those who carry them out; those who impose them may wish to select those likely to succeed, whereas a probation department or a department of corrections doing the selecting would choose those with a higher risk of failure.

There are thus serious budgetary obstacles to be overcome if intermediate punishments are to become an important part of a comprehensive punishment system. One idea relevant to overcoming these obstacles is that of fees for services. Let the convicted offender meet the costs of his intensive supervision, of his electronic or telephonic monitoring, of the collection of his fine, of the supervision of his community service order, and let the obligation to meet these costs be a part of the sentence imposed by the court. Sensitively imposed and vigorously enforced, this type of sentencing is a fine idea. Many courts have accepted it and it has been built into the structure of the federal sentencing guidelines. It has, of course, its limitations, not the least being that many offenders simply lack the resources to pay these costs.

Restitution to the victim should, in our view, take precedence over a fee-for-service order. For similar reasons, a fine and a fee-for-service order should be calculated together by the sentencing court to make the total fiscal sanction realistic and not beyond the reach of the convicted offender. But for those who have the funds to meet such orders and for those for whom community service can be found which will pay enough for them to meet the costs of their supervision there would seem great advantage in this arrangement.

Georgia has recently provided an instructive use of fees for service. Such fees may be imposed on all those sentenced to probation in Georgia. The fees have provided a nest egg for the Georgia probation office to develop a system of intensive probation which has attracted national attention. The costs of intensive probation exceed the fees paid by those under this type of probation supervision, but the budgetary freedom of the total system has allowed for an innovative development which has reassured the courts and financially liberated the department of probation to be creative.

Fees for service underline an important theme in developing a rational system of intermediate punishments: those imposing these sentences must be informed about and sensitive to the realities of the enforcement mechanisms for their implementation.

Two other budgetary ideas relevant to the expansion of intermediate punishments merit consideration: subsidies and privatization. If more than marginal costs can be saved by avoiding net widening and substituting intermediate punishments for incarcerative punishments, there is a strong case for state subsidization of those who supervise these punishments. The experience with the California Probation Subsidy Program, in which the state made cash payments to counties, was ambiguous, but the idea has merit.

Likewise, this is an area where private organizations may well be made responsible for and pay for the implementation of intermediate punishments. In Chapter 5 we argued for the involvement of the private sector in fine collection on grounds of efficiency and economy. Similarly, if, for example, ambulatory drug treatment is ordered as part of an intermediate punishment (as it often is), there is much to be said for the use on a pay-for-service basis of existing community-based drug treatment programs, which are often under the control of private hospitals. Delegation to the private sector here is akin to the use of the private sector in prisons and jails to provide specific services, such as food, health, educational and vocational services; it is not the total delegation of authority involved in the running of a prison or jail by the private sector. There is objection neither in principle nor practice to such arrangements; the essential questions are cost and efficiency.

The involvement of the private sector can also have a positive influence on public attitudes to intermediate punishments. In the longer run, intermediate punishments will have to attract political support if they are to become functioning parts of the punishment system, and this means some degree of acceptance by the public. Public acceptance or rejection may, of course, be based on sound information or on demagoguery; for the moment let us assume a saner world and look critically at how intermediate punishments should be evaluated by those seeking to form a responsible view of their proper role in a comprehensive punishment system.

Evaluation of Intermediate Punishments

What are the criteria for measuring the "success" or "failure" of a particular type of punishment? Cost would be one measure, and this can be calculated with some difficulty. Its efficacy in preventing crime by those to whom it is applied and in deterring crimes by others are measures more difficult of calculation. And there are other relevant measures: community and victim satisfaction, confirming ethical standards, helping to bind the social fabric, and so on. But for the types of intermediate punishments we are considing, two measures stand out: cost and crime prevention. Of these the crime prevention criterion is the value that is most discussed in relation to intermediate punishments, their lesser costs as we have seen being often too easily assumed.

How, then, should one measure the success of intermediate punishments in terms of crime prevention? Their impact as general deterrents compared to sentences that might otherwise be imposed is highly speculative, a matter for argument, but at present levels

of knowledge quite incalculable. Few, however, argue that the
general deterrent difference, if any, is likely to be other than marginal. So it is to specific deterrence, the prevention of repetition of
criminality by an individual, that attention turns. And this too
proves difficult of measurement, more difficult than much of the
literature would suggest.

Consider what at first seems a simple question: How much recidivism do we want from a given type of punishment? None, you
reply. But that is surely wrong. Given existing knowledge of the
efficacy of interventions into human behavior (other than the
really draconic like capital punishment, which clearly profoundly
influences human behavior), such a result would mean that we
must have selected for our punishment a group of offenders of such
low risk of future criminality that our treatment resources must,
previously, have been grossly wasted.

Thus, the immediate insight comes: the "success" of a given
type of punishment in preventing crime must be measured in relation to the alternative punishment that would have been imposed—
if they cost the same and the new one prevents more crime, it is a
"success"; if not, it fails.

With what other punishment is our new intermediate punishment to be compared? The question needs sharpening. Suppose
we are seeking to evaluate the crime prevention effects of a recently introduced intermediate punishment, say, ambulatory drug
treatment under intensive supervision probation for certain addicts
convicted of property crimes? Shall we compare them to a matched
group, if we can do the matching, given six-month jail sentences?
Shall we compare them to a matched group put on ordinary probation? If the former, the short-term results will certainly be
worse, for an appreciable number will commit crimes in the community while their matched brothers in jail will not, at least for six
months. If the latter, the short-term results are likely to be better,
though this is not easy to ascertain because the criminality of our
more intensively treated group will be more observable, more de-
tected, more responded to than the less supervised others. And if
they fail to adhere to the treatment or other conditions of their
intermediate punishment, they will be either revoked and sent to
jail or even more intensively supervised, controlled, and perhaps
assisted.

The temptation is again the temptation of the alternative punishment: if those sentenced to the intermediate punishment commit no more crime over the longer haul (not just the period of incarceration of the others) than those incarcerated, and if the program is cheaper, then it is a "success." But again this perspective on intermediate punishments as alternatives to incarceration should be resisted.

The point can be made by considering the two different perspectives of the chief administrator of a prison system and the chief administrator of a probation system, each considering the group within their control most suitable for a period of community-based ambulatory drug treatment. The prison administrator will select for early release from the prison population a group of addicts who have a low base expectancy rate of future criminality as compared to other addicts convicted of property crimes. He will select his most hopeful cases since his purposes are to relieve the population pressure within his prison system, to reduce its cost, to help those who seem most likely to respond, and to minimize for himself the political embarrassment and adverse publicity that result when released prisoners commit new crime.

By contrast, the probation administrator will select for intensive probation a group of addicts who will increase his costs by necessitating greatly reduced caseloads for the few probation officers supervising high-risk addicted probationers for whom he will arrange a drug treatment program. He will select for this program a high-risk group compared to other addicts on probation, since his purposes are to reduce the overall recidivism rate of all those on probation and in particular to reduce the risk to the community from those whom he selects for the new program. He increases his costs in the cause of crime prevention and he wishes to spend each dollar where it will reduce community danger the most.

Now combine these two perspectives and consider the sentencing judge allocating punishment resources anew for both the prison group and the probation group. What risk category should he select for his new intermediate punishment? The type of offender selected by the prison administrator or the type selected by the probation administrator?

It would be unsafe to assume, given the vagaries of sentencing convicted offenders, that the probation high-risk group matches the prison low-risk group. Hence whatever the outcome of our measures of recidivism (even assuming perfect knowledge in its assessment), we would not know whether the new intermediate punishment was a "success" if the judge made the selection. If the comparison to the prison group favored those on intensive probation with ambulatory drug treatment, all that may have been demonstrated was that the judges were successful in selecting the higher risk group for imprisonment and the lower for the intermediate punishment. If the comparison to those on ordinary probation favored those on ordinary probation, as it likely would, all that may have been shown was that the judges were successful in selecting this higher risk group for the new punishment—not that that punishment had "failed."

To make responsible judgments of crime prevention, then, and even assuming precise knowledge of later criminality, a more global perspective must be taken in which the distribution of all punishments, carceral and noncarceral, must be considered and in which rates of later recidivism are but one of the measures—and a difficult one at that.

Another and briefer way of putting this point is to ask: What is the optimum rate of recidivism for this punishment? Reflection will confirm that given the realities of crime as a relapsing condition in many criminals, given the age distribution of crime and its connection with community tolerances and the resources of the criminal justice system, the question is not easy to answer.

Some would suggest running an experiment to test the answers to these questions. Their experiment would be organized something like this: of the next 100 addicts convicted of property crimes and who lack a record of violence or threat of violence to the person and who are sentenced to between six months and a year of imprisonment, let the computer randomly select 50 for release to intensive probation and ambulatory drug treatment. Then follow both groups, and so on. Even assuming that such an experiment is ethical and would be acceptable to the judiciary, such is the complexity of human interactions that much could go wrong with the experiment. Some of the imprisoned will themselves seek drug treatment on their release; some will be urged to do so. Are they to be denied such assistance in the cause of the experiment? And some of the released group will promptly get into a variety of troubles not immediately connected with their criminality—debts, matrimonial and quasi-matrimonial turbulence, and so on—which the incarcerated group is spared for the time being.

We are not opposing experimental designs in the pursuit of knowledge and the development of a fairer and more efficient punishment system, but we are suggesting that such knowledge is difficult of acquisition and involves larger numbers and larger experiments than have so far been launched in assessing the relative virtues and deficiencies of contending penal methods.

Is this a counsel of despair? Not at all. The case for careful accountability in relation to intermediate punishments and of critical evaluation of the later behavior of those subjected to diverse penal methods is compelling. Gradually knowledge will evolve of the costs and benefits of each type of punishment. But useful knowledge of the applicability of diverse punishments within a comprehensive punishment system, including carceral, community-based, and fiscal sanctions, cannot emerge until a comprehensive system begins to take shape—and that has not yet happened.

We wish to be seen neither as Pollyannas, who propose a complex new system of comprehensive sentencing standards and resources unaware of the many practical impediments to its realization, nor as Cassandras, who see the obstacles to progress as insuperable and the prospects for reform as bleak. The impediments are real, but the prospects need not be bleak. Few people in the 1960s would have predicted with any confidence that the lawlessness and absence of standards for decision making by prosecutors, judges, and parole boards, which were then common, would by 1990 be replaced in many jurisdictions by thoughtful, well-managed systems of plea bargaining, sentencing, and parole guidelines. Intermediate punishments are but a part of a comprehensive sentencing system, and we predict that by early in the next century many impediments to reform will have been overcome and intermediate punishments will, in many jurisdictions, be humane, well-run, fairly administered parts of the correctional system.

▣▣▣▣▣ Bibliographic Note

We have chosen not to clutter the text with references or to distract readers with footnotes. It seems, however, not inappropriate to identify written sources on which we have mainly relied and briefly to introduce readers to them. This note and the reference list that follows are selective, not exhaustive; the major sources cited provide comprehensive lists of references that readers wishing to know more should consult. In this book, we attempt to pull together learning on recent developments, empirical research, and policy options for the future in relation to sentencing and intermediate punishments.

Sentencing

Beginning in the 1960s, indeterminate sentencing in the United States came under attack. One challenge was that indeterminate sentencing did not keep its rehabilitative promises (Allen 1964). A second was that indeterminate sentencing produced arbitrary and capricious decisions and suffered from racial and class bias (American Friends Service Committee 1971). A third was that prosecutorial, sentencing, and parole practices did not comply with minimum procedural safeguards that are common elsewhere in our legal system (Davis 1969). A fourth was that the system was characterized by gross and unacceptable sentencing disparities (Frankel 1972). A fifth was that research on the effectiveness of correctional programs gave no reason to be confident of their effectiveness (Martinson 1974; Lipton, Martinson, and Wilks 1975; in the United Kingdom, Brody 1976). (These pessimistic conclusions were in large part affirmed in two reports of the National Academy of Sciences Panel on Rehabilitative Techniques [Sechrest, White, and Brown 1979; Martin, Sechrest, and Redner 1981]. An earlier National Academy of Sciences Panel on Research on Deterrent and Incapacitative Effects questioned the empirical evidence supporting belief in the deterrent and incapacitative efficacy of modern punishment practices [Blumstein, Cohen, and Nagin 1978].) On the basis of these critiques and others, a number of influential books proposed replacement of indeterminate sentencing with new approaches (Frankel 1972; Morris 1974; Twentieth Century Fund Task Force on Criminal Sentencing 1976; von Hirsch 1976). The same influences underlay the proposed *Model Sentencing and Corrections Act* of the National Conference of Commissioners on Uniform State Laws (1979) and proposed revised sentencing standards from the American Bar Association (1980). Influenced by these critiques and proposals, many states changed their sentencing laws and practices in major respects. Von Hirsch and Hanrahan (1981), the National Academy of Sciences Panel on Research on Sentencing (Blumstein et al. 1983), and Tonry (1987) surveyed sentencing law reform developments in the United States. The only comprehensive state-by-state review of sentencing reform developments is Shane-DuBow, Brown, and Olsen (1985).

Parole Reforms

A model for many later sentencing reform initiatives was provided by research and policy developments leading to the establishment of parole guidelines by the then U.S. Parole Board (Gottfredson, Wilkins, and Hoffman [1978] reviewed these developments). Staff evaluations of the federal parole guidelines' effectiveness are described in Beck and Hoffman (1983, 1984). The General Accounting Office (1982) and Arthur D. Little, Inc. (1981) conducted outside evaluations. Michael Gottfredson (1979) evaluated the federal parole guidelines' effectiveness at reducing sentencing disparities. Many states adopted parole guidelines, though some, including Minnesota and Washington, later abandoned both parole guidelines and parole release. Arthur D. Little, Inc. (1981) evaluated the operation of parole guidelines in Minnesota, Oregon, and Washington. Lombardi (1981) examined the operation of Florida's parole guidelines. Mueller and Sparks (1982) evaluated the Oregon guidelines.

Sentencing Commissions and Presumptive Sentencing Guidelines

Judge Marvin Frankel (1972) first proposed the creation of a specialized administrative agency empowered to devise presumptive guidelines for sentencing. An ad hoc sentencing policy group at the Yale Law School elaborated Judge Frankel's proposals and proposed model legislation (O'Donnell, Curtis, and Churgin 1977) which became the basis for a number of bills introduced into the United States Congress. The National Conference of Commissioners on Uniform State Laws (1979) proposed another, similar, model bill, the *Model Sentencing and Corrections Act*. A variety of states, including notably Minnesota, Washington, and Pennsylvania, and later the United States Congress enacted sentencing commission legislation. The Minnesota experience is described in Parent (1988b). Staff evaluations by the Minnesota Sentencing Guidelines Commission's staff are summarized in Knapp (1984a, 1984b); rationales for specific policy decisions are presented in Knapp (1985) and Parent (1988b). An outsider's view of the political aspects of the Commission's work is contained in Martin (1984). Outside evaluations are reported in Miethe and Moore (1985, 1987); Moore and Miethe (1986); and Miethe (1987). Concern for the increased powers of prosecutors under determinate sentencing led the National Conference of Commissioners on Uniform State Laws (1979) to propose in its *Model Sentencing and Corrections Act* that sentencing be based on "the real offense" as a means to counter-balance prosecutors' ability, through charging and dismissal decisions, to determine the offense to which a plea bargaining defendant pled guilty. For similar reasons, the first set of guidelines proposed by the United States Sentencing Commission called for adoption of "real offense sentencing" (U.S. Sentencing Commission 1986). Neither the Washington state nor the Pennsylvania sentencing guidelines have been the subjects of external evaluations. Boerner (1985) describes the policy rationales underlying key features of the Washington guidelines, as does Washington State Sentencing Guidelines Commission (1983). The Washington Commission's staff have completed a number of internal evaluations (Washington State Sentencing Guidelines Commission 1985, 1986, 1987). The Pennsylvania Commission's major policy decisions are described in Kramer and Scirica (1985). Martin (1984) provides an outsider's view of the political aspects of the Commission's early work. Evaluations of the guidelines' impact by Commission staff are contained in Kramer and Lubitz (1985), Lubitz and Kempinen (1987), and Pennsylvania Commission on Sentencing (1986, 1987). Critical reviews of the evaluation research on the effects of presumptive sentencing guidelines are contained in, as of their respective dates, Cohen and Tonry (1983) and Tonry (1987, 1988). Von Hirsch, Knapp, and Tonry (1987) discuss policy issues implicated by presumptive sentencing guidelines.

Voluntary Sentencing Guidelines

"Voluntary" sentencing guidelines are voluntary in the double sense that they were crafted voluntarily by judges, that is, not acting under legislative mandates, and they were used voluntarily by judges in individual cases. The initial projects in Denver and Vermont were an effort to apply parole guidelines technologies to sentencing. Gottfredson, Wilkins, and Hoffman (1978) provide the rationale for that attempt. Kress (1980) describes early voluntary sentencing guidelines projects in four states. Goldkamp and Gottfredson (1985) recount the experience in Philadelphia applying the voluntary guidelines approach to bail decisions. Rich et al. (1982) evaluated the implementation and operation of early voluntary guidelines systems in Denver, Chicago, Newark (New Jersey), and Philadelphia. Carrow et al. (1985) evaluated voluntary guidelines systems in Maryland and Florida. Sparks (1983) surveyed statistical and methodological issues relating to voluntary sentencing guidelines. Cohen and Tonry (1983) and Tonry (1987, 1988) provide critical reviews of that literature.

Statutory Determinate Sentencing

Maine was the first state to abolish parole release and thereby establish "determinate sentencing." Reports on the only major evaluation of the Maine experience are contained in Anspach (1981) and Anspach, Lehman, and Kramer (1983). California was the first populous state to adopt determinate sentencing. The results were evaluated by the California Department of Corrections (e.g., Brewer, Beckett, and Holt 1980), Abt Associates (Ku 1980), and the Rand Corporation (Lipson and Peterson 1980). Two major California evaluations were funded by the National Institute of Justice, U.S. Department of Justice (Casper, Brereton, and Neal [1982] and, as part of a large, multi-investigator study, Sparks [1981] and Utz [1981]). These and other California evaluations are critically reviewed in Cohen and Tonry (1983). Messinger and Johnson (1978) provide an analysis of the political pressures and interest groups that led to passage of the California Determinate Sentencing Law. Although more than a dozen other states have abolished parole release and thereby established "determinate" sentencing laws, only North Carolina's law has been the subject of published evaluations in Clarke (1984, 1986, 1987) and Clarke et al. (1983). There have been a few outside evaluations of Illinois's determinate sentencing law (e.g., Schuwerk 1984).

Mandatory Sentencing Laws

Mandatory sentencing laws in many states predate the 1970s. By 1983 every state but one had enacted mandatory sentencing laws (Shane-DuBow, Brown, and Olsen 1985). Probably the best-known evaluation concerned the "Rockefeller Drug Laws" in New York State (Joint Committee on New York Drug Law Evaluation 1978). Massachusetts's mandatory firearms sentencing law was the most evaluated mandatory sentencing law (Beha 1977; Rossman et al. 1979; Pierce and Bowers 1981). Evaluators of Michigan's mandatory firearm sentencing statute investigated systems effects on plea bargaining and sentencing (Heumann and Loftin 1979) and deterrent effects on firearms violence (Loftin and McDowall 1981; Loftin, Heumann, and McDowall 1983). Carlson (1982) critically reviewed evaluations of mandatory sentencing laws in several states. Evaluations were also published on Florida's mandatory firearm sentencing law (Loftin and McDowall 1984) and on a variety of mandatory sentencing laws in Pennsylvania (Pennsylvania Commission on Crime and Delinquency 1986). These evaluations are critically reviewed in Cohen and Tonry (1983) and Tonry (1987).

Plea Bargaining

Concern with plea bargaining in an era of determinate sentencing has taken two forms. First, for reasons similar to those underlying proposed limits on judicial discretion, there have been calls for regularization and standardization of the exercise of prosecutorial discretion. Second, since the earliest days of determinate sentencing, observers have suggested that restraints on judicial discretion will increase the powers of prosecutors (e.g., Zimring 1977; Alschuler 1978; Schulhofer 1980; Coffee and Tonry 1983). This seems, indeed, to have happened under Minnesota's sentencing guidelines (Rathke 1982; Knapp 1984a; Miethe 1987). Although proposals have been made for establishment of internal guidelines for the exercise of prosecutorial discretion since the 1960s, the most radical and best-known effort to control plea bargaining occurred in Alaska where it was "abolished" by the state Attorney General (Rubinstein, Clarke, and White 1980). There have been a number of evaluations of the effects of full or partial plea bargaining bans (by the United States Coast Guard: Call, England, and Talarico [1983]; in New York State: Joint Committee on New York Drug Law Evaluation [1978]; in Michigan: Church [1976] and Heumann and Loftin [1979]).

Intermediate Punishments

Except for textbooks and practitioners' manuals, which we do not discuss, there has been even less writing in the United States on intermediate punishments than there has been on sentencing. Ball, Huff, and Lilly (1988) describe a number of house arrest and electronic monitoring programs. McCarthy (1987) and Petersilia (1987a) contain a series of descriptions and evaluations of intensive supervision, house arrest, and electronic monitoring programs. Tonry and Will (1988) examine house arrest, electronic monitoring, intensive supervision, community service, and fiscal penalties. Very little rigorous evaluative research on the operation of intermediate punishment programs has been conducted and reported. There have been a handful of major, federally funded evaluations. A few academics and researchers who have chosen to specialize in community corrections, notably James Byrne of the University of Lowell, Todd Clear of Rutgers University, and Joan Petersilia of the Rand Corporation, have written extensively on a wide variety of intermediate punishment programs. A few of their writings are listed in the reference list. There have been, in addition, large numbers of descriptive reports, brochures, and leaflets issued by state and local governmental departments. Below we cite what we believe are the most important, intellectually respectable, and generally accessible writings on the use of intermediate punishments in the United States.

Financial Penalties

Although there has been some writing by economists on the use of fines as criminal punishments (e.g., Becker 1968; Becker and Landes 1974; Ehrlich 1974; Gillespie 1981; Posner 1977, 1980), there has been very little empirical or evaluative writing on the use of criminal fines in American courts. The General Accounting Office (1985) provides an empirical analysis of imposition, administration, and collection of federal fines. Most of the existing work on criminal fines has been done by researchers associated with the Vera Institute of Justice in New York City; those projects included examinations of fining practices in selected jurisdictions across the country and in selected courts in New York City (Hillsman, Sichel, and Mahoney 1984), a review of fining practices in Western Europe (Casale 1981), and an examination of the relevance to the United States of the extensive English experience with criminal fines (Casale and Hillsman 1986). Cole et al. (1987) conducted a nationwide survey of the attitudes of American trial court judges toward increased use of fines. Hillsman (1990) reports on American research to date on the use of fines. Grebing (1982) provides a descriptive summary of experience with fines as criminal sanctions in 21 countries. Sweden, West Germany, and England are the countries whose use of fines as criminal penalties is most often discussed: on West Germany, see Friedman (1983); on Sweden, see Thornstedt (1985) and Hillsman (1990); and on England, see Casale and Hillsman (1986) as well as Lewis (1988). Mullaney (1988) prepared for the National Institute of Corrections an exhaustive review of fines and other economic sanctions now in use in the United States. Warren et al. (1983) carried out a national survey and evaluation of restitution programs. McGillis (1986) reviewed for the National Institute of Justice the American experience with restitution orders. Morgan and Bowles (1981) reviewed fining experience in the United Kingdom, and Newburn and de Peyrecave (1988) review research on the use of compensation orders in English magistrates' courts; this last publication contains references to the sizable body of research on financial penalties that has been conducted by, or from, the Home Office Research Unit. Baird, Holien, and Bakke (1986) reviewed the then-current state of experience with probation fees.

Community Service

Community service orders are in use throughout the United States. There have been two recent, important reviews of experience with community service. Pease (1985) reviews research and experience up to that year; the emphasis is on Great Britain, but the American, Canadian, and Australian literatures are also examined. Bevan (1983) offers an overview of community service orders in Australia and New Zealand. There have been other reviews of the British experience (e.g., Young 1979; Pease and McWilliams 1980). McDonald (1986) reviews the American experience and provides a detailed evaluation of the operation of the Vera Institute of Justice's celebrated experiment with community service orders in New York City.

Intensive Supervision Probation

Overviews of development of intensive supervision probation (ISP) programs are contained in Byrne (1986), Petersilia (1987a), and Tonry and Will (1988), and Tonry (1990). The January 1990 issue of *Crime and Delinquency* is a special issue on intensive supervision probation. Banks et al. (1977) provide a summary of research findings on use of ISP and differential caseload programs in probation in the 1960s and 1970s. Joan Petersilia of the Rand Corporation is now involved in experimental evaluations of the operation of ISP programs in more than a dozen states; her findings should be available in a year or two. In the meantime, the most extensive evaluations available are those for Georgia (e.g., Erwin 1987; Erwin and Bennett 1987), New Jersey (Pearson 1987, 1988), and Massachusetts (Byrne and Kelly 1988). Less ambitious evaluations of ISP programs have been carried out in New York State (Association of the Bar of the City of New York 1986), Ohio (e.g., Latessa 1979, 1987), Texas (Fields 1984), Cook County, Illinois (Lurigio 1987), and the State of Illinois (Thomson 1987). Clear and Shapiro (1986) describe an Oregon program.

House Arrest

No major independent evaluations have been conducted of house arrest programs. An overview of developments with house arrest and reports on several modest evaluations are contained in Ball, Huff, and Lilly (1988). The best-known, and reportedly most extensive, house arrest program is Florida's community control program. Flynn (1986) and Wainwright (1984) provide descriptions of that program. Descriptive statistics on the program, together with some effort to evaluate its operation, are contained in Florida Department of Corrections (1987) and Florida Mental Health Institute (1987). Blomberg, Waldo, and Burcroff (1987) offer evaluative comments on the Florida program. A number of brief studies and evaluations of house arrest programs are reported in Petersilia (1987a), Ball, Huff, and Lilly (1988), and McCarthy (1987). The best-known house arrest program operating as a prison early release program is Oklahoma's; it is described in Meachum (1986); an evaluation is reported in Sandhu and Dodder (1986). The limited federal prison early release home confinement program is described in Hofer and Meierhoefer (1987). Petersilia (1987a) also describes a number of state house arrest programs.

Electronic Monitoring

Proposals for maintaining electronic controls on offenders' whereabouts have been discussed since the 1960s (e.g., Schwitzgebel, Pahnke, and Hurd 1964; Schwitzgebel 1969). A number of electronic monitoring programs are described in McCarthy (1987); Petersilia (1987a); Huff, Ball, and Lilly (1987); and Tonry and Will (1988). The National Institute of Justice sponsored a monograph on use of electronic monitoring programs in corrections (Friel, Vaughn, and del Carmen 1987). The Office of the California Attorney General has prepared surveys of the use of electronic monitoring (Farley 1987, 1989). Periodic reviews of the extent of use of electronic monitoring are carried out by the National Institute of Justice, U.S. Department of Justice (e.g., Schmidt 1986, 1988; Schmidt and Curtis 1987).

◨◨◨◨◨◨ References

Advisory Council on the Penal System. 1970. *Non-Custodial and Semi-Custodial Penalties.* London: Her Majesty's Stationery Office.

Albrecht, Hans-Jorg. 1980. *Strafzumessung und Vollstreckung bei Geldstrafen.* Berlin: Duncker and Humbolt.

Albrecht, Hans-Jorg, and Elmer H. Johnson. 1980. "Fines and Justice Administration: The Experience of the Federal Republic of Germany." *International Journal of Comparative and Applied Criminal Justice* 4:3–14.

Allen, Francis A. 1964. *The Borderland of Criminal Justice.* Chicago: University of Chicago Press.

Alschuler, Albert W. 1978. "Sentencing Reform and Prosecutorial Power." *University of Pennsylvania Law Review* 126: 550–77.

American Bar Association. 1980. *American Bar Association Standards for Criminal Justice,* Volume 2. Boston: Little, Brown.

American Friends Service Committee. 1971. *Struggle for Justice: A Report on Crime and Punishment in America.* New York: Hill and Wang.

American Law Institute. 1962. *Model Penal Code (Proposed Official Draft).* Philadelphia: American Law Institute.

Anglin, M. Douglas, and Yih-Ing Hser. 1990. "Treatment of Drug Abuse." In *Drugs and Crime,* edited by Michael Tonry and James Q. Wilson. Volume 13 of *Crime and Justice: A Re-*

view of Research, edited by Michael Tonry and Norval Morris. Chicago: University of Chicago Press.

Anglin, M. Douglas, and George Speckart. 1988. "Narcotics Use and Crime: A Multisample, Multimethod Analysis." *Criminology* 26:197–231.

Anspach, Donald F. 1981. *Crossroads of Justice: Problems With Determinate Sentencing in Maine—Interim Report.* Portland: Department of Sociology, University of Southern Maine.

Anspach, Donald F., Peter H. Lehman, and John H. Kramer. 1983. *Maine Rejects Indeterminacy: A Case Study of Flat Sentencing and Parole Abolition.* Unpublished document prepared for the National Institute of Justice. Portland: Department of Sociology, University of Southern Maine.

Armstrong, William L., and Sam Nunn. 1986. "Alternatives to Incarceration: The Sentencing Improvement Act." In *Crime and Punishment in Modern America,* edited by Patrick B. McGuigan and Jon S. Pascale. Washington, D.C.: The Free Congress Research and Education Foundation.

Arthur D. Little, Inc. 1981. *An Evaluation of Parole Guidelines in Four Jurisdictions.* Unpublished document prepared for the National Institute of Corrections, Washington, D.C.

Association of the Bar of the City of New York. 1986. "New York State Probation's Intensive Supervision Program: A Reform in Need of Reform." Unpublished manuscript. New York: Association of the Bar of the City of New York.

Austin, James, and Barry Krisberg. 1982. "The Unmet Promise of Alternatives to Incarceration." *Crime and Delinquency* 28: 374–409.

Australian Law Reform Commission. 1980. *Sentencing of Federal Offenders.* Canberra: Australian Government Publishing Service.

Baird, S. Christopher, Douglas A. Holien, and Audrey J. Bakke. 1986. *Fees for Probation Services.* Madison, Wisc.: National Council on Crime and Delinquency.

Ball, Richard A., C. Ronald Huff, and J. Robert Lilly. 1988. *House Arrest and Correctional Policy: Doing Time at Home.* Newbury Park, Calif.: Sage.

Banks, J. A., L. Porter, R. L. Rardin, T. R. Silver, and V. E. Unger. 1977. *Phase I Evaluation of Intensive Special Probation Projects.* Washington, D.C.: U.S. Government Printing Office.

Beck, James L., and Peter B. Hoffman. 1983. "Reliability in Guideline Application: Initial Hearings—1982." *Research Unit Report 35*. Washington, D.C.: U.S. Parole Commission.

———. 1984. "Reliability in Guideline Application: Initial Hearings—1983." *Research Unit Report 37*. Washington, D.C.: U.S. Parole Commission.

Becker, Gary S. 1968. "Crime and Punishment: An Economic Approach." *Journal of Political Economy* 76:169–217.

Becker, Gary S., and William M. Landes. 1974. *Essays in the Economics of Crime and Punishment*. New York: Columbia University Press.

Beha, James A., II. 1977. " 'And Nobody Can Get You Out': The Impact of a Mandatory Prison Sentence for the Illegal Carrying of a Firearm on the Use of Firearms and on the Administration of Criminal Justice in Boston." *Boston University Law Review* 57:96–146 (Part I), 289–333 (Part II).

Berry, Bonnie. 1985. "Electronic Jails: A New Criminal Justice Concern." *Justice Quarterly* 2(1):1–22.

Bevan, C. R., ed. 1983. *Community Service Orders in Australia and New Zealand*. Canberra: Australian Institute of Criminology.

Blomberg, Thomas G., Gordon P. Waldo, and Lisa C. Burcroff. 1987. "Home Confinement and Electronic Surveillance." In *Intermediate Punishments: Intensive Supervision, Home Confinement and Electronic Surveillance*, edited by Belinda R. McCarthy. Monsey, N.Y.: Willow Tree Press.

Blumstein, Alfred. 1988. "Prison Populations: A System Out of Control?" In *Crime and Justice: A Review of Research*, Volume 10, edited by Michael Tonry and Norval Morris. Chicago: University of Chicago Press.

Blumstein, Alfred, Jacqueline Cohen, Susan E. Martin, and Michael Tonry, eds. 1983. *Research on Sentencing: The Search for Reform*. Washington, D.C.: National Academy Press.

Blumstein, Alfred, Jacqueline Cohen, and Daniel Nagin, eds. 1978. *Deterrence and Incapacitation: Estimating the Effects of Criminal Sanctions on Crime Rates*. Washington, D.C.: National Academy Press.

Blumstein, Alfred, Jacqueline Cohen, Jeffrey Roth, and Christy Visher, eds. 1986. *Criminal Careers and "Career Criminals."* Washington, D.C.: National Academy Press.

Boerner, David. 1985. *Sentencing in Washington—A Legla Analysis of the Sentencing Reform Act of 1981*. Seattle: Butterworth.

Brewer, D., G. E. Beckett, and N. Holt. 1980. *Determinate Sentencing in California: The First Year's Experience.* Chino: California Department of Corrections.

Brody, S. R. 1976. *The Effectiveness of Sentencing—A Review of the Literature.* London: Her Majesty's Stationery Office.

Bureau of Justice Statistics. 1987. *Jail Inmates 1986.* Washington, D.C.: U.S. Department of Justice, Bureau of Justice Statistics.

———. 1988. *Prisoners in 1987.* Washington, D.C.: U.S. Department of Justice, Bureau of Justice Statistics.

———. 1989. *Prisoners in 1988.* Washington, D.C.: U.S. Department of Justice, Bureau of Justice Statistics.

Bynum, Timothy S. 1982. "Prosecutorial Discretion and The Implementation of a Legislative Mandate." In *Implementing Criminal Justice Policies,* edited by Merry Morash. Beverly Hills, Calif.: Sage.

Byrne, James M. 1986. "The Control Controversy: A Preliminary Examination of Intensive Probation Supervision Programs in the United States." *Federal Probation* 50(2):4–16.

Byrne, James M., and Linda M. Kelly. 1987. "The Use of Electronic Surveillance in the Criminal Justice System: The Marketing of Punishment." Paper presented at the annual meeting of the Society for the Study of Social Problems, Chicago, August.

———. 1988. *Restructuring Probation as an Intermediate Sanction: An Evaluation of the Massachusetts Intensive Probation Supervision Program.* Report to the National Institute of Justice, Washington, D.C.

Call, Jack E., David E. England, and Susette M. Talarico. 1983. "Abolition of Plea Bargaining in the Coast Guard." *Journal of Criminal Justice* 11:351–58.

Canadian Sentencing Commission. 1987. *Sentencing Reform: A Canadian Approach.* Ottawa: Canadian Government Publishing Centre.

Carlson, Kenneth. 1982. *Mandatory Sentencing: The Experience of Two States.* U.S. Department of Justice, National Institute of Justice. Washington, D.C.: U.S. Government Printing Office.

Carrow, Deborah M. 1984. "Judicial Sentencing Guidelines: Hazards of the Middle Ground." *Judicature* 68:161–71.

Carrow, Deborah M., Judith Feins, Beverly N. W. Lee, and Lois Olinger. 1985. *Guidelines Without Force: An Evaluation* of the *Multi-Jurisdictional Sentencing Guidelines Field Test.* Cambridge, Mass.: Abt Associates.

Carver, John A. 1986. "Drugs and Crime: Controlling Use and Reducing Risk through Testing." *NIJ Reports,* SNI 199, September/October.

Casale, Silvia G. 1981. *Fines in Europe: A Study of the Use of Fines in Selected European Countries with Empirical Research on the Problems of Fine Enforcement.* New York: Vera Institute of Justice.

Casale, Silvia G., and Sally T. Hillsman. 1986. *The Enforcement of Fines as Criminal Sanctions: The English Experience and its Relevance to American Practice.* New York: Vera Institute of Justice.

Casper, Jonathan D., David Brereton, and David Neal. 1982. *The Implementation of the California Determinate Sentencing Law.* Washington, D.C.: U.S. Department of Justice.

———. 1983. "The California Determinate Sentence Law." *Criminal Law Bulletin* 19:405–33.

Chaiken, Jan M., and Marcia R. Chaiken. 1990. "Drugs and Predatory Crime." In *Drugs and Crime,* edited by Michael Tonry and James Q. Wilson. Volume 13 of *Crime and Justice: A Review of Research,* edited by Michael Tonry and Norval Morris. Chicago: University of Chicago Press.

Church, Thomas, Jr. 1976. " 'Plea' Bargains, Concessions, and the Courts: Analysis of a Quasi-Experiment." *Law & Society Review* 10:377–401.

Clarke, Stevens H. 1984. "North Carolina's Determinate Sentencing Legislation." *Judicature* 68:140–52.

———. 1986. *Indeterminate and Determinate Sentencing in North Carolina, 1973–85: Effects of Presumptive Sentencing Legislation: Preliminary Draft.* Chapel Hill: Institute of Government, University of North Carolina.

———. 1987. *Felony Sentencing in North Carolina 1976–1986: Effects of Presumptive Sentencing Legislation.* Chapel Hill: Institute of Government, University of North Carolina.

Clarke, Stevens H., Susan Turner Kurtz, Glenn F. Lang, Kenneth L. Parker, Elizabeth W. Rubinsky, and Donna J. Schleicher. 1983. *North Carolina's Determinate Sentencing Legislation: An Evaluation of the First Year's Experience.* Chapel Hill: Institute of Government, University of North Carolina.

Clear, Todd R. 1987. "The New Intensive Supervision Movement."

Paper presented at the 39th Annual Meeting of the American Society of Criminology, Montreal, November.

———. 1988. "A Critical Assessment of Electronic Monitoring in Corrections." *Policy Studies Review* 7(3):671–81.

Clear, Todd, Suzanne Flynn, and Carol Shapiro. 1987. "Intensive Supervision in Probation: A Comparison of Three Projects." In *Intermediate Punishments: Intensive Supervision, Home Confinement and Electronic Surveillance,* edited by Belinda R. McCarthy. Monsey, N.Y.: Willow Tree Press.

Clear, Todd, and Carol Shapiro. 1986. "Selecting Offenders for Intensive Supervision in Probation: The Oregon Model." *Federal Probation* 50(2):45–52.

Cochran, Donald, R. P. Corbett, Jr., and James Byrne. 1986. "Intensive Probation Supervision in Massachusetts: A Case Study in Change." *Federal Probation* 50(2):35–41.

Coffee, John C., Jr., and Michael Tonry. 1983. "Hard Choices." In *Reform and Punishment,* edited by Michael Tonry and Franklin E. Zimring. Chicago: University of Chicago Press.

Cohen, Jacqueline. 1983. "Incapacitation as a Strategy for Crime Control: Possibilities and Pitfalls." In *Crime and Justice: An Annual Review of Research,* Volume 5, edited by Michael Tonry and Norval Morris. Chicago: University of Chicago Press.

Cohen, Jacqueline, and Michael Tonry. 1983. "Sentencing Reforms and Their Impacts." In *Research on Sentencing: The Search for Reform,* Volume 2, edited by Alfred Blumstein, Jacqueline Cohen, Susan E. Martin, and Michael Tonry. Washington, D.C.: National Academy Press.

Cole, George F., Barry Mahoney, Marlene Thornton, and Roger A. Hanson. 1987. *The Practices and Attitudes of Trial Court Judges Regarding Fines as a Criminal Sanction.* Final report submitted to the National Institute of Justice, U.S. Department of Justice, Washington, D.C.

Criminal Courts Technical Assistance Project. 1980. *Overview of State and Local Sentencing Guidelines and Sentencing Research Activity.* Washington, D.C.: American University Law Institute.

Curtis, Christine, and Susan Pennell. 1987. "Electronic Monitoring of Offenders: Methodological Considerations." Paper presented at the 39th Annual Meeting of the American Society of Criminology, Montreal, November.

Davies, Robertson. 1970. *Fifth Business.* New York: Viking.

Davis, Kenneth Culp. 1969. *Discretionary Justice: A Preliminary Inquiry.* Baton Rouge: Louisiana State University Press.

D.C. Superior Court, Sentencing Guidelines Commission. 1987. *Initial Report of the Superior Court Sentencing Guidelines Commission—The Development of Felony Sentencing Guidelines.* Washington, D.C.: District of Columbia Superior Court.

del Carmen, Rolando V., and Joseph B. Vaughn. 1986. "Legal Issues in the Use of Electronic Surveillance in Probation." *Federal Probation* 50(2):60–69.

Doob, Anthony N., and P. Diane Macfarlane. 1984. *The Community Service Order for Youthful Offenders: Perceptions and Effects.* Toronto: Centre of Criminology, University of Toronto.

Du Pont, Pete. 1986. "A Governor's Perspective on Sentencing." In *Crime and Punishment in Modern America,* edited by Patrick B. McGuigan and Jon S. Pascale. Washington, D.C.: Free Congress and Research Foundation.

Ehrlich, I. 1974. "Participation in Illegitimate Activities: A Theoretical and Empirical Investigation." In *Essays in the Economics of Crime and Punishment,* edited by Gary S. Becker and William M. Landes. New York: Columbia University Press.

Erwin, Billie S. 1987. *Final Evaluation Report: Intensive Probation Supervision in Georgia.* Atlanta: Georgia Department of Corrections.

Erwin, Billie S., and Lawrence A. Bennett. 1987. *New Dimensions in Probation: Georgia's Experience with Intensive Probation Supervision (IPS).* Research in Brief (January). Washington, D.C.: U.S. Department of Justice, National Institute of Justice.

Farley, Barbara. 1987. *The Use and Effectiveness of Electronic Monitoring Programs.* Sacramento: Office of the Attorney General.

———. 1989. *The Use and Effectiveness of Electronic Monitoring—An Update.* Sacramento: Office of the Attorney General.

Fields, Charles B. 1984. *The Intensive Supervision Probation Program in Texas: A Two-Year Assessment.* Ph.D. dissertation. Sam Houston State University, College of Criminal Justice, Huntsville, Texas.

Florida Department of Corrections. 1987. *Community Control "House Arrest" Program: A Three Year Longitudinal Report.* Tallahassee: Florida Department of Corrections, Probation and Parole Services.

Florida Mental Health Institute. 1987. "Evaluation of Florida Community Control 'House Arrest' Program." Summarized in

Community Control "House Arrest" Program: A Three Year Longitudinal Report. Tallahassee: Florida Department of Corrections, Probation and Parole Services.

Flynn, Leonard E. 1986. "House Arrest: Florida's Alternative Eases Crowding and Tight Budgets." *Corrections Today* 48(4): 64–68.

Frankel, Marvin E. 1972. *Criminal Sentences: Law Without Order.* New York: Hill and Wang.

Friedman, Gary M. 1983. "The West German Day-Fine System: A Possibility for the United States?" *University of Chicago Law Review* 50:281–304.

Friel, Charles M., Joseph B. Vaughn, and Rolando V. del Carmen. 1987. *Electronic Monitoring and Correctional Policy.* Washington, D.C.: U.S. Department of Justice, National Institute of Justice.

Gable, Ralph K. 1986. "Application of Personal Telemonitoring to Current Problems in Corrections." *Journal of Criminal Justice* 14:173–86.

General Accounting Office. 1982. *Federal Parole Practices: Better Management and Legislative Changes Are Needed.* Washington, D.C.: U.S. Government Printing Office.

———. 1985. *After the Criminal Fine Enforcement Act of 1984— Some Issues Still Need to be Resolved.* Washington, D.C.: U.S. Government Printing Office.

Gillespie, Robert W. 1980. "Fines as an Alternative to Incarceration: The German Experience." *Federal Probation* 44(4):20–26.

———. 1981. "Sentencing Traditional Crimes with Fines: A Comparative Analysis." *International Journal of Comparative and Applied Criminal Justice* 5(2):197–204.

———. 1982. "Economic Penalties as Criminal Sanctions: A Pilot Study of Their Use in Illinois." Paper presented at the 34th Annual Meeting of the American Society of Criminology, Toronto, November.

Goldkamp, John S., and Michael R. Gottfredson. 1985. *Policy Guidelines for Bail.* Philadelphia: Temple University Press.

Goldstein, Paul J. 1987. "Drugs and Violent Crime." In *Drugs and Crime: Workshop Proceedings,* edited by Jeffrey A. Roth, Michael Tonry, and Norval Morris. Report of the 1986 National Academy of Sciences Conference on Drugs and Crime Research, National Research Council, Washington, D.C.

Gottfredson, Don M., Leslie T. Wilkins, and Peter B. Hoffman. 1978.

Guidelines for Parole and Sentencing. Lexington, Mass.: Lexington Books.

Gottfredson, Michael R. 1979. "Parole Guidelines and the Reduction of Sentence Disparity." *Journal of Research in Crime and Delinquency* 16:218–31.

Grebing, Gerhardt. 1982. *The Fine in Comparative Law: A Survey of 21 Countries.* Occasional Papers No. 9. Cambridge, England: Institute of Criminology, University of Cambridge.

Greenwood, Peter W., with Allan Abrahamse. 1982. *Selective Incapacitation.* Santa Monica, Calif.: Rand.

Harris, M. Kay. 1980. *Community Service by Offenders.* Washington, D.C.: American Bar Association, Basics Program.

Hart, H. L. A. 1968. *Punishment and Responsibility: Essays in the Philosophy of Law.* Oxford: Oxford University Press.

Heumann, Milton, and Colin Loftin. 1979. "Mandatory Sentencing and the Abolition of Plea Bargaining: The Michigan Felony Firearm Statute." *Law & Society Review* 13:393–430.

Hillsman, Sally T. 1990. "Fines and Day-Fines." In *Crime and Justice: A Review of Research,* Volume 12, edited by Michael Tonry and Norval Morris. Chicago: University of Chicago Press.

Hillsman, Sally T., and Judith Greene. 1988. "Tailoring Criminal Fines to the Financial Means of the Offender." *Judicature* 72:38–45.

Hillsman, Sally T., Joyce L. Sichel, and Barry Mahoney. 1984. *Fines in Sentencing: A Study of the Use of the Fine as a Criminal Sanction.* New York: Vera Institute of Justice.

Hofer, Paul J., and Barbara S. Meierhoefer. 1987. *Home Confinement: An Evolving Sanction in the Federal Criminal Justice System.* Washington, D.C.: The Federal Judicial Center.

Home Office. 1981. *Criminal Statistics: England and Wales.* London: Her Majesty's Stationery Office.

———. 1983. *Criminal Statistics: England and Wales.* London: Her Majesty's Stationery Office.

Hudson, Joe, and Burt Galaway, eds. 1980. *Victims, Offenders, and Alternative Sanctions.* Lexington, Mass.: D. C. Heath.

Huff, C. Ronald, Richard A. Ball, and J. Robert Lilly. 1987. "Social and Legal Issues of Home Confinement." In *House Arrest and Correctional Policy,* edited by J. Inciardi. Newbury Park, Calif.: Sage.

Iowa Law Review. 1975. "The Elimination of Plea Bargaining in Black Hawk County: A Case Study." *Iowa Law Review* 61:1053.

Ives, G. 1914. *A History of Penal Methods.* London: Stanley Paul.

James, William. 1902. *The Varieties of Religious Experience.* New York: Longmans, Green.

Joint Committee on New York Drug Law Evalution. 1978. *The Nation's Toughest Drug Law: Evaluating the New York Experience.* A project of the Association of the Bar of the City of New York and the Drug Abuse Council, Inc.

Knapp, Kay A. 1984a. *The Impact of the Minnesota Sentencing Guidelines—Three Year Evaluation.* St. Paul: Minnesota Sentencing Guidelines Commission.

———. 1984b. "What Sentencing Reform in Minnesota Has and Has Not Accomplished." *Judicature* 68:181–89.

———. 1985. *Minnesota Sentencing Guidelines and Commentary Annotated.* St. Paul: Minnesota CLE Press.

Kramer, John H., and Robin L. Lubitz. 1985. "Pennsylvania's Sentencing Reform: The Impact of Commission-Established Guidelines." *Crime & Delinquency* 31:481–500.

Kramer, John H., and Anthony J. Scirica. 1985. "Complex Policy Choices: The Pennsylvania Commission on Sentencing." Paper presented at the annual meeting of the Academy of Criminal Justice Sciences, Las Vegas, Nevada, April.

Kress, Jack M. 1980. *Prescription for Justice: The Theory and Practice of Sentencing Guidelines.* Cambridge, Mass.: Ballinger.

Ku, R. 1980. *American Prisons and Jails: Volume 4, Case Studies of New Legislation Governing Sentencing and Release.* Washington, D.C.: U.S. Department of Justice, National Institute of Justice.

Latessa, Edward J. 1979. *Intensive Probation: An Evaluation of the Effectiveness of an Intensive Diversion Unit.* Ph.D. dissertation. Sam Houston State University, College of Criminal Justice, Huntsville, Texas.

———. 1987. "Intensive Supervision: An Eight Year Follow-up Evaluation." Paper presented at the annual meeting of the Academy of Criminal Justice Sciences, St. Louis, Missouri, March.

Lewis, Donald E. 1988. "A Linear Model of Fine Enforcement with Application to England and Wales." *Journal of Quantitative Criminology* 4:19–37.

Lilly, J. Robert, Richard A. Ball, and J. Wright. 1987. "Home Incarceration with Electronic Monitoring in Kenton County, KY: An Evaluation." In *Intermediate Punishments: Intensive Supervision, Home Confinement and Electronic Surveillance,* edited by Belinda R. McCarthy. Monsey, N.Y.: Willow Tree Press.

Lipson, Albert J., and Mark A. Peterson. 1980. *California Justice Under Determinate Sentencing: A Review and Agenda for Research*. Santa Monica, Calif.: Rand.

Lipton, Douglas, Robert Martinson, and Judith Wilks. 1975. *The Effectiveness of Correctional Treatment: A Survey of Treatment Evaluation Studies*. New York: Praeger.

Loftin, Colin, and David McDowall. 1981. " 'One With a Gun Gets You Two': Mandatory Sentencing and Firearms Violence in Detroit." *Annals of the American Academy of Political and Social Science* 455:150.

————. 1984. "The Deterrent Effects of the Florida Felony Firearm Law." *Journal of Criminal Law and Criminology* 75:250–59.

Loftin, Colin, Milton Heumann, and David McDowall. 1983. "Mandatory Sentencing and Firearms Violence: Evaluating an Alternative to Gun Control." *Law & Society Review* 17:287–318.

Lombardi, John Harold. 1981. *Florida's Objective Parole Guidelines: Analysis of the First Year's Implementation*. Ph.D. dissertation. Florida State University, Department of Criminology, Gainesville.

Lubitz, Robin L., and Cynthia A. Kempinen. 1987. *The Impact of Pennsylvania's Sentencing Guidelines: An Analysis of System Adjustments to Sentencing Reform*. State College: Pennsylvania Commission on Sentencing.

Lurigio, Arthur. 1987. "Evaluating Intensive Probation Supervision: The Cook County Experience." *Perspectives* 1987:17–19.

McCarthy, Belinda R., ed. 1987. *Intermediate Punishments: Intensive Supervision, Home Confinement and Electronic Surveillance*. Monsey, N.Y.: Willow Tree Press.

McDonald, Douglas C. 1986. *Punishment Without Walls*. New Brunswick, N.J.: Rutgers University Press.

McGillis, Daniel. 1986. *Crime Victim Restitution: An Analysis of Approaches*. National Institute of Justice, Issues and Practices. Washington, D.C.: U.S. Government Printing Office.

McGuigan, Patrick B., and Jon S. Pascale, eds. 1986. *Crime and Punishment in Modern America*. Washington, D.C.: The Free Congress Research and Education Foundation.

Martin, Susan. 1984. "Interests and Politics in Sentencing Reform:

The Development of Sentencing Guidelines in Pennsylvania and Minnesota." *Villanova Law Review* 29:21–113.

Martin, Susan E., Lee E. Sechrest, and R. Redner, eds. 1981. *New Directions in the Rehabilitation of Criminal Offenders.* Washington, D.C.: National Academy Press.

Martinson, Robert. 1974. "What Works?—Questions and Answers About Prison Reform." *Public Interest* 35(2):22–54.

Meachum, Larry R. 1986. "House Arrest: Oklahoma Experience." *Corrections Today* 48(4):102ff.

Messinger, Sheldon, and Phillip Johnson. 1978. "California's Determinate Sentencing Laws." In *Determinate Sentencing: Reform or Regression.* Washington, D.C.: U.S. Government Printing Office.

Miethe, Terance D. 1987. "Charging and Plea Bargaining Practices Under Determinate Sentencing: An Investigation of the Hydraulic Displacement of Discretion." *Journal of Criminal Law and Criminology* 78:155–76.

Miethe, Terance D., and Charles A. Moore. 1985. "Socioeconomic Disparities Under Determinate Sentencing Systems: A Comparison of Preguideline and Postguideline Practices in Minnesota." *Criminology* 23:337–63.

———. 1987. *Evaluation of Minnesota's Felony Sentencing Guidelines.* Report to the National Institute of Justice, Washington, D.C.

Minnesota Citizens Council on Crime and Justice. 1982. *Juvenile Court Dispositional Guidelines: Handbook for Advisory Sanction Levels.* Minneapolis: Minnesota Citizens Council on Crime and Justice.

Monahan, John, and Henry J. Steadman. 1983. "Crime and Mental Disorder: An Epidemiological Approach." In *Crime and Justice: An Annual Review of Research,* Volume 4, edited by Michael Tonry and Norval Morris. Chicago: University of Chicago Press.

Moore, Charles A., and Terance D. Miethe. 1986. "Regulated and Unregulated Sentencing Decisions: An Analysis of First-Year Practices under Minnesota's Felony Sentencing Guidelines." *Law and Society Review* 20:253–77.

Morgan, Rod, and Roger Bowles. 1981. "Fines: The Case for Review." *Criminal Law Review* (April):203–14.

Morris, Norval. 1974. *The Future of Imprisonment.* Chicago: University of Chicago Press.

———. 1976. "Punishment, Desert, and Rehabilitation." In *Equal*

Justice Under Law: U.S. Department of Justice Bicentennial Lecture Series. Washington, D.C.: U.S. Government Printing Office.

Mueller, Julia M., and Richard F. Sparks. 1982. "Some Statewide Statistics—Oregon." In *Report on Strategies for Determinate Sentencing.* Unpublished document prepared for the National Institute of Justice, Washington, D.C.

Mullaney, Fahy G. 1988. *Economic Sanctions in Community Corrections.* Washington, D.C.: National Institute of Corrections.

National Academy of Sciences Panel on Rehabilitative Techniques. 1979. See Sechrest et al. 1979.

National Academy of Sciences Panel on Rehabilitative Techniques. 1981. See Martin et al. 1981.

National Academy of Sciences Panel on Research on Sentencing. 1983. See Blumstein et al. 1983.

National Advisory Commission on Criminal Justice Standards and Goals. 1973. *Task Force Report: Courts.* Washington, D.C.: U.S. Government Printing Office.

National Commission on Reform of Federal Criminal Law. 1971. *Report.* Washington, D.C.: U.S. Government Printing Office.

National Conference of Commissioners on Uniform State Laws. 1979. *Model Sentencing and Corrections Act.* Chicago: National Conference of Commissioners on Uniform State Laws.

National Swedish Council for Crime Prevention. 1986. *Bulletin No. 3.* Stockholm: Swedish National Council for Crime Prevention.

Newburn, T., and H. de Peyrecave. 1988. *The Use and Enforcement of Compensation Orders in Magistrates' Courts.* London: Her Majesty's Stationery Office.

Nozick, Robert. 1981. *Philosophical Explanations.* Cambridge, Mass.: Harvard University Press.

O'Donnell, Pierce, Dennis Curtis, and M. Churgin. 1977. *Toward a Just and Effective Sentencing System.* New York: Praeger.

Ogletree, J. Charles, Jr. 1988. "The Death of Discretion? Reflections on the Federal Sentencing Guidelines." *Harvard Law Review* 101:1938–60.

Parent, Dale. 1988a. *Shock Incarceration: An Assessment of Existing Programs.* June 13, 1988 draft. Cambridge, Mass.: Abt Associates.

———. 1988b. *Structuring Sentencing Discretion: The Evaluation of Minnesota's Sentencing Guidelines.* Stoneham, Mass.: Butterworth.

Paton, Alan. 1948. *Cry, the Beloved Country.* New York: Charles Scribner's Sons.

Pearson, Frank S. 1987. *Research on New Jersey's Intensive Supervision Program.* Washington, D.C.: U.S. Department of Justice, National Institute of Justice.

———. 1988. "Evaluation of New Jersey's Intensive Supervision Program." *Crime & Delinquency* 34:437–48.

Pease, Ken. 1985. "Community Service Orders." In *Crime and Justice: An Annual Review of Research,* Volume 6, edited by Michael Tonry and Norval Morris. Chicago: University of Chicago Press.

Pease, Ken, S. Billingham, and I. Earnshaw. 1977. *Community Service Assessed in 1976.* Home Office Research Study, No. 39. London: Her Majesty's Stationery Office.

Pease, Ken, and W. McWilliams, eds. 1980. *Community Service by Order.* Edinburgh: Scottish Academic Press.

Pease, Ken, and Martin Wasik, eds. 1987. *Sentencing Reform: Guidance or Guidelines.* Manchester: Manchester University Press.

Pennsylvania Commission on Crime and Delinquency. 1986. *The Effects of Five-Year Mandatory Sentencing in Pennsylvania.* Harrisburg: Pennsylvania Commission on Crime and Delinquency.

Pennsylvania Commission on Sentencing. 1981. *Sentencing Guidelines. Pennsylvania Bulletin.* January 24, pp. 463–76.

———. 1984. *1983 Report: Sentencing in Pennsylvania.* State College: Pennsylvania Commission on Sentencing.

———. 1985. *1984 Report: Sentencing in Pennsylvania.* State College: Pennsylvania Commission on Sentencing.

———. 1986. *1985 Annual Report.* State College: Pennsylvania Commission on Sentencing.

———. 1987. *1986–1987 Annual Report.* State College: Pennsylvania Commission on Sentencing.

Petersilia, Joan. 1986. "Exploring the Option of House Arrest." *Federal Probation* 50(2):50–55.

———. 1987a. *Expanding Options for Criminal Sentencing.* Santa Monica, Calif.: Rand.

———. 1987b. "Georgia's Intensive Probation: Will the Model Work Elsewhere?" In *Intermediate Punishments: Intensive Supervision, Home Confinement and Electronic Surveillance,* edited by Belinda R. McCarthy. Monsey, N.Y.: Willow Tree Press.

———. 1987c. *House Arrest*. Crime File Study Guide. Washington, D.C.: U.S. Department of Justice, National Institute of Justice.

Petersilia, Joan, Susan Turner, James Kahan, and Joyce Peterson. 1985. *Granting Felons Probation: Public Risks and Alternatives*. Santa Monica, Calif.: Rand.

Pierce, Glen L., and William J. Bowers. 1981. "The Bartley-Fox Gun Law's Short-Term Impact on Crime in Boston." *Annals of the American Academy of Political and Social Science* 455: 120–32.

Polonoski, M. I. 1981. *Community Service Order Programme in Ontario, Number 4, Summary*. Scarborough: Ontario Ministry of Correctional Services Planning and Research Branch.

Posner, Richard. 1977. *Economic Analyses of Law*. 2d ed. Boston: Little, Brown.

———. 1980. "Optimal Sentences for White-Collar Criminals." *American Criminal Law Review* 17:409–18.

President's Commission on Law Enforcement and Administration of Justice. 1967. *The Challenge of Crime in a Free Society*. Washington, D.C.: U.S. Government Printing Office.

Rathke, Stephen C. 1982. "Plea Negotiating Under the Sentencing Guidelines." *Hamline Law Review* 5:271–91.

Read, Edward. 1987. "The Alcoholic, the Probation Officer, and AA: A Viable Team Approach to Supervision." *Federal Probation* 51(1):11–15.

Rich, William D., L. Paul Sutton, Todd D. Clear, and Michael J. Saks. 1982. *Sentencing by Mathematics: An Evaluation of the Early Attempts to Develop Sentencing Guidelines*. Williamsburg, Va.: National Center for State Courts.

Rook, M. K. 1978. *Practical Evaluation of the Tasmanian Work Order Scheme*. M.A. thesis, University of Tasmania.

Rossman, David, Paul Froyd, Glen L. Pierce, John McDevitt, and William J. Bowers. 1979. *The Impact of the Mandatory Gun Law In Massachusetts*. Report to the National Institute of Law Enforcement and Criminal Justice, Law Enforcement Assistance Administration, U.S. Department of Justice, Washington, D.C.

Roth, Jeffrey A., Michael Tonry, and Norval Morris, eds. 1987. *Drugs and Crime: Workshop Proceedings*. Report of the 1986 National Academy of Sciences Conference on Drugs and Crime Research. Washington, D.C.: National Research Council.

Rubinstein, Michael L., Stevens H. Clarke, and Teresa J. White. 1980.
    Alaska Bans Plea Bargaining. Washington, D.C.: U.S. De-
    partment of Justice, National Institute of Justice.
Sandhu, Harjit S., and Richard A. Dodder. 1986. "Community Based
    Alternatives to Incarceration: A Comparison of Their In-
    Program Success or Failure." Paper presented at the 38th
    Annual Meeting of the American Society of Criminology,
    Atlanta, November.
Saunders, Daniel, and Sandra T. Azar. 1989. "Treatment Programs
    for Family Violence." In *Family Violence,* edited by Lloyd
    Ohlin and Michael Tonry. Volume 11 of *Crime and Justice:
    A Review of Research,* edited by Michael Tonry and Norval
    Morris. Chicago: University of Chicago Press.
Schmidt, Annesley K. 1986. "Electronic Monitors." *Federal Probation*
    50(2):56–59.
———. 1988. "The Use of Electronic Monitoring by Criminal Justice
    Agencies." Washington, D.C.: U.S. Department of Justice,
    National Institute of Justice.
Schmidt, Annesley, and Christine E. Curtis. 1987. "Electronic Moni-
    tors." In *Intermediate Punishments: Intensive Supervision,
    Home Confinement and Electronic Supervision,* edited by
    Belinda R. McCarthy. Monsey, N.Y.: Willow Tree Press.
Schulhofer, Stephen. 1980. "Due Process of Sentencing." *University
    of Pennsylvania Law Review* 128:733–828.
Schuwerk, Robert P. 1984. "Illinois' Experience with Determinate
    Sentencing: A Critical Reappraisal. Part 1: Efforts to Struc-
    ture the Exercise of Discretion in Bargaining for, Imposing,
    and Serving Criminal Sentences." *DePaul Law Review* 33:
    631–739.
Schwitzgebel, Ralph K. 1969. "Issues in the Use of an Electronic
    Rehabilitation System with Chronic Recidivists." *Law &
    Society Review* 3:597–615.
Schwitzgebel, Ralph K., Walter N. Pahnke, and William S. Hurd.
    1964. "A Program of Research in Behavioral Electronics."
    Behavioral Science 9:233–38.
Sechrest, Lee B., Susan O. White, and Elizabeth D. Brown, eds. 1979.
    *The Rehabilitation of Criminal Offenders: Problems and
    Prospects.* Washington, D.C.: National Academy Press.
Shane-DuBow, Sandra, Alice P. Brown, and Erik Olsen. 1985. *Sen-
    tencing Reform in the United States: History, Content, and
    Effect.* Washington, D.C.: U.S. Government Printing Office.
Sherman, Michael, and Gordon Hawkins. 1981. *Imprisonment in*

America: Choosing the Future. Chicago: University of Chicago Press.

Softley, Paul, and David Moxon. 1982. *Fine Enforcement: An Evaluation of Practices in Individual Courts.* Home Office Research and Planning Unit Paper No. 12. London: Her Majesty's Stationery Office.

Sparks, Richard S. 1981. "Sentencing Before and After DSL: Some Statistical Findings." In *Report on Strategies for Determinate Sentencing.* Unpublished document prepared for the National Institute of Justice, Washington, D.C.

———. 1983. "The Construction of Sentencing guidelines: A Methodological Critique." In *Research on Sentencing: The Search for Reform,* Volume 2, edited by Alfred Blumstein, Jacqueline Cohen, Susan Martin, and Michael Tonry. Washington, D.C.: National Academy Press.

Speckart, George, and M. Douglas Anglin. 1986. "Narcotics and Crime: A Causal Modeling Approach." *Journal of Quantitative Criminology* 2:3–28.

Tevelin, David. 1986. "Fines Research Paper." Unpublished manuscript. Washington, D.C.: The U.S. Sentencing Commission.

———. 1987. "Summary of Draft 'Just Punishment' Approach to Calculating Size of Fine to be Imposed on Convicted Defendants." Unpublished manuscript. Washington, D.C.: The U.S. Sentencing Commission.

Thomson, Douglas R. 1987. "Intensive Probation Supervision in Illinois." Unpublished manuscript. University of Illinois at Chicago, Center for Research in Law and Justice.

Thornstedt, Hans. 1985. "The Day Fine System in Sweden." *Criminal Law Review* (June):307–12.

Tonry, Michael. 1987. *Sentencing Reform Impacts.* National Institute of Justice, Issues and Practices. Washington, D.C.: U.S. Government Printing Office.

———. 1988. "Structuring Sentencing." In *Crime and Justice: A Review of Research,* Volume 10, edited by Michael Tonry and Norval Morris. Chicago: University of Chicago Press.

———. 1990. "Latent and Overt Functions of Intensive Supervision Probation." *Crime and Delinquency* (January).

Tonry, Michael, and Richard Will. 1988. *Intermediate Sanctions.* Report submitted to the National Institute of Justice, Washington, D.C.

Twentieth Century Fund Task Force on Criminal Sentencing. 1976. *Fair and Certain Punishment.* New York: McGraw-Hill.

U.S. Sentencing Commission. 1986. *Sentencing Guidelines, September 1986—Preliminary Draft.* Washington, D.C.: U.S. Sentencing Commission.

———. 1987. *Manual: Sentencing Guidelines.* Washington, D.C.: U.S. Sentencing Commission.

Utz, Pamela. 1981. "Determinate Sentencing in Two California Courts." In *Report on Strategies for Determinate Sentencing.* Unpublished document prepared for the U.S. National Institute of Justice, Washington, D.C.

Vass, A. A. 1980. "Law Enforcement in Community Service: Probation, Defense and Prosecution." *Probation Journal* 27: 114–17.

von Hirsch, Andrew. 1976. *Doing Justice: The Choice of Punishments.* New York: Hill and Wang.

———. 1985. *Past or Future Crimes.* New Brunswick, N.J.: Rutgers University Press.

von Hirsch, Andrew, and Kathleen Hanrahan. 1981. "Determinate Penalty Systems in America: An Overview." *Crime & Delinquency* 27:289–316.

von Hirsch, Andrew, Kay A. Knapp, and Michael Tonry. 1987. *The Sentencing Commission and its Guidelines.* Boston: Northeastern University Press.

von Hirsch, Andrew, Martin Wasik, and Judith Greene. 1989. "Punishments in the Community and the Principles of Desert." *Rutgers Law Review* 20:595–618.

Vonnegut, Kurt. 1968. *Welcome to the Monkey House.* New York: Delacorte Press/Seymour Lawrence.

Wainwright, Louis L. 1984. *Preliminary Report on Community Control.* Tallahassee: Florida Department of Corrections, Probation and Parole Services.

Warren, Marguerite, A. Harland, E. Brown, M. Buckman, K. Heide, K. Maxwell, P. Van Voorhis, and J. Simon. 1983. *Restitution in Law and Practice: The Experience of Ten Programs.* Report to the National Institute of Justice, U.S. Department of Justice, Washington, D.C.

Washington State Sentencing Guidelines Commission. 1983. *Report to the Legislature.* Olympia: Washington Sentencing Guidelines Commission.

———. 1984. *Report to the Legislature.* Olympia: Washington State Sentencing Guidelines Commission.

———. 1985. *Sentencing Practices Under the Sentencing Reform*

Act: A Preliminary Report. Olympia: Washington State Sentencing Guidelines Commission.

————. 1986. *Report to the Legislature—January 1, 1986.* Olympia: Washington State Sentencing Guidelines Commission.

————. 1987. *Preliminary Statistical Summary of 1986 Sentencing Data.* Olympia: Washington State Sentencing Guidelines Commission.

Wasik, Martin, and Andrew von Hirsch. 1988. "Noncustodial Sentences and the Principles of Desert." *Criminal Law Review* 1988:555–72.

West, Donald J. 1983. "Sex Offenses and Offending." In *Crime and Justice: An Annual Review of Research,* Volume 5, edited by Michael Tonry and Norval Morris. Chicago: University of Chicago Press.

Wexler, Harry K., and Douglas S. Lipton. 1986. "Interventions that 'Work' with Drug-involved Offenders." Washington, D.C.: National Institute of Justice.

Wilkins, Leslie T., Jack M. Kress, Don M. Gottfredson, Joseph C. Calpin, and Arthur M. Gelman. 1978. *Sentencing Guidelines: Structuring Judicial Discretion—Report on the Feasibility Study.* Washington, D.C.: U.S. Department of Justice.

Wish, Eric D., Elizabeth Brady, and Mary Cuadrado. 1986. "Urine Testing of Arrestees: Findings from Manhattan." Paper presented at the National Institute of Justice-sponsored conference on Drugs and Crime: Detecting Use and Reducing Risk, Washington, D.C., June.

Wish, Eric D., and Bruce D. Johnson. 1986. "The Impact of Substance Abuse on Criminal Careers." In *Criminal Careers and "Career Criminals,"* Volume 2, edited by Alfred Blumstein, Jacqueline Cohen, Jeffrey A. Roth, and Christy Visher. Washington, D.C.: National Academy Press.

Wootton, Barbara. 1978. *Crime and Penal Policy.* London: Allen and Unwin.

Young, Warren A. 1979. *Community Service Orders.* London: Heinemann.

Zimring, Franklin E. 1977. "Making the Punishment Fit the Crime: A Consumer's Guide to Sentencing Reform." *Hastings Center Report* 6(6):13–21.

Index